Mobilising Teacher Researchers

'[A] really important book [. . .] the growth of interest in teachers in England taking part in educational research is significant.'

John Furlong, Emeritus Professor of Education,
Oxford University, UK

Mobilising Teacher Researchers brings together the results of a research project carried out over a two-year period, commissioned by the National College for Teaching and Learning and involving over 650 schools in England.

An internationally renowned group of contributors present crucial and intriguing lessons learnt from the 'Closing the Gap: Test and Learn' project aimed at identifying ways in which to close the attainment gap, raise the achievement of disadvantaged children in England and introduce new research methods into schools. From the project's policy origins to its implementation, the book captures the diverse range of outcomes from the project, both intended and unexpected. It reveals the ways and extent to which teachers were mobilised as researchers, and how analysis will impact on the future of research-informed practice in schools.

This resulting collection of evolutionary debates focuses on topics such as new forms of governance, teacher engagement and the effectiveness of Randomised Controlled Trials. It foregrounds new approaches to school-based educational research, and is crucial reading for anyone concerned with educational research, and seeking to understand education for social mobility.

Ann Childs is Associate Professor of Science Education at the Department of Education, University of Oxford, UK.

Ian Menter is Emeritus Professor of Teacher Education at the Department of Education, University of Oxford, UK.

Mobilising Teacher Researchers

Challenging Educational Inequality

Edited by Ann Childs
and Ian Menter

Routledge
Taylor & Francis Group

LONDON AND NEW YORK

First published 2018
by Routledge
2 Park Square, Milton Park, Abingdon, Oxon OX14 4RN

and by Routledge
711 Third Avenue, New York, NY 10017

Routledge is an imprint of the Taylor & Francis Group, an informa business

British Library Cataloguing-in-Publication Data
A catalogue record for this book is available from the British Library

Library of Congress Cataloging-in-Publication Data
Names: Childs, Ann, 1957– editor. | Menter, Ian, 1949– editor.
Title: Mobilising teacher researchers : challenging educational inequality / edited by Ann Childs and Ian Menter.
Description: Abingdon, Oxon ; New York, NY : Routledge, 2018. | "This book emerges from a major innovative project carried out in England during 2013–15. The project was called 'Closing the Gap: test and learn'." | Includes bibliographical references.
Identifiers: LCCN 2017028729| ISBN 9781138064607 (hbk) | ISBN 9781138064638 (pbk) | ISBN 9781315160320 (ebk)
Subjects: LCSH: Action research in education – England | Academic achievement – England. | Educational equalization – England. | Children with social disabilities – Education – England.
Classification: LCC LB1028.24 .M63 2018 | DDC 370.72 – dc23
LC record available at https://lccn.loc.gov/2017028729

ISBN: 978-1-138-06460-7 (hbk)
ISBN: 978-1-138-06463-8 (pbk)
ISBN: 978-1-315-16032-0 (ebk)

Typeset in Bembo and Gill Sans
by Florence Production Ltd, Stoodleigh, Devon, UK

Printed and bound by CPI Group (UK) Ltd, Croydon, CR0 4YY

Contents

PART 2
Teachers and research methods: some wider issues

PART 3
New approaches to school-based educational research

Tables

Figures

Abbreviations

AfA	Achievement for All
ANCOVA	Analysis of Co-Variance
ANOVA	Analysis of Variance
BERA	British Educational Research Association
CfBT	CfBT Education Trust (now EDT, see below)
CPD	Continuing Professional Development
CPDL	Continuing Professional Development and Learning
CtG	Closing the Gap: Test and Learn
CUREE	Centre for the Use of Research Evidence in Education
DfE	Department for Education
EBPQ	Evidence-Based Practice Questionnaire
EDT	Education Development Trust (formerly CfBT)
EEF	Education Endowment Foundation
FSM	Free School Meals
HEI	Higher Education Institution
NCTL	National College for Teaching and Leadership
NFER	National Foundation for Educational Research
NGRT	New Group Reading Test
NIP	Numicon Intervention Programme
OUDE	Oxford University Department of Education
PiM	Progress in Mathematics
R&D	Research and Development
RCT	Randomised Controlled Trial
RDNE	Research and Development Networking Event
RLS	Research Lesson Study
RSA	Royal Society for the Arts
RTI	Response to Intervention
SAS	Standard Age Scores
SEN	Special Educational Needs
TDT	Teacher Development Trust
TSA	Teaching School Alliance
UDSE	University of Durham School of Education
URN	Unique Reference Number

Notes on contributors

Sanne F. Akkerman is Professor of Higher Education at Leiden University Graduate School of Teaching in Leiden, the Netherlands.

Larike H. Bronkhorst works as Assistant Professor at Leiden University Graduate School of Teaching in Leiden, the Netherlands.

Juliet Brookes, formerly at the Department for Education – National College for Teaching and Leadership, is now Research and Development Lead at Kyra Teaching School Alliance.

Ann Childs is Associate Professor of Science Education at the Department of Education, University of Oxford.

Richard Churches is Lead Adviser – Education Reform and Evidence-Based Practice at the Education Development Trust.

Paul Connolly is Professor of Education at the School of Education, Queen's University Belfast.

Philippa Cordingley is the Chief Executive of the Centre for the Use of Research & Evidence in Education.

Bart Crisp is Senior Manager (Research in Practice) of the Centre for the Use of Research & Evidence in Education.

Paul Crisp is the Managing Director of the Centre for the Use of Research & Evidence in Education and its Chief Information Officer.

Nigel Fancourt is Associate Professor of Education at the Department of Education, University of Oxford.

Roger Firth is Associate Professor of Geography Education at the Department of Education, University of Oxford.

Trevor Gale is Professor of Education Policy and Social Justice at the School of Education, Glasgow University.

Robin Hall is School-based Research and Development Manager at the Department for Education, National College for Teaching and Leadership.

Steve Higgins is Professor of Education at the School of Education, University of Durham.

Els Laroes is Teacher Educator and Manager in the Teacher Education Programme at Utrecht University, the Netherlands.

Ian Menter is Emeritus Professor of Teacher Education at the Department of Education, University of Oxford.

Ian Thompson is Associate Professor of English Education at the Department of Education, University of Oxford.

Theo Wubbels is Professor of Education at Utrecht University, the Netherlands.

Introduction

Ann Childs and Ian Menter

This book emerges from a major innovative project carried out in England during 2013–2015. The project was called Closing the Gap: Test and Learn. It is our belief that the significance of the work reported here (the central project is described in detail in Chapter 2) goes far beyond the borders of this country because two of the major themes of the book – improving educational attainment, especially for disadvantaged children, and developing the research skills of teachers as part of their professionalism – are themes of great interest in most parts of the world.

These years were certainly very important in the history of school governance and educational research, as the influences of neoliberalism and neoconservatism were played out under a government that was a frequently uneasy coalition between the Conservatives and the Liberal Democrats (Coalition government 2010–2015). We have written elsewhere about the impact of this period of government on initial teacher education (Childs and Menter, 2013). However, what this book is concerned with is a scheme designed to introduce a major set of interventions across hundreds of Teaching Schools. The idea of Teaching Schools in England had been developed early on in that government's term of office, as part of its commitment to school improvement. These were to be schools that had achieved a high level of success in terms of their exam results and their inspection gradings (see Gu et al., 2015). They were to work on 'six big ideas', one of which was Research and Development. Teaching Schools were established as networks in particular settings, described as Teaching School Alliances (TSAs). TSAs were a significant element of the overall approach to school governance which was to give schools greater freedom and to facilitate the creation of a 'school-led system' of state education.

The interventions within Closing the Gap: Test and Learn (hereafter CtG) were selected because they were educational approaches which sought (among other things) to close the attainment gap between the highest and lowest achieving pupils. Because the lowest achieving pupils were often those from socioeconomically disadvantaged backgrounds, this element of the scheme was very much underpinned by a motive of improving social – and educational – justice.

But the scheme was also radical and innovative in seeking to introduce new research skills into the teaching workforce. The project was designed along the lines of a Randomised Controlled Trial (RCT), and the teachers who were coordinating the work in schools were to be supported and trained in the application of appropriate research methods through their engagement in the project.

One of the themes to emerge from the global recognition of the importance of the teaching profession in the improvement of educational outcomes (Mourshed and Barber, 2007) has been that of 'evidence-based practice'. In England the Department for Education (DfE) has been promoting evidence-based teaching since at least 2010, and this was more recently reinforced in the 2016 White Paper *Educational Excellence Everywhere* (DfE, 2016).

These developments coincide with trends in the USA and internationally (Lingard and Gale, 2010) to view Randomised Controls Trials (RCTs) as the ' "gold standard" for assessing educational research', which Lingard and Gale (2010: 33) suggest fails to recognise 'the significance of theory to social explanation in educational research'. In England this trend is also apparent in the Department of Education's very strong commitment to the use of RCTs in educational research, demonstrated by the commissioning of a paper by Ben Goldacre in 2013 (Goldacre, 2013) and also by the approach taken by the Education Endowment Foundation (https://educationendowmentfoundation. org.uk/), which has received large-scale funding from the Government.

The project

This volume therefore focuses on a highly innovative and unique project which sought to introduce a new level of research engagement and capacity building by schools and teachers. The project was initiated by the National College for Teaching and Leadership (NCTL). The NCTL is an arm's-length 'executive' agency of government which aims to improve academic standards by recruiting and developing a workforce to meet the needs of the school system and to help schools to help each other to improve. The project sought to involve Teaching Schools and their partners in a major educational experiment. The project involved 673 schools (Teaching Schools and their Alliance Schools) over a period of two years conducting RCTs on seven teaching interventions, which had been identified as having promise in the first phase of the experiment, to see if they 'worked' to 'close the gap'. The project connects with the strong espoused commitment to education for social mobility – another global phenomenon echoed in English government policies – through the concept of 'closing the gap', a reference to the persistent differences in attainment between socially advantaged and disadvantaged learners in schools.

The chapters in this book therefore relate to a number of key contemporary themes in education of wide and international relevance, including:

- new forms of governance under neoliberal approaches to education and teacher education (Sleeter, 2008; Zeichner, 2010);
- teacher engagement in research practice in schools and the development of the teaching profession (Berry, 2012);
- education and social mobility (Brown et al., 2013);
- the effectiveness of RCTs and quasi-experimental research methodologies in education, including ethical dimensions (Lingard and Gale, 2010).

The project was undertaken for the NCTL by a consortium led by CfBT (now called the Education Development Trust). A team of five from the University of Oxford's Department of Education (of which we were a part) was involved in supporting the development of research skills for teachers in the participating schools and in researching aspects of the processes of the whole project. The other partners were the University of Durham and CUREE – the Centre for the Use of Research and Evidence in Education – (their respective roles are described in later chapters).

All of the lead partners working in the consortium were invited to write chapters for this collection, and we have been delighted by the enthusiasm with which this invitation was accepted. Readers who work their way through the book will detect a number of different perspectives on the project as a whole, which very much reflect the particular authors' own experiences, work settings and contributions to the project. There was great debate and discussion during the development and delivery of the project and this is reflected in what follows.

In order to ensure that our work was considered critically and independently, we also invited authors who were not involved in the project to comment on what had emerged, and the book therefore includes three chapters written from 'elsewhere'. We are very grateful to Theo Wubbels and his colleagues in the Netherlands, to Paul Connolly, based in Northern Ireland, and to Trevor Gale, an Australian based in Scotland, for their diligence in offering critical perspectives on the work of the core team.

Outline of the book

Each chapter offers an analysis that relates to one or more of the key themes above. This introduction has just signalled some of the key issues that are explored in much greater depth in what follows. For example, questions we have touched on and which are considered in much greater depth in what follows include: the management of national educational developments in a 'school-led system'; the quality (rigour, reliability, etc.) of research undertaken by teachers; questions of fidelity in intervention-based RCTs in education; the deconstruction of 'closing the gap' in education; and the implications that arise for teacher learning and development.

The book is structured in three main parts. The first part, consisting of four chapters, has the task of setting out the background, the development and implementation of the project. The second part also has four chapters, all written by members of the core team. But in these chapters the authors step back from the immediate CtG project to place it in various wider contexts. The third and final part consists of the three 'external' responses or commentaries which bring a set of independent and critical voices to our attention. As editors of the book, we then offer a brief concluding review in which we set out some of the implications that we believe this work has for the future of education and educational research.

Part I: Closing the Gap: Test and Learn

The first chapter, by three Oxford colleagues, Ann Childs, Roger Firth and Ian Thompson, seeks to identify the 'policy origins' of the entire scheme, and to identify the agenda and motivations of those who originally conceived the scheme. It considers the ways in which CtG emerged out of: the development of Teaching Schools; the 'closing the gap' objective of the Coalition government; the desire to increase research capacity within the teaching workforce, as well as other elements. Through tracking changes that occurred during the period of the project, attention is given to the dynamic nature of an ambitious project of this sort and how policy is enacted in a major national but yet 'school-led' initiative.

This is followed by a chapter based on the official research report of the whole project which was published by the Department for Education (Churches, 2016). The chapter, written by colleagues at the Education Development Trust (Richard Churches) and at the NCTL (Robin Hall and Juliet Brookes), provides a summary of that research report (Churches, 2016) and seeks to draw out the main features of the programme, the different phases of delivery and the developments that took place in response to the increasing levels of engagement that schools demonstrated. It also summarises the large-scale trial results for the seven interventions and the governmental learning from these. Additionally, a total of 48 teacher-led experimental studies (including RCTs designed and conducted by schools) were grant funded and these are discussed. The chapter concludes by suggesting some of the learning that was achieved from developing teachers' scientific literacy in the school-led research programme and a discussion of the efficacy of system-led research approaches such as the ones embedded within the initiative.

In Chapter 3, Ian Menter and Ian Thompson, from Oxford, seek to explore the extent to which the overall methodology can indeed be described as a randomised controlled trial. Although this was a very large-scale initiative, the actual interventions were each carried out with relatively small numbers of pupils in a very diverse range of contexts. Policymakers during the recent past have expressed enormous enthusiasm for RCTs, not least in the wake of Ben Goldacre's paper commissioned by a former Secretary of State for Education (Goldacre, 2013) and with the promotion of RCTs by the Education

Endowment Foundation (referred to above). However, there are some conceptual and technical difficulties which were encountered in this project which call some of the RCT precepts into question.

The final chapter in Part 1 was written by colleagues based at CUREE, Phillippa Cordingley, Paul Crisp and Bart Crisp. The chapter explores the conceptual, practical and research issues involved in developing a large-scale, randomised control-like intervention to enhance research and development and close gaps for vulnerable learners across nearly 700 schools. The chapter explores three key issues: the short and longer term impacts of preparing for a large-scale intervention via consultation with schools; the nature of interventions capable of being implemented through a trial-like programme; and the emerging centrality of Continuing Professional Development and Learning (CPDL) for teachers and for school leaders to interventions with strong prior evidence. The chapter draws on extensive evidence from the intense consultation process and from the identification, systematic evaluation, short listing and final selection of interventions that all paved the way for the implementation of the programme.

Part 2: Teachers and research methods: some wider issues

In Chapter 5, Steve Higgins, from Durham University, considers the role of randomised trials in education as a necessary but not sufficient design for drawing conclusions about effective educational practice. Using a toolbox metaphor, he identifies what kinds of questions are appropriate for different RCT designs in terms of supporting causal inference as part of a wider set of tools for educational inquiry. Higgins argues that trials have one key feature, randomisation, which uniquely addresses some aspects of potential bias in evaluative educational research. The chapter then reviews the designs of the trials used in the CtG project to identify some strengths and weaknesses, particularly in relation to the internal and external validity of the findings. A contrast is drawn between the large-scale and micro-scale designs in CtG in response to Biesta's (2007) challenges about the democratic deficit in notions of 'what works' which restrict opportunities for participation in educational decision making. By contrast, Higgins argues that causal evidence is necessary, but not sufficient, for the normative professional judgements of teachers.

The next chapter is a collaboration between Churches, Hall and Higgins, and examines more closely the role of teachers in RCTs. They draw on several strands of activity which have involved giving teachers in England, Dubai and Wales experimental research design training based on research methods from psychology and education. Central to this was a strand of CtG. With grant funding, 48 teachers from Teaching School Alliances in England designed and completed small-scale randomised controlled trials and other forms of experimental research (such as non-randomised case-matched designs). The investigations explored the effectiveness of a number of teaching and learning strategies where the focus of the inquiry was determined by the teachers themselves, such as strategies to develop the quality of talk or children's decoding skills, or aspects of feedback and marking. The chapter presents an overview of the research investigations, their designs and a meta-analysis of teacher findings, with additional evidence from focus groups and findings from teacher completion of a questionnaire.

In Chapter 7, Ann Childs and Nigel Fancourt, both from Oxford, assess the extent to which evidence emerged from the project to suggest that teachers in schools were becoming increasingly research-literate (to use the phrase adopted in the report from BERA-RSA, 2014), and that the 'school-led system' was developing research capacity through engagement in a scheme such as this. The focus therefore is on schools as 'centres of research'. The chapter concludes by seeking to draw out implications for teachers, schools, university departments, policy makers and other key stakeholders, and to indicate what the experience of this programme has revealed about the development of professional practice and the nature of policy change in such a system.

Finally, in Chapter 8, Nigel Fancourt considers various aspects of research ethics in randomised controlled trials in education. First the chapter explores how research ethics are addressed in recent policy documents supporting the use of randomised controlled trials in schools. Then there is an account of the ethical issues in the CtG project and their pragmatic solutions. Five stages are identified: choice of interventions; the use of control groups; data collection; use of interim data; and subsequent research. The problems posed by two of these – choice of interventions and sharing of interim data – are then reviewed in detail in the light of the notion of equipoise, and particularly in identifying the appropriate expert community given the range of organisations involved, including schools themselves. The need for more attention to equipoise in educational research ethics, both in terms of governance and deliberation, is discussed.

Part 3: New approaches to school-based educational research

Part 3 then offers three external perspectives. In the first of these Theo Wubbels and some of his colleagues at Utrecht University in the Netherlands, discuss a project in which they were involved which has some similarities with CtG. This was an alternative but nevertheless systematic approach to securing teachers' engagement in research activity. A number of interesting differences emerge from this work including the realisation for many teachers that educational research which is qualitative in nature can be as valuable to schools as that which is predominantly quantitative.

Secondly, Paul Connolly, who leads an important research centre at Queen's University, Belfast, which specialises in RCT studies in educational practices, offers a critical perspective on the achievements of CtG. He notes the increasing priority being given to using RCTs to assess the effectiveness of interventions, but does caution that there is a danger that the outcomes of RCTs may be simplistically interpreted. For example, where an intervention is found not to be effective, the funding may be hastily removed before a fuller evaluation of the project may be undertaken. He also emphasises the importance of very careful design in such studies if their outcomes are to be valid and reliable.

Finally, Trevor Gale, now at the University of Glasgow (formerly at Deakin University, Australia), offers a highly sceptical view on the value of RCT approaches to educational research. Adopting a sociological perspective, he argues that not only are RCTs not sufficient – as their proponents, such as Higgins in Chapter 5, readily attest – but they are actually misleading and potentially dangerous, especially if they are used to inform the development of policy and practice. He suggests that RCTs are intended as a method to assess interventions in the physical world, whereas education is in essence a social process, for which RCTs are inappropriate. He makes reference to many of the earlier chapters in the book to argue the case, and brings to the fore some of the tensions that have been alluded to (more than being explicitly discussed) in these earlier chapters.

We are very grateful to all three of these authors and authorial teams for devoting such care and commitment to offering these perspectives. In the final brief concluding 'Afterword' we reflect, as editors of the volume, on what we have learned and what may be some of the implications, not only for schools and universities, or for teachers and researchers in England, but for the development of educational and research policy and practice around the world.

References

BERA-RSA. (2014). *Research and the teaching profession: building the capacity for a self-improving education system*. London: BERA.

Berry, J. (2012). Teachers' professional autonomy in England: are neo-liberal approaches incontestable? *Forum*, 54(3), 397–410.

Biesta, G. (2007). Why 'what works' won't work: evidence-based practice and the democratic deficit in educational research. *Educational Theory*, 57(1), 1–22.

Brown, P., Reay, D. and Vincent, C. (2013). Education and social mobility. *British Journal of Sociology of Education*, 34(5–6): 637–643.

Childs, A. and Menter, I. (2013). Teacher education in the 21st century in England: a case study in neo-liberal policy. *Revista Espanola de Educacion Camparada (Spanish Journal of Comparative Education)*, 22, 93–116.

Churches, R. (2016). *Closing the gap: test and learn: research report*. London: Department for Education/National College for Teaching and Leadership. Available at: https://www.gov.uk/government/publications/closing-the-gap-test-and-learn (accessed on 8 March 2016).

Department for Education (DfE). (2016). *Educational excellence everywhere* (White Paper). London: DfE.

Goldacre, B. (2013). *Building evidence into education*. London: DfE. Downloaded from: https://www.gov.uk/government/news/building-evidence-into-education (accessed on 3 May 2017).

Gu, Q., Rea, S., Smethem. L., Dunford, J., Varley, M. and Sammons, P. with Parish, N., Armstrong, P. and Powell, L. (2015). *Teaching schools evaluation – final report*. Downloaded from: https://www.gov.uk/government/uploads/system/uploads/attachment_data/file/503333/Evaluation_of_Teaching_schools_FINAL_FOR_PUB_25_feb_final_.pdf (accessed on 3 May 2017).

Lingard, B. and Gale, T. (2010). Defining educational research: a perspective of/on presidential addresses and the Australian Association for Research in Education. *The Australian Educational Researcher*, 37(1), 21–49.

Mourshed, M. and Barber, M. (2007). *How the world's best performing schools come out on top*. McKinsey & Co. Dowloaded from: https://mckinseyonsociety.com/how-the-worlds-best-performing-schools-come-out-on-top/ (accessed on 3 May 2017).

Sleeter, C. (2008). Equity, democracy, and neoliberal assaults on teacher education. *Teaching and Teacher Education*, 24, 1947–1957.

Zeichner, K. (2010). Competition, economic rationalization, increased surveillance, and attacks on diversity: neo-liberalism and the transformation of teacher education in the U.S. *Teaching and Teacher Education* 26, 1544–1552.

Part I

Closing the Gap

Test and Learn

Chapter 1

Who, how and why?

Motives and agendas for key stakeholders in Closing the Gap

Ann Childs, Roger Firth and Ian Thompson

Introduction

This chapter looks at the motives and agendas of key stakeholders in their initial and continuing involvement in the Closing the Gap: Test and Learn project (hereafter CtG). The chapter draws on training materials and interviews with respondents from: the National College of Teaching and Leadership (NCTL); the Education Development Trust (formerly CfBT Education Trust, hereafter EDT); the Centre for the Use of Research and Evidence in Education (CUREE); Durham University, School of Education (DUSE); the University of Oxford, Department of Education (OUDE); and the trial coordinators in the Teaching School Alliances (all teachers). Key ministerial speeches and policy documents associated with the setting up of this scheme are also drawn on. Bowe, Ball and Gold's (1992) 'policy cycle' model of the policy process and approach to policy analysis is used as a heuristic to ascertain the motives and agendas of stakeholders' involvement in CtG. These stakeholders had their own motives for involvement in the project, but were also representatives of their particular educational organisation. The first section of the chapter looks at the policy origins of CtG based on three strands in government policy. The second section draws particularly on the interview data to look at the motives and agendas of the stakeholders in becoming involved in the scheme. The third section focuses on the policy text production, and the final section then examines how the original motives, particularly of the Teaching Schools, evolved and changed over the lifetime of the scheme as they became involved in the 'complex and differentiated activities' that constitute the 'policy work' of CtG (Ball, Maguire, Braun and Hoskins, 2011a: 625). These sections emphasise the 'policy work' of the stakeholders, focusing on the roles and positions through which the stakeholders engage with policy and policy enactment, as well as the differentiated nature of their involvement as both implementers and agents of policy (Ball, Maguire, Braun and Hoskins, 2011b).

The policy cycle approach envisaged by Bowe et al. (1992) rejected previous top-down linear models of education policy which separated the generation and implementation phases of policy. They 'challenge[d] the separation of policy, politics and practice' (White and Crump, 1993: 415) by drawing attention to the work of policy recontextualisation that goes on in schools and more widely, as well as the need to investigate how interested parties interact and interpret policy. They 'viewed policy analysis as a process that identified policy as an interactive process rather than an end product that involved a "cycle"' (Naidu, 2011: 6). Bowe et al. (1992) drew attention to three primary policy contexts: the 'context of influence' 'where public policy is normally initiated' (p. 19); 'the context of policy text production' where policy texts are produced that *represent* policy (p. 20); and 'the context of practice' where 'policy is not simply received and implemented within this arena, rather it is subject to interpretation and then "recreated"'' (p. 22). In this way, policy can be:

> thought of as texts constituted by discourses. Policy is thus seen as a repre-sentation which is encoded and decoded in complex ways. Policy texts may be 'readerly' or 'writerly', according to the degree of interpretation allowed to the reader, but always and inevitably texts are interpreted and thus contested, adopted and adapted in different contexts of work. Thus, policy is constantly being made or remade at different educational sites.
>
> (Bowe et al., 1992: 22)

We are mindful that this approach has not escaped criticism. Hatcher and Troyna (1994), for example, in their critical appraisal of the 'policy cycle thesis' and the use of Barthes' notion of 'readerly' and 'writerly', argue that the approach 'obscures more than it illuminates' (p. 163). While acknowledging processes of reinterpretation, Hatcher and Troyna give much greater weight to the ability of the state to control outcomes and the need for 'opposition to government education policy ... to extend beyond the level of pragmatic micro-political action at the level of the individual and the school' (p. 168). Here, however, the model is being used as a means of gaining a better purchase on the nuances of the stakeholders' involvement in CtG and the complexities of the relationships that characterise the policy process within a specific gov-ernment 'intervention scheme' in its cross-sectional micro-political contexts. Our concern is not with opposition/resistance to government policy, but rather with 'taking context seriously' (Braun, Ball, Maguire and Hoskins, 2011) through our interest in stakeholders' motives and agendas for involvement in CtG and the mediated character and complex determinations of policy work within the policy community.

Context of influence

The CtG scheme was described on the DfE website in 2013 as being:

> a new scheme from the National College of Teaching and Leadership providing grants for schools and teachers to get involved in rigorous

research. The goal is to help improve the evidence-base for what works in closing the attainment gap (CTG) for disadvantaged pupils and also to stimulate robust research and development in schools. The scheme should also strengthen relationships between schools and higher education institutions.

Three strands in government policy seem to have come together to influence the setting of the CtG scheme: a stated commitment to social mobility and improving the attainment of disadvantaged students; a preference for randomised controlled trials (RCTs) in educational research; and the ambition to develop Teaching Schools and Teaching School Alliances into 'robust' leaders on research and development.

Strand 1: Government stated commitment to social mobility and improving the attainment of disadvantaged students

The Coalition Government made a clear commitment to social mobility as the principal goal of their social policy, which complemented the agenda for social justice. Together, they were seen as 'inseparable components in [the] fight against poverty and disadvantage' (HM Government, 2011: 11). Five broad principles underpinned the government's policy:

- a long-term view;
- a progressive approach;
- an evidence-based approach;
- a life cycle approach from the foundation years through school life and into the working world;
- and a recognition that Government does not have all the answers.

The aim of the life cycle approach was to 'make life chances more equal at the critical points for social mobility', the 'crucial moments, where government can make the most difference' (HM Government, 2011: 6).

A research review published by the Centre for Excellence and Outcomes in Children and Young People's Services (funded by the DfE) emphasised that:

> There is an extensive amount of research in the UK analysing the link between poverty and attainment, and in relation to other factors (gender, ethnicity, schools etc). However, there is much less quantitative evidence available in terms of 'what works' for specific interventions and strategies. There is a much larger evidence base available internationally in this area.
>
> (Sharples, Slavin, Chambers and Sharp, 2011: 1)

The aim was to summarise the best available evidence to help the government and service providers improve services and, ultimately, outcomes for children, young people and their families.

Work to close gaps in attainment between pupils from disadvantaged backgrounds and their peers is a high priority for schools. There is targeted additional funding available for schools, through the Pupil Premium (introduced in 2011), and accountability, through greater scrutiny from the new Ofsted inspection framework (2012). The growth in Teaching School Alliances (see below) and the steady rise in the numbers of national leaders of education is at the forefront of the move to a 'self-improving school system' (Rea, Hill and Dunford, 2013: 3).

Key political figures in the coalition government (2010–2015) from the Conservative Party (Michael Gove, Education Secretary) and the Liberal Democrats (David Laws, Schools Minister and Nick Clegg, Deputy Prime Minister) were seen to consistently express concerns over social mobility and a failure of schools to educate the poor and most disadvantaged in society. For example, in a speech to the Association of School and College Leaders, David Laws stated:

> Over the last decade, there has been a welcome focus on raising standards in English education. Schools with poor levels of performance have been under great pressure to improve – and rightly so. We still have some way to go to raise levels of attainment to acceptable levels in all schools. Only half of the journey is yet completed. But today I want to focus particularly on the issue of closing the achievement gap. Even as overall attainment has risen over the last decade, the attainment gap has remained stubbornly wide. It is unacceptable that in our country there is such an enormous gap between the life chances of children from poor backgrounds and other children. Last year only 38% of disadvantaged pupils achieved 5 good GCSEs, including English and Maths, or equivalent qualifications, versus 65% of other pupils. That is one of the widest achievement gaps in the world, and it is one of this Government's key objectives to dramatically narrow that gap. We want schools, local authorities and Academy chains to focus not only on overall attainment but on narrowing the attainment gaps.
>
> (Laws, 2013)

The need to 'close the gap' in educational attainment was also a recurrent and passionate theme for the then Education Secretary, Michael Gove. For example, in a speech in 2010 Gove said:

> The gap in attainment between rich and poor, which widened in recent years, is a scandal. For disadvantaged pupils, a gap opens even before primary school. Leon Feinstein's research has shown that the highest early achievers from deprived backgrounds are overtaken by lower achieving children from advantaged backgrounds by age five. Schools should be

engines of social mobility – the places where accidents of birth and the unfairness of life's lottery are overcome through the democratisation of access to knowledge. But in the school system we inherited the gap between rich and poor just widens over time.

(Gove, 2010)

This view of schools as potential 'engines of social mobility' was also echoed by David Laws:

Breaking this stubborn attainment gap between richer and poorer pupils is my party's key objective in the Department for Education. It is what drives me as a minister.

(Laws, 2014)

However, respondents from the National College had slightly different perceptions of who was actually the key player in the Coalition government that influenced the setting up of the CtG scheme. One respondent perceived that a speech from Nick Clegg in May 2012 was the key influence. As Clegg put it:

And we need teachers to help in this effort too - they're the real experts. One idea I'm keen on, and I'm looking at, is giving more teachers the chance to do some proper research with universities. When an individual teacher excels at breaking this link between poverty and educational failure they'll help maybe 5, 10, 15 pupils. But if we can turn their real life successes into hard research, into lessons that can be shared we can massively multiply the benefits - helping thousands of pupils. And, in the process, we can build new links between state schools and universities too.

(https://www.gov.uk/government/speeches/delivering-
educations-progressive-promise-using-the-pupil-
premium-to-change-lives)

However, another respondent from the NCTL perceived David Laws as the chief instigator.

Nevertheless, what certainly seems to be the case is that the Liberal Democrats in the coalition had a key influence in promoting policies that had the potential to close the gap and Michael Gove would most likely have been supportive given his clear commitment, in numerous speeches in his time as Education Minister, to social mobility and reducing educational inequity.

Strand 2: The preference for randomised controlled trials (RCTs) in educational research

A second key influence in the formulation of the CtG scheme was a focus on the use of randomised control trials (RCTs) in educational research. This focus was heavily influenced by a paper by Dr Ben Goldacre (2013) titled *Building Evidence into Education*. This paper was commissioned by the then Education Secretary Michael Gove and examined the role of research evidence on practice in the education sector. Goldacre, a medical physician, academic and journalist, had been helping the Department for Education with their Analytical Review, which looked at the role of research and evidence within the DfE and in schools and children's services. Previously, Goldacre along with others, had published the paper 'Test, learn, adapt', which set out an argument for the use of Randomised Controlled Trials (RCTs) as a basis for social policy across the public service (Haynes, Service, Goldacre and Torgerson, 2012).

In *Building Evidence into Education*, Goldacre set out to persuade educators that 'a revolution in the production and use of evidence' could and should happen in education. He argued that RCTs, as used in medicine, were the best way to find out which interventions will work best for all, and outlined what he perceived they could achieve:

> I think there is a huge prize waiting to be claimed by teachers. By collecting better evidence of what works best, and establishing a culture where this evidence is used as a matter of routine, we can improve outcomes for children, and increase professional independence.
>
> (Goldacre, 2013)

Goldacre confronted several 'myths' about RCTs including the argument that it is unethical to randomly assign children to one educational intervention or another or, indeed, to deprive them of the new intervention. He acknowledged that ethical issues associated with random allocation to interventions need to be worked through, and also, amongst other points, that RCTs are good at showing that something works but not why, which often requires qualitative research to answer.

Goldacre recognised the importance of systems to disseminate and communicate results and for professional development to enable teachers to understand and appraise the quality of the research that is done. In addition, he perceived that RCTs in education have the potential to empower teachers rather than constrain them:

> (E)vidence based practice isn't telling teachers what to do: in fact, quite the opposite. This is about empowering teachers, and setting a profession free from governments, ministers and civil servants who are overly keen on sending out edicts, insisting their new idea is the best in town.
>
> (Goldacre, 2013: 7)

We will return to the issue of teacher empowerment, through the use of RCTs, later in the chapter.

Strand 3: The ambition to develop Teaching Schools and Teaching School Alliances into 'robust' leaders in research and development

A third strand that may have influenced the development of the CtG scheme was a policy initiative, coordinated by the NCTL, to develop a network of Teaching Schools and their Alliance Schools.

> Teaching schools are seen as the transformative leaders of groups of 25 or more schools that choose to be allied to them. Together with strategic partners – other high-quality schools, higher education institutions (HEI) and other organisations – teaching schools are expected to identify, demonstrate and disseminate best practice through their role in initial teacher training, the professional development of teachers, leadership development, succession planning, school-to-school support, and research and development (R&D), so as ultimately to improve outcomes for children.
>
> (Mathews and Berwick, 2013: 5)

Teaching Schools and their alliances are part of a changing and increasingly diverse educational landscape and initiative that had been evolving for several years and was formalised by the 2010 Government white paper, *The Importance of Teaching* (DfE, 2010). 'The system has seen the emergence and proliferation of groups of schools in federations, academy chains and co-operatives of maintained and autonomous schools; system-leading schools such as national support schools (NSSs); free schools, university technical colleges (UTCs) and studio schools, and independent schools' (Mathews and Berwick, 2013: 5). Teaching Schools 'are the designated leaders of school alliances in which building knowledge and social capital and sharing leadership across partners are important ingredients of success' (ibid.).

The following statements from *Teaching Schools: First among Equals?* (Mathews and Berwick, 2013) are indicative of the thinking behind the policy:

> 'Modelling teaching schools on teaching hospitals is an idea whose time has come' (p. 9).

> 'They also need, like teaching hospitals, to conduct and draw from research' (p. 19).

> 'One well-rehearsed criticism of the British educational research effort over many years is the lack of a mechanism for integrating that research knowledge into the system. We perceive a gap between the knowledge of what works in, say, school improvement and what actually happens in schools at large' (p. 19).

Respondent 2 from the NCTL stated that the key purpose for the first cohort of Teaching Schools 'was focused on developing school-to-school support and ITT (*initial teacher training*)'. However, when the second cohort of Teaching Schools joined, all Teaching Schools were then given six core responsibilities of which research and development was one. These six responsibilities were:

1   School-led initial teacher training;
2   Continuing professional development;
3   Supporting other schools;
4   Identifying and developing leadership potential;
5   Specialist leaders of education;
6   Research and development.

Information from the DFE outlined that the scope of the research and development responsibility was to:

- build on existing research and contribute to alliance and wider priorities;
- base new schemes within your alliance on existing evidence and ensure you can measure them;
- work with other Teaching Schools in your area, or nationally, where appropriate;
- ensure that your staff use existing evidence;
- allow your staff the time and support they need take part in research and development activities;
- share learning from research and development work with the wider school system (https://www.gov.uk/guidance/teaching-schools-a-guide-for-potential-applicants#research-and-development).

Respondent 1 from the NCTL perceived that although there was a lot of research already going on in schools, principally action research, being involved in CtG and its RCT focus would:

> get more and more teachers involved in high quality research and broaden the types of research that they were doing as well as at the same time helping them to hopefully provide some of the answers around some of the things they could do.
>
> (Respondent 1, NCTL)

In summary, analysis of the data suggests therefore that it is likely that these three strands (support for closing the gap and for teacher development from the Liberal Democrats alongside proposals for using RCTs in education and, finally, the setting up of a national network of Teaching Schools charged with using research to develop their practice) were influential in supporting the development of the CtG scheme. CUREE summarised the scheme as:

a new scheme from the National College of Teaching and Leadership providing grants for schools and teachers to get involved in rigorous research. The goal is to help improve the evidence-base for what works in closing the attainment gap (CTG) for disadvantaged pupils and also to stimulate robust research and development in schools. The scheme should also strengthen relationships between schools and higher education institutions.

(http://www.curee.co.uk/ctg/overview)

Initial motives and agendas of key stakeholders for their involvement in CtG

This section again draws on interviews with key stakeholders in the CtG scheme from the NCTL, EDT, CUREE, Oxford University, Durham University and the trial coordinators in ten geographically spread Teaching School Alliances. It examines the motives and agendas of the key participants for their decisions to become involved in CtG, particularly those of the Teaching Schools and their Alliance Schools whose involvement was arguably through choice rather than by government mandate.

Being involved in a nationwide randomised controlled trial

For almost all of the respondents, the opportunity to be involved in the first nationwide randomised controlled trial in education was a significant motivating factor for three reasons. Firstly, respondents were committed to or interested in seeing how a nationwide RCT, at such a significant scale in education, would work in practice. For example, the respondent from Durham University reported that being involved in CtG built on smaller scale work on RCTs with school teachers with the group at Durham. CtG would allow them to see 'whether that (RCTs) would be feasible or beneficial at a much larger scale' as envisaged in the CtG scheme. CUREE had already 'been closely involved in the idea of randomised control trials in the education system being underused' so again, like Durham University, the opportunity to be involved in a large-scale RCT was a key motivating factor. For EDT, like Durham University, being involved in a large-scale RCT in education also built on previous work. For example, respondent 1 from EDT said that EDT had already 'funded one of the first RCTs in education which was led by Susan Greenfield'. In addition, EDT had been involved for years in working with teachers to build their capacity to do action research, and the opportunity to extend this work by the involvement of teachers in such a large-scale RCT was again a key motivating factor for their involvement. Finally, the University of Oxford also has a long standing commitment and background in supporting teachers in research-informed perspectives. The OUDE team saw their involvement in CtG as an important move 'towards teacher engagement in research . . . and this seemed like a structured opportunity to move forward on that agenda'.

Secondly, being involved in CtG at nationwide level was perceived by some of the respondents as being prestigious for the organisation concerned. As the respondent from CUREE said:

> We were conscious that as an independent organisation our standing in the system was insecure. People didn't quite know who we were. We were quite interested therefore in being associated with a serious structured piece of research, which we thought, if it came off, would be good for our reputation.
>
> (Respondent 1, CUREE)

Thirdly, the financial advantages afforded to stakeholders were perceived by some of the respondents as a key motivating factor because of the increased likelihood of significant school and teacher involvement. For example, for schools the payments for pupils to take the literacy and numeracy tests and for staff to go to training events for the interventions were significant factors in schools deciding to be involved in CtG. Funding was also important for other independent stakeholders and was particularly mentioned by respondent 1 from CUREE:

> Okay so we are an independent research organisation so – the money, having people pay for it. We were conscious that as an independent organisation our standing in the system was insecure.
>
> (Respondent 1, CUREE)

CtG as a vehicle to meet Teaching School responsibilities in R&D and other school priorities

As discussed above, involvement in CtG was perceived by many respondents as helping them better meet or extend their responsibilities in developing the research and development strand of being a Teaching School. For example, one Teaching School felt unsure about how to develop this research and development responsibility and CtG was seen to be able to meet this need. As the respondent said, 'what better than to start with a national research programme?' Many of the respondents in Teaching Schools also already reported that they were involved in doing significant amounts of research and development, principally through action research, but they were looking for more and/or different opportunities to be involved in research and development. Therefore, CtG was perceived to be a key way to achieve this. For example, in one Teaching School Alliance the opportunity of being involved in a nationwide RCT was consistent with the partner schools' priority of developing a wider evidence base to inform practice that had 'a deeper validity'. For another Teaching School, which already had a research and development ethos firmly established, being involved in CtG offered the school the opportunity to 'explore and develop new areas that would help us identify the best possible practices for our children'. Furthermore, for one school the actual intervention chosen, and then carried out, was perceived to be integral to meeting a key area of development of practice within the school. For another, being involved in CtG not only added another strand to their commitment to research and development but research and development was seen to be a key means to move the school's Ofsted grading to 'beyond outstanding'.

Commitment to social justice and closing the gap

Only two of our respondents offered the aim of closing the attainment gap (CTG) for disadvantaged pupils as an explicit motivation for being involved. For example, respondent 1 from CUREE was:

> very pleased to encounter something quite early on in the policy frame-work (of the newly elected coalition government) which represented an explicit acknowledgement of the distribution of disadvantage within the education system.

Furthermore, another Teaching School Alliance's mission was already focused on 'supporting children in challenging circumstances', and so CtG offered a further opportunity to develop this mission.

Developing Teaching School Alliances

Analysis of the data also gave interesting insights into the diversity of the ways in which Teaching Schools and their alliances worked. Many were well established with clearly identifiable school alliance networks with significant amounts of research and development, particularly action research, already taking place as indicated above. However, one respondent talked about how she saw the CtG scheme as a means to establish links and to develop her Teaching School's alliance with other schools in her area. Her school became a Teaching School in the second wave and came into an already crowded 'market' of Teaching Schools in her area. Schools that her school had been allied to historically were now linked to other Teaching School Alliances that had come in on the first wave. Therefore, for this respondent, a strong moti-vator was the aim to use the CtG as a means to attract schools to become part of her Teaching School Alliance. This aim had been achieved through the scheme and her school was now allied for the first time to new schools in the area that they had never worked with before.

Empowering teachers

Two of our respondents perceived that a key reason to be involved in CtG was that the evidence produced had the potential to empower teachers. For example, the respondent from Durham University perceived that teachers involved in RCTs would be able 'to take ownership of evidence rather than having it done to them'. A respondent from one of the Teaching School Alliances also saw RCTs as being a means for schools to provide:

> a bank of evidence-based research in order for what actually works to be done in schools, rather than the whim of a minister.

These motives also resonate strongly with the rationale offered by Goldacre (2013) above about RCTs being empowering for teachers rather than teachers always having to respond to ministers' 'edicts'.

Other motives

Finally, two other motives emerged from the analysis of the data. The first was a teacher respondent who perceived that colleagues in different positions in the school had different motives for being involved:

> Classroom teachers . . . very much want to see whether there were new things that would . . . improve achievement for children.

She also attributed this particular motivation to her head teacher. However, she felt as trial coordinator that, although she was interested in children's achievement, her role was to look at the bigger picture and how CtG was being run in the whole alliance.

Secondly, one respondent also had a strong personal rationale for being involved. She expressed a strong interest in research in education and a knowledge already of using RCTs from her particular degree background, and so she said:

> CtG and I thought here's a project with random control trials and things and that would be great and I'd love to get involved in that.

Context of policy text production

In CtG, the policy roles and agency of the stakeholders combined to make policy happen. The roles of the stakeholders, which inevitably give contours to their agency, are described first.

CtG had two phases: a consultation and initiation phase to decide which interventions would be trialled and to launch the scheme (involving four regional launch events) and a two-year programme of testing in schools. CUREE and UDSE had lead responsibility for the first phase of the scheme, overseen by the NCTL. They consulted widely within the education system to identify the interventions to be trialled (January–August 2013). CUREE and EDT, under the supervision of the NCTL, took responsibility for the launch events. EDT then took lead responsibility, under the supervision of the NCTL, for taking the project forward into the second phase with its principal partners, OUDE and CUREE (September 2013–November 2015). The testing or capacity phase involved three elements:

1   the design (CUREE and OUDE with final approval by NCTL) and delivery (OUDE) of comprehensive research training for Teaching School trial coordinators;
2   the provision of support to Teaching School trial coordinators (EDT);
3   intervention delivery training and testing within trial site schools (see Table 1.1).

The intervention delivery training and testing were carried out by the intervention developers and a provider of assessment services to schools; these stakeholders were not participants in the research carried out on the CtG scheme. The trial coordinators represented their Teaching School/Teaching School Alliance and were generally members of staff of the Teaching School, though changes of personnel were quite common across the life cycle of the scheme.

Bowe et al. (1992) describe two types of policy text as those which are 'readerly' and those which are 'writerly'. The more readerly texts have characteristics where the 'signifier/signified relationship is clear and inescapable' and where 'there is minimum opportunity for creative interpretation by the writer' (p. 11); writerly texts offer more opportunity for 'critical and creative response to the text' which 'opens up possibilities for "gaps" and moments' of 'progressive radical insertion' (p. 12). Of course, these categorisations are a matter of degree as policy texts may involve both readerly and writerly characteristics in different contexts. Nevertheless, the concept of a more writerly policy text has important implications for the agency of teachers and schools responding to policy.

The challenge for the scheme, given the demands raised above by a nationwide RCT trial, was how to minimise 'the possibility of misunderstandings' and to give as 'exhaustive' guidance as possible. The scheme seemed to be set up to achieve this high level of control in two principal ways. Firstly, face-to-face events (see Table 1.1) were held, supported by extensive PowerPoints and support materials, and secondly, the scheme generated highly detailed tools and protocols to prescribe, for example, how pupils would be selected by the trial.

In the initial stages of the CtG scheme, the policy texts which guided the implementation of the RCTs were highly structured and prescriptive and could be characterised as more readerly. For example, the launch events and their materials were formulated and presented 'in the language of general public good' (Bowe et al., 1992: 20). Their appeal was based upon claims about improving the evidence-base for what works in closing the attainment gap

Table 1.1 Characteristics of policy texts at CtG events

Timing	Event	Characteristics of policy texts
June/July 2013	Launch events in Nottingham, London, Bristol and Manchester	Readerly
October/November 2013	Training Round 1 in locations around the UK	Readerly
November 2013	Intervention training	Readerly
December/January 2013–2014	The research and development networking events (RDNEs)	At first readerly and then more writerly
June/July 2014	Training Round 2	Writerly
April/May 2015	Training Round 3	Writerly

for disadvantaged pupils and the importance of stimulating 'robust research' and development in schools. In addition, it was emphasised that the scheme should also strengthen relationships between schools and higher education institutions. The events encompassed the intention of incorporating schools and teachers into the government's scheme; it was not an invitation to creatively reinterpret it.

The fact that the training materials, co-designed by CUREE and OUDE, were given final approval by NCTL also emphasises the readerly nature of the policy texts. The delivery of research training for trial coordinators involved three one-day regional training events administered by OUDE and overseen by the NCTL. The first training event covered the nature, purposes and benefits of randomised controlled trials, the principles of randomisation and their operationalisation. The event also introduced the key tools and protocols developed to ensure fidelity in the RCTs. There was particular emphasis on the pupil identification tool, which gave step-by-step procedures by which pupils had to be selected for the trials. The training event sought to ensure that schools were able to contribute effectively to the trials and that coordinators and teachers in different contexts were able to deliver the interventions under trial in a consistent manner.

This level of control is consistent with the fact that the scheme required a diverse range of Teaching Schools and their Alliance Schools to conduct randomised control trials for a range of interventions where issues of accurate identification of sample students, fidelity of implementation of the intervention, for example, were of crucial importance. Indeed, the RCT methodology *itself* demanded readerly texts which tightly controlled what the participant schools did and which were subject to minimal levels of interpretation.

After the first training event, once schools had been assigned as control or intervention schools, the intervention group were then trained by the intervention providers in how to deliver the intervention. The provision of support for trial coordinators was delivered through research development and networking events (RDNEs) run by EDT, which focused on delivering the interventions and also training teachers in the delivery of small-scale RCTs. This immediately generated school-level activity. An 'Early Adopters' scheme was set up, which supported and funded 50 schools/school alliances in the design and running of their own experimental research designs involving small-scale RCTs. This early adopter micro-enquiry activity focused on school concerns, and it was apparent that schools' involvement in CtG was both shaped by and shaping their attitudes to and capacity for research more generally. The RDNEs seemed to catalyse changes in schools' engagement with and in research.

As the scheme developed, more writerly texts seemed to emerge, specifically the materials for the second and third training events. At the time of the second training round, the intervention schools had carried out the intervention(s) and the assessment (post-test). The second training event aimed to feedback on progress and strengthen research and development capacity in Teaching Schools and their alliances. This involved: sharing and analysing experiences and understandings; a consideration of the second year of the scheme and action planning; consideration of alternative and possible future strategic research and development issues to connect with school agendas; and dissemination and/or knowledge exchange of the intervention trials. The final training event in April/May 2015 involved thinking back and looking forward, as well as further consideration of dissemination. It was therefore seen as appropriate for participating schools to begin to explore their own ways to enhance the RCT research, for example, with more qualitative research, within the context of their research and development responsibilities, as well as to think of ways to disseminate the aspects of the scheme.

Context of practice – how did motives and practice play out during implementation?

> The key point is that policy is not simply received and implemented within this arena rather it is subject to interpretation and then 'recreated'.
>
> (Bowe et al. 1992: 22)

This section focuses on the way the CtG scheme played itself out in practice. In particular, this section examines the ways and the extent to which the policy was 'subject to interpretation' and recreated by the Teaching Schools and their alliances. The first part looks at how certain Teaching Schools and alliances exhibited some degree of agency and adapted the scheme according to their own specific circumstances. The second part identifies different motives within the schools with regards to how the CtG scheme was perceived and would be taken forward. The third part discusses the emergence of a sub-group of 50 schools, the early adopters, who undertook 'their own micro-enquiry projects' (Churches, 2016: 15) and who, we will argue, evolved during the course of the scheme from 'policy subjects . . . to policy actors' (Ball et al., 2011b: 622).

Adaptation and agency

As discussed earlier, once Teaching Schools had opted to take part in the CtG scheme, the policy texts to implement the RCTs gave very little room for flexibility or creativity. However, evidence from the training rounds, interviews and the report on the scheme (Churches, 2016) shows that schools did adapt the different interventions. As Churches said:

> Teacher qualitative evidence supplied during the two end-of-year surveys, and from the national event focus group data suggested that teachers had adapted interventions to suit their context.
>
> (Churches, 2016: 18)

Specific examples of this came from the second training round sessions and the interviews conducted for this book. For example, schools reported that the Numicon interventions, planned to be carried out by teaching assistants in one school, were actually carried out by experienced teachers. In addition, one trial coordinator involved in AfA talked about how the school had adapted the structured conversations and made them more useful as AfA was very much being used as a means to meet a key school development priority of developing closer links to parents. This school, however, went further than just adjusting the intervention by testing all pupils in that they felt that the NGRT would be valuable for all their students.

How then can we understand these adaptations? Bowe et al. (1992) talk about 'resistance' or indeed 'subterfuge' in the implementation process and go on to say:

> Parts of text will be rejected, selected out, ignored, deliberately misunderstood, responses may be frivolous.
>
> (Bowe et al., 1992: 22)

However, the examples given here do not seem to show resistance, subterfuge or even rejection. It could be argued in the case of the Numicon and AfA example that instructions for the implementation of interventions were 'deliberately misunderstood', 'selected' or 'ignored', and these changes seem to have been done for reasons of professional concern to adapt the scheme to fit better with the particular context in which the intervention was being implemented. This lack of the more negative connotations of implementation such as resistance, subterfuge or rejection might be explained by the fact that schools had chosen to take part (with the reservations about choice indicated above).

In addition, the policy texts and the nature of the scheme were, as we have argued, more 'readerly' giving 'a minimum of opportunity for creative interpretation by the reader' (Bowe et al., 1992: 10), but the adaptation here and agency shown in these examples were modest and were shaped, as Braun et al. (2011) argue, by 'school-specific factors' (p. 585).

There was, however, one voice of dissent from a Teaching School and its Alliance Schools who were initially engaged and enthusiastic in the CtG scheme. This seems to be because they perceived that the scheme was poorly organised and implemented, and when they came into the scheme they already had a strong and vibrant research culture which they felt was not recognised and that there was 'a false assumption that schools were new to the principles of evidence based research'. Therefore, their commitment to CtG 'dwindled' over the two-year course of the scheme as they became more and more disillusioned with the scheme. Could this response then be described as 'resistance', 'subterfuge' or even 'rejection' of the policy (Bowe et al., 1992)? Their response does look very much like rejection. However, one could argue that rejection, in Bowe et al.'s typology, occurs in relation to a policy that has been imposed in a top-down way, which may have significant implications for a school in a high accountability system. In this example, rejection could be argued to be qualitatively different in that involvement in CtG was voluntary and rejection may have had little or no implications for this strong, confident and united Teaching School Alliance that already had a vibrant research culture.

Different motives that developed in schools during the course of the scheme

The initial importance attached to being involved in the RCT trial and the hard evidence it would provide for 'what works' became less important for some respondents over the course of the CtG scheme. Some respondents perceived that, in their schools, the importance of the nationwide results became less prominent as the scheme proceeded and that the benefits that the intervention at school/classroom level had come more into focus. For example, one respondent, whose school was trialling AfA (where no national results were yet available at the time of the interview), indicated that the school had already seen benefits in the school, for example, in the use of an audit tool and the more effective use of structured conversations with parents. Therefore, he perceived that they would continue with the intervention regardless of the results of nationwide trial results. Taking this point further, respondents also perceived that, because of the different positions of professionals within their schools, different motivations and responsibilities emerged during the course of the scheme about how it would be taken on into the future. As one respondent said:

> I don't think individual teachers will respond to that (the results of the RCTs) if I am honest. I think it's more of a leadership response to then

make whole school decisions based on evidence and that's where the report will have an influence. Teachers are exposed to loads of different CPD, loads of different agenda, loads of different information coming at them and if they pick up on something and become enthused by it will have a positive impact because of the way they use it and are enjoying using it. But making big decisions about how to organise the curriculum and whether you have a day a week where you do growth mindsets that's where you need the results of trials like these.

In agreement with this, another respondent perceived that the head teacher of the school would be interested in the trial findings because the head teacher makes the strategic/financial decisions for their school. Therefore, the results from RCTs, she believed, would be compelling for the head teacher in making those larger policy decisions about whether to adopt/fund an intervention at whole school and/or alliance level. However, she also perceived that the classroom teachers in her school, and other teachers in the Alliance Schools, had seen considerable benefits in using the interventions with individual pupils and may, even if the national results show negative gains for a particular intervention, want to continue to use the interventions they had trialled. Indeed, another respondent, a Teaching School leader with over 300 schools in their alliance, recognised herself the difference in her responses to the interventions as opposed to the classroom teachers in her school involved in implementing them. She contended that the classroom teachers:

> were looking specifically at their classes. So they were looking for a very child led sort of focus, whereas I'm looking from their co-coordinator's point of view. . . But I was looking at the bigger picture.

These findings resonate with literature on policy enactment in schools, for example in Ball et al.'s (2011a) case study of four schools in the UK where they argued that 'Actors in schools are positioned differently and take up different positions in relation to policy' (Ball et al., 2011a: 625). Further, Bowe et al. in their study of the introduction of the Education Reform Act in 1988 in England and Wales into schools stated that:

> Practitioners do not confront policy texts as naive readers, they come with their histories, with experience, with values and purposes of their own, they have vested interests in the meaning of policy.
>
> (Bowe et al., 1992: 22)

In our case, the senior leaders in these schools often had different values, purposes and vested interests from the teachers in the classroom. For example, their vested interests as senior leaders were in making decisions for the school and potentially its Alliance Schools which, as demonstrated above, would have significant economic implications for the alliance. For this reason, they perceived they needed 'hard' evidence of what works. In contrast the teachers' values, purposes and vested interests were located much more in their class-rooms and in 'seeing' the immediate benefits of the intervention for these pupils. Therefore, as we have shown, they perceived the policy and its implementation in very different ways from their leaders.

Early adopters' grants programme

A sub-group of schools formed within the nationwide RCT which were called 'Early Adopters'. As well as being involved in the large-scale trial, they also conducted mini RCTs themselves in school. These mini trials were funded by grants from the NCTL. This programme developed from four half-day training modules on RCTs which were conducted in the research and development networking events (RDNEs). The initial aim of these modules was for the trial co-coordinators to better understand the RCT process and:

> to understand the terminology to know what they were a part of and then to feel more comfortable.
>
> (Respondent 1, EDT)

Respondent 1, from EDT, facilitated these training modules and said:

> immediately after the first event a small group of teachers went off and did a trial. So Teacher X in the north of England, she did a quick within subject RCT over a couple of lessons with her A level students.
>
> (Respondent 1, EDT)

Once the enthusiasm and the potential for schools to do their own mini RCTs through work in these network meetings became apparent, EDT sought funds from the NCTL for schools to run their own mini RCTs. This funding was secured and some 50 schools who were interested applied for funds to join the Early Adopters scheme. In one Teaching School Alliance their involvement in the Early Adopters scheme, and running their own RCTs, had been extended to other Alliance Schools. As Respondent 1 reports, some schools collaborated to increase sample sizes for these school-led RCTs:

> However if you start to collaborate, you can do it (increase sample size) so Teacher X's trial that he's finished one of the first ones from our grant managed to do across 11 schools and has 213 in his study altogether by taking a collaborative approach.
>
> (Respondent 1, EDT)

Respondents from four Teaching School Alliances who received grants from the Early Adopters programme talked about its many benefits, for example: increase in collaboration in research and development between Alliance Schools; empowering of schools in having control over their own research agenda and determining 'what works' within their own contexts; and more focused and systematic research and the development of teachers responsible for leading research across alliances. Indeed, for one group, RCTs had now superseded action research in their schools and, as one respondent said, 'the action researchers have become RCT[ers]'. However, although many of the Early Adopter schools became very committed to RCTs as a major or 'the' form of doing research-informed practice, there were others who perceived that RCTs, whilst valuable, were part of a whole toolkit of ways in which they could engage in research-informed practice in their schools.

The emergence of the Early Adopter scheme seems to show that it did genuinely create ' "space" for manoeuvre' (Bowe et al., 1992: 14). In contrast to the case of the more 'readerly' policy text of the main trial where there was 'minimum opportunity for creative interpretation', the early adopter programme allowed for creativity and innovation to flourish. There seems to be three key reasons for this: firstly, the provision of funds allowed schools to invest in staff time and resources to carry out the mini RCTs. Secondly, Respondent 1's (EDT) role in the programme seems to have been absolutely crucial in initiating the programme and then in supporting it. Ball et al. (2011b), in identifying policy actors in schools, talk about policy actors who are outsiders and act as entrepreneurs and partners. They contend that 'some policies in schools can only be "brought off" by including outsiders in the policy process', and Respondent 1 seems to have fulfilled this role. Our respondent talked about how he encouraged schools to apply for the Early Adopter programme, provided individual support to conduct the mini RCTs, helped schools analyse their data and provided opportunities for schools to disseminate their findings to wider audiences, for example:

> And you know Respondent 1, he allowed me so many opportunities you know going to Bradford and presenting at the University there as well about what I'd done, and things like that. That was beyond what I would have thought you know being a teacher I would be doing. So it was a brilliant opportunity, and hopefully the teachers that we've had during this time of what we've been doing research do go on and use it or kind of promote it to then these schools.

A third reason why this programme flourished was that the leaders in these Early Adopter programmes had characteristics as policy actors themselves of being 'entrepreneurs', 'enthusiasts' and 'translators' with their colleagues (Ball et al., 2011a). Indeed, Ball et al. describe entrepreneurs, for example, as 'forceful agents of change, who are personally invested in and identified with policy ideas and their enactment' (p. 628), and certainly the evidence from the interviews with all the respondents involved in the early adopter scheme show they possessed all these qualities.

Finally, taking the scheme as a whole, the Early Adopter scheme seems to have emerged as the most surprising and perhaps the most significant positive outcome in terms of teacher professional learning and development from the CtG scheme. To sum this point up, Respondent 2 from EDT said:

> That has been interesting to see how schools have taken experimental research forward and which areas they would focus on and to encourage them to focus on their own school improvement agenda. This aspect has been quite important for us as an organisation as it was unexpected. It has signalled what teachers are capable of and they can use a number of research methods and not just the ones they are more familiar with and have used in the past . . . I think it is where people have tried to do it themselves, on a small scale, *that we have seen the most learning* [our emphasis]. They are then faced with the challenges of what is your research design, how are you going to test the intervention, who is going to participate, how you are going to organise it and how you are going to randomly allocate children to the intervention and the control groups. It is where people have had to do this on the ground that they have had to get to grips with these questions as a result.

Conclusion

The motives for the key stakeholders of Durham, the NCTL, CUREE and EDT involved in setting up the scheme remained consistent throughout the scheme: the opportunity to implement what they perceived as an RCT done at scale; the development of research capacity in schools; and the extension of evidence-based practice through teachers' and schools' collaboration in research. OUDE shared the last two objectives, whilst perhaps because of their involvement after the initial design phase were more interested in mixed-method research evidence than the introduction of RCTs as a schools research methodology. For Teaching School Alliances, and the teachers within them, the picture was much more mixed. All were committed to evidence-based practice to close the gap through understanding research, but there was a wide range of motives and indeed existing practice. For some teachers, either as trial coordinators or as teachers from schools allied to a Teaching School, the scheme was an important part of establishing a working relationship across the alliance. Others, mostly from the Early Adopters group, started to believe that the real importance of the scheme was in developing their capacity to implement either a mini RCT or more mixed-methods approaches to research. Finally, as the scheme developed, there also seemed to be a suggestion of the divergence of motives with classroom teachers implementing the interventions valuing the outcomes they could see in their classrooms and head teachers valuing the results of the RCTs in their decision-making roles.

In terms of the other two policy strands – developing research and development capacity in Teaching Schools and CtG for the most disadvantaged students – the findings do seem to indicate that the involvement of Teaching Schools did allow them to address their research and development responsibilities, learn from the involvement and use this as a basis for extending their research repertoire, particularly those who were involved in the Early Adopter scheme. However, only two of the respondents expressed as an explicit motive the opportunity to be involved in a scheme whose aim was to close the educational gap for the most disadvantaged students. The principal motivation expressed seemed to be focused on the opportunity to be involved in a nationwide RCT for all the reasons outlined in the paragraph above.

Finally, the findings also gave some insights into the Teaching Schools themselves and their alliances and how this particular government initiative was being implemented. The findings indicate that all of the respondents in the Teaching Schools were engaged in some form of research, principally action research, which seemed to be more embedded in some Teaching Schools than others. However, the findings also indicate that the strength of the alliance associated with the Teaching Schools varied considerably from those with strong, well-linked Alliance Schools to those whose alliances were much more unstable and fluctuating. For these, as indicated above, CtG became a key vehicle for establishing and then developing relationships with their Alliance Schools.

References

Ball, S.J., Maguire, M., Braun, A. and Hoskins, K. (2011a) Policy actors: doing policy work in schools. *Discourse: Studies in the Cultural Politics of Education* 32(4): 625–639.

Ball, S.J., Maguire, M., Braun, A. and Hoskins, K. (2011b) Policy subjects and policy actors in schools: some necessary and insufficient analyses. *Discourse: Studies in the Cultural Politics of Education* 32(4): 611–624.

Bowe, R., Ball, S.J. and Gold, A. (1992) *Reforming Education and Changing Schools*. London: Routledge.

Braun, A., Ball, S., Maguire, M. and Hoskins, K. (2011) Taking context seriously: towards explaining policy enactments in the secondary school, *Discourse: Studies in the Cultural Politics of Education*, 32(4): 585–596.

Churches, R. (2016) *Closing the Gap: Test and Learn: research report*. Winter 2016, Nottingham: NCTL.

Department for Education (DfE) (2010) *The Importance of Teaching: The Schools White Paper 2010*. Available online: https://www.gov.uk/government/uploads/system/uploads/attachment_data/file/175429/CM-7980.pdf

Goldacre, B. (2013) *Building Evidence into Education*. Available online: http://aka.education.gov.uk/inthenews/a00222740/building-evidence-into-education

Gove (2010) Speech to the Westminster Academy, 9 September 2010. Available online: https://www.gov.uk/government/speeches/michael-gove-to-westminster-academy

Hatcher, R. and Troyna, B. (1994) The 'policy cycle': a ball by ball account. *Journal of Education Policy* 9(2): 155–170.

Haynes, L., Service, O., Goldacre, B. and Torgerson, D. (2012) *Test, Learn, Adapt: Developing Public Policy with Randomised Controlled Trials*. https://www.gov.uk/government/publications/test-learn-adapt-developing-public-policy-with-randomised-controlled-trials

HM Government (2011) *Opening Doors, Breaking Barriers: A Strategy for Social Mobility*. Available online: https://www.gov.uk/government/uploads/system/uploads/attach ment_data/file/61964/opening-doors-breaking-barriers.pdf

Laws, D. (2013) Speech on 'closing the achievement gap' to the Association of School and College Leaders, 5 March. Available online: https://www.gov.uk/government/speeches/closing-the-achievement-gap

Laws, D. (2014) Speech on grammar schools. 19 June. Available online: https://www.gov.uk/government/speeches/david-laws-speech-on-grammar-schools

Mathews, P. and Berwick, G. (2013) *Teaching Schools: First Among Equals?* Nottingham: National College for Teaching and Leadership.

Naidu, S. (2011) *Teachers and the Policy Reform Agenda: The Changing Emphasis in Educational Policy Analysis*. Available online: http://files.eric.ed.gov/fulltext/ED526 977.pdf

Ofsted (2012) *The Framework for School Inspection*. London: Ofsted. Available online: https://www.gov.uk/government/publications/the-framework-for-school-inspection

Rea, S., Hill, R. and Dunford, J. (2013) *Closing the Gap: How System Leaders and Schools Can Work Together*. Nottingham: National College for Teaching and Leadership. Available online: http://www.isospartnership.com/uploads/files/ctg-how-system-leaders-and-schools-can-work-together-full-report.pdf

Sharples, J., Slavin, R., Chambers, B. and Sharp, C. (2011) *Effective Classroom Strategies for Closing the Gap in Educational Achievement for Children and Young People Living in Poverty, Including White Working-class Boys*. London: Centre for Excellence and Outcomes in Children and Young People's Services. Available online: https://www.york.ac.uk/media/iee/documents/Closing%20the%20Gap.pdf

White, C. and Crump. S. (1993) Education and the three 'p's: policy, politics and practice. A review of the work of S.J. Ball. *British Journal of Sociology of Education* 14(4): 415–429.

Chapter 2

Closing the Gap

Test and Learn – an unprecedented national educational research project

Richard Churches, Robin Hall and Juliet Brookes

Introduction

This chapter provides a summary of the final Department for Education research report from Closing the Gap: Test and Learn (Churches, 2016) and seeks to draw out the main features of the programme, the different phases of delivery and the developments that took place in response to the increasing levels of engagement that schools demonstrated. It also summarises the large-scale trial results and learning from these. Closing the Gap: Test and Learn was the first programme in the world to trial multiple interventions simultaneously using a wholly collaborative approach across a large number of schools. Seven interventions were chosen through an extensive and systematic consultation and review of interventions seen as most likely to close the attainment gap for pupils with achievement below the national average in literacy and numeracy. Collaborative randomised controlled trials (RCTs) were then conducted to evaluate these interventions and four of the interventions were replicated. Alongside this, teachers were trained in a range of research methods. A total of 50 teacher-led experimental studies (including RCTs designed and conducted by schools) were grant funded. This report describes the programme and its delivery. It also outlines the findings from the large-scale trials, learning from developing teachers' scientific literacy through the school-led research programme and conclusions regarding the efficacy of system-led research approaches such as the ones embedded within the initiative.

Programme management

From the outset, the programme had an innovative and collaborative structure that evolved as the programme progressed. The National College for Teaching and Leadership (NCTL), an executive agency of the Department for Education (DfE), commissioned an extended partnership to manage the implementation of the programme through a competitive tender. CfBT Education Trust (now rebranded as Education Development Trust) acted as the lead provider for the implementation and dissemination phase of the programme. They worked in partnership with the Centre for the Use of Research Evidence in Education

(CUREE), Oxford University and Durham University. This partnership worked on materials development, training and support for the schools that were involved, including launch events, three training rounds across the country, research development and networking events, online events and contributions to the final report. CUREE and Durham University also led the initial extensive consultation during which over 70 interventions nominated by Teaching Schools were scrutinised to determine the seven interventions that would form the heart of the large-scale RCT programme.

All Teaching Schools in England were invited to participate in the scheme, and a further recruitment round was conducted prior to the start of the second year and the replication programme. In this second round, Teaching Schools that had not previously had the opportunity to join were approached and new starters brought on board to increase sample size during the replications. In total, over the two-year implementation phase, the programme worked with 206 Teaching Schools. A total of 673 groups of children in trial site schools completed pre- and post-tests.

The role of the Teaching Schools themselves was also highly innovative, as (following training) they were given the role of directly managing the trials and the testing processes from their schools. Their role included:

- appointing a trial co-ordinator;
- recruiting trial site schools from within their alliances and networks;
- purchasing places on the training courses provided by the intervention providers;
- passing on training and administration details;
- managing the fidelity of the trials in the trial site schools, a role with increasing challenge in the year 2 replications as the schools had to manage separation between a control group and intervention group within the same school.

In the first year, 387 trial sites schools took part in the trials, with 15,292 pupils tested. In the second year, 286 schools (5,530 pupils) completed the trials. Intervention providers maintained their natural roles within the trials ensuring high levels of mundane realism (everyday activity). Although in some cases special events had to be put on to accommodate the volume of Closing the Gap: Test and Learn participants, in many cases programme participants attended training alongside other teachers from schools outside the programme who had also purchased the commercial training. Importantly, no additional efforts were made to change the nature of the commercial products beyond the way in which they were normally trained and had been trained prior to inclusion within the trials. The exceptions to the above were RTI (RTI was originally used with year 6 pupils, but was adapted for this programme for use with a broader range of ages), a programme developed in partnership with AfA for an Education Endowment Foundation (EEF) sponsored trial and the version of RLS which was written specifically for use on the programme by CUREE. There was, at the time that the programme commenced, no comparable commercial version of RLS available at scale in England. The materials produced by this process were developed as Crown Copyright.

Unlike many of the other RCTs that have taken place in education, a different approach to the provision of intervention was taken. The schools themselves were required to contact the commercial provider, book their teachers onto the training (within prescribed time windows) and attend the training without DfE/NCTL direct oversight. The same approach was taken with regard to the purchasing of the pre- and post-tests from GL Assessment. The schools also managed the administration of the testing, choosing the date that they would do this (also within a window that was prescribed centrally). This required schools to identify and book suitable facilities to allow the children to take the online test, a function which was challenging for some smaller primary schools that lacked onsite computer facilities at scale.

Adopting this approach meant that the research programme as a whole had a high level of mundane realism, improving the programme's external validity and arguably the generalisability of the findings. In other words, the programme was able to create the type of general conditions that might occur in normal daily life where a school had decided to purchase a place for their teachers on a commercial programme with a view to cascading and implementing that training in their schools – whilst evaluating it with an externally purchased standardised test.

With this, of course, came a possible risk to the internal validity of the trials (particularly with regard to whether the protocol delivery was a fitting representation of the provider's product), as considerable levels of trust were being placed on the schools themselves. Indeed, teacher qualitative evidence supplied during the two end-of-year surveys, and from the national event focus group data, suggested that teachers had adapted interventions to suit their context. Again, however, this is something that would be expected in normal everyday circumstances. There is always a tension in experimental research between external and internal validity. Where a laboratory-style trial can generate high levels of internal validity, its external validity (generalisability of the findings) may be questioned. The opposite is likely to be true for larger-scale, more extended studies that aim to create real-world conditions.

Programme phases, support and materials

There were three phases to the programme:

- a consultation phase (January to August 2013);
- a capability phase in which the research programmes and training of schools took place (September 2013 to July 2015);

- a dissemination phase involving an event for early adopters of teacher-led experimental research (as they became known) and a national dissemination event involving focus groups (October and November 2015).

The purpose of the consultation phase, described in detail in Chapter 4, was to identify a set of interventions which the current evidence supported as being effective in closing the attainment gap for lower-performing pupils, with a view to evaluating them using large-scale RCTs. It was also during the consultation phase that the research design for the first phase of trialling and timelines for pre- and post-testing were determined. The first part of the consultation took the form of online surveys and focus groups with partner Teaching Schools and schools that had expressed an interest in contributing. A total of 233 responses were received to the survey and 19 teachers were involved in focus groups and discussions. NCTL also asked school leaders to nominate interventions and received 24 suggestions. The survey and focus group data offered a list of over 70 potential interventions. The team from CUREE and Durham University used a process designed to select a long list (of 12–18 interventions) most suitable for trialling on the basis of:

- an ability to assess the intervention's planned outcomes and its suitability for use within an RCT;
- the manageability of the intervention within the programme timescales, resource levels and the likely demands on participating schools;
- the extent to which the intervention matched the criteria identified by schools in the consultation process and, hence, the likelihood of take-up by them.

The Teaching Schools' research and development (R&D) advisory group then carried out a ranking exercise for the long-list interventions, considering them in terms of likely take-up and manageability for large-scale trialling. This process, combined with the technical scores identified by the Durham University and CUREE team, produced a provisional final list of interventions which was confirmed as the final list after a number of technical and logistical uncertainties were resolved.

The final list of interventions selected was as follows:

- 1stClass@Number (1stClass)
- Achievement for All (AfA)
- Growth mindsets
- Inference training
- Numicon intervention programme (NIP)
- Research lesson study (RLS)
- Response to intervention: breakthroughs in literacy (RTI).

The final element of the first phase of the project aimed to help establish the conditions for its successful implementation by the school-based R&D team at NCTL and the phase 2 capability partnership (CfBT Education Trust supported by Oxford University, CUREE and Durham University). This involved:

- establishing (sometimes, negotiating) with the intervention providers the detail of their provision and, in particular, how training would be provided for the trial site schools;
- producing broad descriptions of each of the interventions for the benefit of the Teaching School leaders who would have the first-line responsibility for co-ordinating the interventions in their participating schools;
- devising (drawing extensively on Durham University's expertise) the protocols for managing the interventions to provide the most robust environment for conducting RCTs given the programme's distributed leadership context;
- providing advice and guidance to the NCTL school-based R&D team on other features of the programme, particularly the selection, design and logistics of testing and the management of the randomisation process;
- documenting the process and creating guides and other resources for trainers, Teaching School co-ordinators and staff in the trial site schools.

There were three elements to the capability phase of the programme:

1   the delivery of comprehensive training for Teaching Schools;
2   the provision of support to Teaching School trial co-ordinators;
3   Teaching School testing and intervention delivery within trial site schools.

The delivery of comprehensive training for Teaching Schools participating in the Closing the Gap: Test and Learn programme covered rigorous and robust research methods appropriate for use in schools, including quantitative research methods such as RCTs, so that teachers gained an awareness of research methodologies (set-up, design and evaluation) and were able to contribute effectively to the trials. This also ensured that teachers in different contexts were able to deliver the interventions under trial in a consistent manner. The strand of work delivered through the Research Development and Networking Events (RDNE) focused on training teachers in the delivery of small-scale RCTs (and other forms of experimental research) and immediately yielded school-level activity. In response to this, the NCTL made available 50 'early adopter' grants to support participating Teaching Schools and their alliances in delivering their own small-scale RCTs. These studies were presented at a conference poster event at NCTL in Nottingham on 21 October 2015. The teacher-led research is reported on in detail in . Teacher poster examples can be found in the reports from NCTL (2016b–g).

All materials supplied to Teaching Schools were presented in a format that supports cascading and re-delivery to teachers in the wider body of trial site schools. For example, the launch event and training round 1 materials were included on a CD-ROM and Teaching Schools were supplied with a binder to help them organise the materials. As new materials were delivered these were all made available in an online 'Dropbox', which included a video of the first launch event to support schools to share the vision· and aims of the programme within their networks. Using the materials supplied at the launch events and during training round 1, participating Teaching Schools and trial site schools carried out a programme of testing over a period of two academic years (September 2013–July 2015). This focused on assessing whether the seven selected interventions made a positive difference and whether such effects may be replicable and transferable.

Two dissemination events took place – on 21 October 2015 in Nottingham and on 18 November 2015 in London. The first event was attended by teachers who had conducted their own teacher-led RCTs (and other forms of experimental research) ('early adopters') together with some invited guests. The second event was open to all participating Teaching Schools and included presentations summarising the large-scale trial findings and the small-scale teacher-led studies alongside two teacher research presentations. Both of these events included focus group sessions. The final project report was drafted with contributions from CfBT Education Trust, the Oxford University partner team, CUREE, Durham University and NCTL. Large-scale trial results analyses were undertaken by analysts from the DfE.

In order to implement the programme, a broad range of support was developed. This included launch events, training round training days, research development and networking events (RDNEs), materials and a helpline. In relation to the delivery of support in year 1, participating Teaching School trial co-ordinators (who were leading the delivery of the research across their nominated trial site schools) were offered attendance at a launch event, two one-day training events (training rounds 1 and 2) and two RDNEs. A further training event (training round 3) was delivered in the second academic year, as well as two further RDNEs. The content of training events (rounds 2 and 3) and RDNEs (rounds 1–4) included learning about research methods along with expert input that ensured the project remained engaging and developmental for the schools.

The four RDNEs, as well as providing the opportunity for participating Teaching Schools to network and learn from one another's experience, were designed to provide a comprehensive programme of learning that enabled schools to design and deliver their own small-scale RCTs. Thus, in turn, they sought to develop teachers' scientific literacy within the context of the programme. The programme, embedded within the four events, covered the following:

- designing an RCT and exploring different research designs. For example, the advantages and disadvantages of between-subject versus within-subject designs, choosing and designing tests to ensure validity and reliability and pre- and post-test designs and when to use them. Teachers were also taught about quasi-experimental designs and the testing of more than one intervention at once;
- implementation, sampling, sample size and randomisation (using Excel). This included managing a trial to avoid confounding variables that might arise as a result of delivery;
- statistical analysis and interpretation of findings. This included how to conduct preliminary assumption testing, calculating effect sizes, selecting the right test and reporting levels of significance. CfBT Education Trust's Excel StatsWizard, which can conduct the main tests teachers needed to use, was made available during the programme. Teachers with more complex designs were given support by the Programme Director;
- writing up quantitative research and understanding the conventions that apply to this style of research. This session also sought to develop schools' capacity to critique such research and included the use of poster design, building on the extremely well-received training delivered by Oxford University at training event 2.

All programme materials designed by the programme were provided in hard-copy format to delegates and made available in an online 'Dropbox' access point. A1-sized trials timeline posters outlining key dates during the first and second years of the programme were designed, produced and circulated to trial co-ordinators (see Churches, 2016 for an illustration). A Closing the Gap: Test and Learn information leaflet aimed at informing higher educational institutes (HEIs) about the programme was developed and disseminated via participating Teaching Schools. In respect of the trialled interventions, the standard materials used by the various commercial suppliers were given to schools in the inter-ventions as part of the payment made by the schools directly to those suppliers. A dedicated email address and telephone helpline for use by participating Teaching Schools were operational throughout the programme.

The large-scale trials

Six of the seven interventions trialled were existing programmes, owned, licensed or managed by charities supported by chargeable training courses. The exception to this was RLS, which was designed specifically for the programme by CUREE based on the practice of lesson study that was developed in Japan. Whereas all the other interventions were immediately available, enabling participants to purchase places on the training programme within a specified date window, RLS needed to be adapted for the purposes of the programme. The developed protocol was then piloted in year 1 of the programme with 20 schools.

AfA is a whole-school improvement framework lasting two years focused on the lowest achieving 20 per cent of learners. It was developed and is delivered by Achievement for All 3As. The intervention works through four dimensions: leadership of achievement for all, teaching and learning, parental engagement and wider outcomes. AfA was evaluated using an RCT over two years. 1stClass@Number is delivered by trained teaching assistants (TAs) to small groups of pupils in year 3 who have fallen behind in mathematics. The intervention was designed and is delivered by Edge Hill University. TAs work with pupils for eight weeks using detailed lesson plans and adapting them according to information gained from structured assessments. Growth mindsets is a training programme developed by the University of Portsmouth. It uses approaches to teaching and learning aimed at creating 'growth mindsets' developed from the research by Carol Dweck (Blackwell, Trzesniewski and Dweck, 2007) which indicates that teachers' and students' beliefs about intelligence have an impact on learning. Inference training was developed by Leicester City Council based on Yuill and Oakhill's research (Yuill and Oakhill, 1988). It claims to help students make meaning as they read. This involves learning vocabulary, using their background knowledge, making inferences and building up meaning. The NIP approach develops conceptual understanding in mathematics using multi-disciplinary/multi-sensory approaches, making use of apparatus and focusing on action, imagery and conversation. NIP is normally aimed at year 2 pupils working below age-related expectations.

A version of RLS was developed in partnership with schools during the first year of the programme by CUREE. This was trialled in year 2 of the programme. RLS is a structured professional development process in which teachers systematically examine their practice and work together to improve it. Teachers worked collaboratively on a small number of 'study lessons' in a plan-teach-observe-critique cycle. To provide focus and direction to this work, teachers selected an overarching goal and related research question that they wanted to explore. The intervention ran for one term and was suitable for early years right through to year 12. The training for participating teachers was one full day and two half-days.

RTI is a multi-tier approach to the early identification and support of targeted pupils from years 5 to 8 with learning and behaviour needs who are not achieving the age-expected level in reading and writing. Literacy interventions are selected by teachers on the basis of close case analysis of pupils' reading and writing needs. The intervention is delivered by CUREE.

Research design

A cluster-randomised, between-subject pre- and post-test design was chosen for use within the large-scale RCTs. In addition to the use of a pre-test, the trial design also sought to build a large sample size where possible (another common approach used to reduce between-participant variation). In the case of the year 1 trials (where schools, rather than individual pupils, were randomly allocated to the control or intervention), stratified randomisation was used. Stratified (or blocked) randomisation involves identifying, in advance, factors (or characteristics) in the participant group that may result in an imbalance between the control group and the intervention group participants. Following the identification of these factors, randomisation is modified to ensure that there is an equal balance of these characteristics in the control and intervention groups. Random allocation at school level removed the risk of control group test performance being affected by the intervention.

Learning from the year 1 interim results, four of the interventions that were assessed in year 1 were replicated in year 2. To reduce some of the between-participant variation that resulted in differing pre-test scores, randomisation to control or intervention took place within each school. Teachers selected two similar-sized groups of disadvantaged pupils which were then randomly allocated to either the control group or intervention group. Such an approach ensured that there was no longer any between-school variation, as every school had a control group and an intervention group taking part in each of the trials. However, individual pupils were not randomly allocated, meaning that there was still a degree of clustering within the process.

The programme design incorporated one additional feature based on the wait list control group design which is sometimes used in clinical studies. Control schools were given enough grant and the opportunity to purchase one of the available interventions in year 2. This is slightly different to the definition of a wait list control group design as the control group schools and specific children within them did not necessarily go on to be exposed to the same treatment for which they had previously been the control group. In a wait list control group design, participants in the control group go on to be exposed to the intervention that they were compared to in the first phase of the programme. Such designs are seen as having the ethical advantage of having a control group whilst at the same time allowing participants to also receive treatment.

The provisional analysis of the year 1 results showed that there were sometimes differences in pre-test scores (probably resulting from cluster randomisation at school level). This aspect of the programme design was modified for efficiency and to facilitate replications in which randomisation could be done within each school (with each school having a control and intervention group). In this way, schools that had been 'waiting' to purchase an intervention for use in their schools were not only able to receive the training but were also able to make a contribution by increasing the number of trial results from seven trials to eleven (seven trials plus four replications). In total, 23 new starter schools who began the programme at the start of the academic year 2014/2015 joined the replication groups. Inference Training was not replicated in year 2 because of adverse effect size findings suggested in the preliminary analysis of year 1 results.

One final variation in the design above was necessary with regard to the evaluation of AfA. AfA is a two-year programme. To ensure that schools who were in the control group for year 1 had an opportunity to experience AfA in year 2, the following structure was adopted (see Figure 2.1).

A pre-test (test A) was first taken by all the pupils in both the control and intervention groups, then the control group continued with existing school practice during the first year whilst the intervention group implemented the first year of the AfA protocol. At the end of the first year a 'mid-test' (test B) was taken by all pupils. At this point it was possible to compare the effectiveness of the AfA year 1 protocol with existing Teaching School associated practice. This 'mid-test' was then considered to be the pre-test for the second year of AfA. In this second year, the schools that had previously been in the control group moved forward to implement the AfA year 1 protocol, whilst the schools that had previously implemented AfA year 1 now moved to implement the AfA year 2 protocol. The mid-test (test B) then acted as a pre-test for the second year of AfA in which the effectiveness of the first year of AfA could now be compared to the effectiveness of the second year of AfA through the conducting of a final post-test (test C). When interpreting the results it is important, therefore, for the reader to recognise that where test B allows for an assessment of the first year of AfA against existing Teaching School associated practice, test C is assessing the effectiveness of AfA year 1 against AfA year 2, as the control group is now implementing AfA year 1 as an active control condition.

Intention-to-treat was applied. This is a method of analysing RCTs in which all of the participants who have been randomly allocated to either the control or intervention are analysed together, irrespective of whether they completed or received the treatment or not. Intention to treat is a complex area, and there are a number of competing definitions as to what constitutes intention-to-treat.

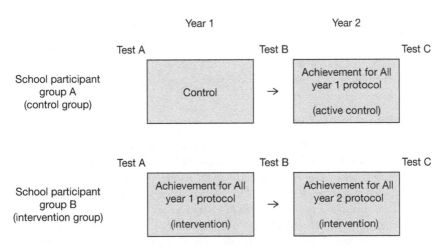

Figure 2.1 The adapted design used with Achievement for All

Because of the complexity of the present study design with regard to the different stages of recruitment, the point at which intention-to-treat was seen as commencing was the point at which pupils took the pre-test. We know, however, that in some cases teachers did not necessarily go on to expose all of these pupils to the interventions, a fact which no doubt also contributed to the levels of attrition within the trials (see NCTL, 2016b).

Pupil attrition rates in the trials where cluster randomisation was conducted at whole-school level ranged from 24 to 48 per cent, with an average of 33 per cent. By far the strongest levels of attrition occurred during the two years of the AfA trial (67 per cent overall). It is likely that this level of attrition was caused by pupil and teacher transition during the long timescales of the trial. Attrition rates in the year 2 replications, where randomisation was conducted at school level (with a control and intervention group in each school), were much lower. The range of attrition in these trials was between 17 per cent and 66 per cent, with the average attrition rate 23 per cent. One test was severely affected by attrition (the additional writing test for RTI). Removing this test from the attrition results indicates an average of 20 per cent.

Participating schools

The scheme was initially advertised through the NCTL member website and the Teaching School newsletter. NCTL's regional associates also promoted the scheme to Teaching School Alliances. Teaching Schools that expressed interest in the scheme were invited to attend launch events at four locations around England. Each Teaching School nominated schools from within its alliance to take part in individual trials. Teaching School trial co-ordinators were responsible for booking teachers from the intervention trial site schools onto the commercially available training programmes. Schools were given a grant to cover the costs of paying for this training, cover and travel expenses. Schools also purchased the tests used in the trials directly from the supplier and were then reimbursed for these costs. No attempt was made to influence the content of the training programmes provided by the suppliers.

Allocation and randomisation

In the last couple of weeks of the summer term 2013, the participating Teaching Schools (and their nominated schools) were sent details of the seven interventions and were asked to rank them in their preference order (and to identify any which they specifically did not want to trial). Around half the nominated schools responded to that invitation and these were allocated to either their first or second choice of intervention. For AfA, the team tried to ensure that only first-choice schools were allocated to it as it was longer (a two-year programme where the others could be completed in around a term), required a higher level of effort on the school's part and needed to start more promptly than the other interventions. All remaining unallocated schools (who had expressed preferences) were allocated to the other six interventions – aiming to have a broad spread of schools across all six – using the criteria in the following order:

- first or second choice preferences;
- interventions with low numbers of first or second preferences;
- phase-specific interventions (NIP and 1stClass@Number);
- all the remaining interventions and schools.

The overall goal was to end up with seven pools of schools allocated to interventions, each of roughly similar size. The exception to this was AfA. Due to the more stringent requirements and higher cost, the final pool for AfA was designed to be slightly smaller than the others.

After completing the allocation for all schools that expressed preferences, the programme set about randomly allocating pools of interventions to Teaching School Alliances so that choices could be made on the ground whilst maintaining the overall size of the intervention pools. Databases were checked for accuracy and duplication and used the resulting master list as the basis for computerised randomisation. NIP and 1stClass@Number, as phase-specific interventions, were given priority and allocated first. We first filtered the list to include only primary schools and then randomly allocated the required number of schools. Finally, the remaining interventions were allocated, randomly, to bring them up to the same pool size as NIP and 1stClass@Number. Trial site schools were grouped by Teaching School Alliance and then randomly allocated to control or intervention using the RAND() function in Excel. The blocking ensured a balance of control and intervention schools by geographical location and phase. The schools taking part in the RLS trial were randomised in the same way as the schools that took part in the trials in year 1. For the year 2 replicated trials, A and B groups of pupils in each school were randomly allocated to control or intervention using the RAND() function in Excel. Simple randomisation was conducted without stratification.

Research ethics and the large-scale trials

The Closing the Gap: Test and Learn project raised various ethical considerations and challenges at the planning stage, during the trials and during the analysis. They were broadly reviewed in the light of the British Educational Research Association guidelines (BERA, 2011), although the involvement of several intervention providers, nearly 900 schools (if Teaching Schools and trial sites school numbers are considered together) and over 20,000 pupils clearly raised some practical issues.

Initial concerns were around voluntary informed consent, confidentiality and anonymity. The most rigorous position would be for explicit parental and individual consent for every pupil involved. However, it was decided that consent from the headteacher would be appropriate, given that under current legislation teachers have some legal responsibility for pupils' welfare anyway, that schools could choose to adopt the interventions without parental consent and that the main sponsor was the DfE (through NCTL), which already handled attainment data on all pupils. This decision did not undermine the UN Convention on the Rights of the Child to act in the best interests of the child (UNICEF, 1989). Further, whilst the project aimed at addressing the needs of educationally disadvantaged pupils, this group were not so vulnerable that special consent was needed, especially as their data were often nested within whole class data.

Pupil data were stored securely by the research team at NCTL on an encrypted and password-protected basis. At the analysis stage, no pupil, school or alliance was identified. However, as schools and alliances became involved in further projects, such as 'early adopters', their involvement voluntarily became public. The research team was initially concerned that schools would raise ethical concerns about being a control group and not an intervention group, in that it might be argued that pupils were 'missing out'. This was therefore addressed at the initial training sessions, first by pointing out that the interventions should be compared with best existing practice, and indeed encouraging the control group schools to teach as well as they could since the interventions needed to be as good as or better than such practice. Second, a utilitarian argument about the value of system-level gains in understanding what works was also proffered. There was no evidence that schools or alliances withdrew from the project on ethical grounds – probably because of the nature of the control condition (existing practice) and the extensive consultation process used to identify the interventions.

The research team was also aware of its ethical obligations to the providers of the interventions. These included treating the relevant data for each provider confidentially, until the research was complete, rather than presenting a partial or distorted picture, for instance by releasing data or analysis, whether positive or negative, before the research was completed. Finally, additional research by Oxford University into the project itself was conducted in accordance with the university's research ethics procedures of consent, anonymity and confidentiality.

Measures

The large-scale trials used two standardised tests:

•   progress in maths (PiM) tests. PiM, developed by GL Assessment and the National Foundation for Educational Research (NFER), covers all current

UK national curriculum content and assesses mathematical skills and concepts;

- new group reading test (NGRT), to measure literacy levels. Developed by GL Assessment and NFER, it assesses the reading and comprehension aspects of literacy.

PiM 6–14 is part of a selection of standardised tests available in both paper and digital editions from GL Assessment. Much of the content of the digital tests is the same as in the paper equivalents. However, some content was changed to take advantage of digital technology and to eliminate items which did not perform well in digital format. The test questions can be grouped in two ways: curriculum content or mathematical processes. The digital edition of PiM can be administered to students across the age range of 6–14 years. The purpose of PiM is to enable regular assessment of students, usually carried out once a year (which provides year-on-year progress), and the test content samples the UK curricula.

NGRT is also part of a selection of standardised tests, available in both paper and digital editions from GL Assessment. The NGRT digital edition contains unaltered content from the paper tests but is presented in a way which allows students' reading to be tested according to their performance as they are taking the test, rather than by age or year group, in an adaptive, digital test. The test comprises three sections: phonics, sentence completion and passage comprehension, in two relevant forms (A and B) which can be administered to students across the age range of 7–16 years. The purpose of NGRT is to enable regular assessment of students and can be carried out year-on-year or at the beginning and end of a single academic year as there is an equivalent form. Applying standardised tests like those above (which produce a standard age score), allowed for the combination of different age groups within each trial.

Hypotheses and analytical approaches

The nature of cluster RCTs inevitably produces results which are harder to interpret than studies with more tightly controlled randomisation. Such challenges are further amplified as the length of treatment period increases and variations in the populations being studied become increasingly likely to attenuate any effects. Taking this into account, a number of different analyses were conducted on the trial data in order to evaluate six distinct but related hypotheses (see Table 2.1). Separate analyses were conducted on all pupil data and on a sub-group of pupils who were eligible for FSM at the point that they took the pre-test. One of the trials (growth mindsets – year 2 replication) involved the assessment of pupil data from both NGRT and PiM. The RTI year 2 replication was assessed using an additional writing test as well as NGRT.

Table 2.1 Hypotheses

Experimental hypothesis 1a	Adjusting for pre-test scores, there will be an improvement in post-test scores for pupils exposed to the intervention for: (i) all pupils and (ii) FSM pupils.
Experimental hypothesis 1b	Adjusting for both the design effect caused by cluster randomisation and pre-test scores, there will be an improvement in post-test scores for pupils exposed to the intervention for: (i) all pupils and (ii) FSM pupils.
Experimental hypothesis 2a	There will be an improvement in the progress rates of pupils exposed to the intervention for: (i) all pupils and (ii) FSM pupils.
Experimental hypothesis 2b	Adjusting for the design effect caused by cluster randomisation, there will be an improvement in the progress rates of pupils exposed to the intervention for: (i) all pupils and (ii) FSM pupils.
Experimental hypothesis 3a	There will be a relationship between exposure to intervention and post-intervention test scores, taking into account pre-test scores, gender, age, FSM status, school Ofsted band and proportion of FSM pupils in the school for: (i) all pupils and (ii) FSM pupils.
Experimental hypothesis 3b	There will be a relationship between exposure to intervention and post-intervention test scores, taking into account pre-test scores, gender, age, FSM status, school Ofsted band, proportion of FSM pupils in the school and clustering of participants for: (i) all pupils and (ii) FSM pupils.

Preliminary assumption testing and the inferential tests used

Prior to analysis, the principle was adopted that it is not acceptable to drop an outlier, just because it is an outlier, in order to use a parametric test. There was no evidence to suggest that any outliers were caused by data error, deliberate or accidental misreporting, sampling error or the non-maintenance of the research protocol. To ensure that the correct statistical test is used, a number of assumptions about the data need to be tested. As a result of these tests, the following statistical tests were used for each hypothesis.

A non-parametric form of ANCOVA (Quade's F [Quade, 1967]) was used to test hypotheses 1a (i–ii) and 1b (i–ii). To test hypotheses 2a (i–ii) and 2b (i–ii), gain scores were first calculated from pre- and post-test scores and the Kruskal-Wallis one-way ANOVA was applied. Finally, in relation to hypotheses 3a (i–ii) and 3b (i–ii), the data were evaluated according to the requirements for conducting regression modelling with standard multiple regression. The majority of the data were satisfactory; however, two of the analyses had sample sizes that were too small for effective regression modelling to take place. Using this variety of tests meant that the first two assessments were able to consider the effectiveness of the interventions with regard to the assessment of attainment, the second two relative progress and the final pair of assessments were able to provide a validation of the other findings with regard to the effect of a range of individual differences at cluster and pupil level.

Adjustment for design effect caused by cluster randomisation

Adjustment for the design effect resulting from clustering in the testing of hypotheses 1b (i–ii) and 2b (i–ii) was carried out using the approach recommended and discussed by Campbell and colleagues (Campbell, Mollison, Steen, Grimshaw and Eccles, 2000). This approach has been applied to primary healthcare where randomisation has had to take place at GP surgery level. It involves using a formula to calculate the effective sample size taking into account the number of clusters and intracluster dependence. The p-value for the result is then adjusted accordingly. Hypotheses 1a (i–ii) and 2a (i–ii) form an assessment of the effect of interventions without taking into account this design effect, whilst hypotheses 1b (i–ii) and 2b (i–ii) represent adjustments to the results found in the preceding hypotheses. Interpretation of these two sets of results allowed for an estimation of the effect of cluster randomisation across the whole programme of RCTs. In the year 1 trials, teachers were asked to identify 'target' pupils (pupils they believed were most in need of having their attainment gap closed). Unfortunately, these data had reliability issues with regard to pupil identification and therefore analysis was not conducted. There were no issues with regard to target pupil data in year 2 replications, as by definition all the pupils involved in these trials were the target group. Teacher identification was not felt to be secure enough for any other intervention data to be re-analysed.

Results

Full statistical appendices can be found in NCTL (2016a). Pooling the converted Cohen's d effect sizes from hypotheses 1a and 1b produces a map of relative effect sizes as shown in Figures 2.2 and 2.3. Effect sizes range widely (from d = 0.51 to d = -0.43). Interpretation of this combined table, however, needs to bear in mind the wide variety of interventions, different treatment periods and the fact that the confidence interval bars are partly a product of sample size – with there being a wide range of pupil numbers across the trials and sub-groups within the trials. Following concern about cross-contamination in one year 2 replication, results were re-analysed, with schools of concern removed; however, the results remained broadly the same.

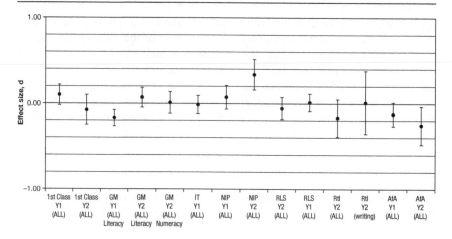

Figure 2.2 Combined effect sizes (generated from ANCOVA results) for all pupils involved in the trials

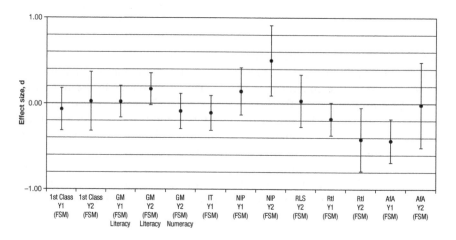

Figure 2.3 Combined effect sizes (generated from ANCOVA results) for FSM pupils involved in the trials

Some trials may have been affected by cluster randomisation and/or between-school differences, but not all were affected. In particular, AfA results may have been affected by a range of differences. This said, the design did not allow for the assessment of whether school-level differences were at the teacher or pupil level. RTI may have been affected by clustering.

Overall, Teaching School associated existing practice (the control conditions for all of the large-scale trials) appears to be at least equal to six of the top seven interventions identified in the consultation, but better than growth mindsets when used with an average group of pupils. Existing Teaching School practice may also be better than the first year of AfA with regard to the exposure of FSM pupils to this treatment. The exception to the above was NIP which consistently appeared to improve mathematics attainment and progress rates, particularly for FSM pupils, and irrespective of the analytical model used to assess its efficacy. There may also be gap closure benefits in the use of RLS; however, in the context of the present study design, none of the assessments produced significant results.

Although finding that the majority of the interventions showed no effect greater than existing good practice is useful, it is but a starting point for further investigation. The established practice in other fields (e.g., medicine) would be to undertake further trials in different circumstances to see if the benefits of these interventions are revealed in different contexts (for example, in struggling schools, with a more tightly defined group of students, or particular age groups).

Additional evaluation of the extent to which the pupils' attainment gap (compared to expected pupil progress) had been closed

GL Assessment standard age scores (SAS) are based on the student's raw score adjusted for age and placed on a scale that makes a comparison with a nationally representative sample of UK students of the same age. The national average score is 100. Using the GL Assessment SAS national average score as a baseline, the following charts show how the attainment gaps between FSM pupils and other pupils changed over the period of the trials. In the trial design used in year 1, schools selected whole classes of pupils for each trial. It was therefore possible to compare mean standard age scores for FSM pupils with mean standard age scores for pupils who were not eligible for free school meals, in the same way that the government has reported the attainment gap for dis-advantaged pupils at the end of key stage 2 and key stage 4. In the design used in year 2, schools only selected pupils that they felt were disadvantaged. In this case, the gap was calculated as the difference between the mean standard age scores for the FSM pupils and the standard mean of 100.

As described above, the AfA trial ran over the full two years of the scheme. In this trial, the intervention group began implementing AfA in the first year, while the control schools carried on as normal. In the second year, the control schools began implementing the first year of the AfA programme, while the intervention schools moved into the second year of the programme. The bars in Figures 2.4 and 2.5 show the change in the attainment gap. A positive score indicates that the attainment gap has been reduced for pupils eligible for FSM. A negative score indicates that the attainment gap has increased.

Assessment of the SAS points reduction in attainment gap for the year 1 trials and RLS (Figure 2.4) shows that in the case of Inference Training, RTI and 1stClass@Number the control condition (existing Teaching School

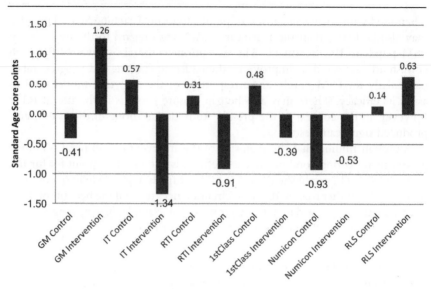

Figure 2.4 SAS points reduction in attainment gaps for the year 1 trials and RLS (trialled for the first time in year 2 of the programme) – control and intervention

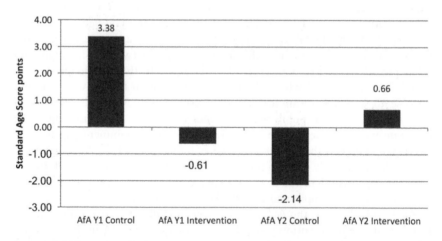

Figure 2.5 SAS points reduction in attainment gaps for AfA (year 1 and year 2) – control and intervention

associated practice) appeared to have closed attainment gaps more effectively than the interventions. The exceptions to this were growth mindsets, NIP and RLS, which appeared to achieve more relative gap closure than existing practice. With regard to the first year of the AfA trial (Figure 2.5), the first year of AfA implementation closed attainment (relatively) far less than existing

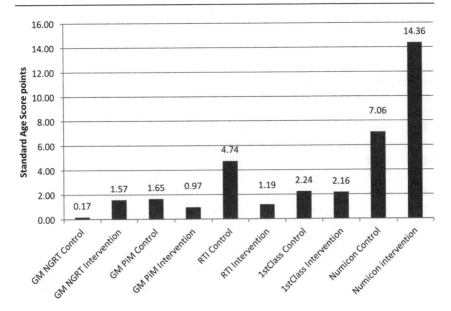

Figure 2.6 SAS points reduction in attainment gaps for the year 2 replicated trials –
control and intervention

practice. The year 2 control (which was the repetition of the first year of AfA)
continued to produce lower gains in gap closure, although there was a small
positive gain achieved for the year 2 AfA protocol.

The replicated year 2 trials (Figure 2.6) yielded positive gains across the board
although a similar pattern was evident with RTI and 1stClass@Number,
which produced less gap closure than existing practice. This was also the case
with regard to mathematics attainment in the growth mindsets replication,
although growth mindsets appeared to close attainment gaps more effectively
with regard to improvement in literacy. NIP, paralleling the inferential test
results and effect sizes resulting from the testing of hypotheses 1a–3b, closed
the attainment gap of pupils substantially, even compared to a control group
that was itself making substantial gains.

Limitations and important considerations when interpreting the results

As has been discussed earlier, all experimental research has limitations. With
regard to the large-scale trials within the Closing the Gap: Test and Learn
programme, these limitations were mainly the product of cluster randomisation
and internal validity issues arising from the collaborative school-led approach,
which reduced the degree to which extraneous variables could be controlled
for. There were also limitations with regard to some of the trials caused by

the fact that, to some degree, the use of standardised literacy and numeracy tests (such as when used with growth mindsets and AfA) could be considered to have reduced the design's sensitivity in detecting changes caused by these interventions. Neither growth mindsets nor AfA claim to directly affect mathematics or literacy attainment. At the same time RLS is not a direct literacy approach but rather one which can be tailored for such use. Similarly, RTI is not a direct pedagogical intervention but rather a flexible targeting approach. This meant that although teachers had a choice between targeting the reading or writing skills of their pupils, it was not possible to match the assessment to reflect this level of teacher in-class usage.

It is also important to acknowledge the wide variation in the nature of the interventions which had in some cases very different focuses, breadth and emphases with regard to target pupils. In this respect, the fact that a teacher-identified sub-group of target pupils (in the year 1 trials) lacked reliability and therefore the main analysis reverted to the analysis of effects on the FSM sub-group may have affected some interventions such as RTI. It is also important to remember that some of the interventions had a long delivery history (such as NIP) and have had a far longer time to become established and improve through feedback and revision. In contrast, for example, RLS was a new training programme which was only piloted the previous year with 20 of the participating schools.

Despite the fact that some trials may have been affected by cluster randomisation, this was by no means the case with the vast majority of trials. Finally, where such between-school effects appear to have occurred, it was not possible to determine the extent to which these may have been caused by teacher-level differences or school-context differences, as the programme collected no teacher performance data with which to make comparisons.

Conclusions

The programme has clearly demonstrated the capacity of schools to engage in research through large-scale multi-arm trials and micro-RCTs; this also increased engagement with research and discussion of research findings. Contrary to assumptions made at the start of the programme, schools were not resistant to the use of control groups, engagement in statistical research or to the use of RCTs in general. Furthermore, teachers can take a more active role in the delivery of RCTs. However, this form of approach requires investment in training and careful control of the communication structure and engagement protocols to ensure that individual trial sites do not become too distant from any middle-tier process used to build scale. The teaching profession already has a deep and available resource of individuals with experience of quantitative methods and their application outside of education research (such as science teachers and psychology teachers). The challenge going forward will be to connect these people with one another and provide them with models of how such approaches can be taken forward in school-led education research projects.

The results can be seen as emphasising the challenge of diagnosis within education – in that it is hard to find general things which improve outcomes across the board (except for NIP). Schools therefore need to think carefully about how their adoption and embedding of research-based approaches will stand more chance of success ('be above average'). Effective use of large-scale evidence is likely to require good diagnosis and targeting – and training of school leaders to understand how to do this.

References

Blackwell, S., Trzesniewski, K.H. and Dweck, C.S. (2007) 'Implicit theories of intelligence predict achievement across an adolescent transition: a longitudinal study and an intervention', *Child Development*, 78(1): 246–262.

British Educational Research Association (BERA) (2011) *Ethical guidelines for educational research*. London: BERA.

Campbell, M.K., Mollison, J., Steen, N., Grimshaw, J.M. and Eccles, M. (2000) 'Analysis of cluster randomized trials in primary care: a practical approach', *Family Practice*, 17: 192–196.

Churches, R. (2016) *Closing the Gap: Test and Learn: Research Report*. London: Department for Education/National College for Teaching and Leadership. Available at: https://www.gov.uk/government/publications/closing-the-gap-test-and-learn (accessed on 8th March 2016).

NCTL (2016a) *Closing the Gap: Test and Learn – Technical Annex: A Statistical Analysis*. London: Department for Education/National College for Teaching and Leadership. Available at: www.gov.uk/government/publications/closing-the-gap-test-and-learn (accessed on 19th July 2019).

NCTL (2016b) *Closing the Gap: Test and Learn: Teacher Led Randomised Controlled Trials – Digital Applications Case Studies*. London: Department for Education/National College for Teaching and Leadership. Available at: www.gov.uk/government/publications/closing-the-gap-test-and-learn (accessed on 19th July 2019).

NCTL (2016c) *Closing the Gap: Test and Learn: Teacher Led Randomised Controlled Trials – Feedback Case Studies*. London: Department for Education/National College for Teaching and Leadership. Available at: www.gov.uk/government/publications/closing-the-gap-test-and-learn (accessed on 19th July 2019).

NCTL (2016d) *Closing the Gap: Test and Learn: Teacher Led Randomised Controlled Trials – Literacy Case Studies*. London: Department for Education/National College for Teaching and Leadership. Available online: www.gov.uk/government/publications/closing-the-gap-test-and-learn (accessed on 19th July 2019).

NCTL (2016e) *Closing the Gap: Test and Learn: Teacher Led Randomised Controlled Trials – Numeracy Case Studies*. London: Department for Education/National College for Teaching and Leadership. Available online: www.gov.uk/government/publications/closing-the-gap-test-and-learn (accessed on 19th July 2019).

NCTL (2016f) *Closing the Gap: Test and Learn: Teacher Led Randomised Controlled Trials – Organisation of Learning Case Studies*. London: Department for Education/National

College for Teaching and Leadership. Available online: www.gov.uk/government/publications/closing-the-gap-test-and-learn (accessed on 19th July 2019).

NCTL (2016g) *Closing the Gap: Test and Learn: Teacher Led Randomised Controlled Trials – Resilience*. London: Department for Education/National College for Teaching and Leadership. Available online: www.gov.uk/government/publications/closing-the-gap-test-and-learn (accessed on 19th July 2019).

Quade, D. (1967) 'Rank analysis of covariance', *Journal of the American Statistical Association* 62: 1187–1200.

UNICEF (1989) *The United Nations Convention on the Rights of the Child*. London: UNICEF.

Yuill, N. and Oakhill, J. (1988) 'Effects of inference awareness training on poor reading comprehension', *Applied Cognitive Psychology* 2(1988): 33–45.

Chapter 3

Closing the evidence gap?

The challenges of the research design of the Closing the Gap: Test and Learn project

Ian Menter and Ian Thompson

Firstly, evidence based practice isn't about telling teachers what to do: in fact, quite the opposite. This is about empowering teachers, and setting a profession free from governments, ministers and civil servants who are often overly keen on sending out edicts, insisting that their new idea is the best in town. Nobody in government would tell a doctor what to prescribe, but we all expect doctors to be able to make informed decisions about which treatment is best, using the best currently available evidence. I think teachers could one day be in the same position.

(Goldacre, 2013: 7)

Introduction

In this chapter, building upon the previous chapters, we consider how the overall design of the Closing the Gap: Test and Learn project relates to the concept of a Randomised Controlled Trial (RCT). In particular, we take the notions of RCTs as proposed by Goldacre (2013) and as commissioned and implemented by the Education Endowment Foundation (EEF). We then consider the extent to which this project has been a major innovation in school-led research development, as has been claimed by its designers. There are several 'design issues' which were revealed during the implementation of the programme, and we critically examine these before concluding with a discussion of some of the implications for future large-scale but dispersed educational research initiatives.

The research design of Closing the Gap: Test and Learn

At an early stage in the implementation of the project Closing the Gap: Test and Learn, some significant claims were made about its overall design. It was suggested that it was the largest ever school-based research initiative 'of its kind', at least in Britain and possibly anywhere. As we saw in Chapter 1, there were two main conceptions behind the whole project, building research capacity in schools and addressing educational disadvantage, respectively.

From the point of view of the national Teaching Schools initiative, the project was an attempt to really accelerate research capacity development within the schools. It had been suggested in the early evaluations of the Teaching Schools that research and development (R&D) was one of the weakest of the six 'big ideas' as the programme was being developed. More recent reports on Teaching Schools (Glover et al., 2014; Greany and Brown, 2015; Gu et al., 2014) and the literature on school self-improvement (Greany, 2015) suggest that the evidence on R&D implementation remains mixed. Whilst Teaching Schools increasingly value R&D, and there are examples of some innovative practice within alliances, there are also challenges of lack of funding and capacity (Gu et al., 2014). Some alliances appear to view R&D as central to their work and have forged effective research partnerships with universities, whilst in others R&D is viewed as 'time consuming and can seem initially daunting for teachers' (Gu et al., 2014: 7). Given this mixed picture on R&D, from the point of view of the NCTL and Durham University who helped to design the project, a major driver for this project was to pursue the Teaching Schools' R&D agenda. When interviewed, a member of NCTL staff pointed out that the NCTL was 'doing this mainly to increase the research capacity in the system and particularly try and strengthen the R&D element of the teaching schools' remit'.

However, as discussed in more detail in Chapter 1, in order to gain ministerial support for the initiative, it was important that it connected with other policy strands as well, and so the focus on Closing the Gap was a way of ensuring that the project did indeed attract a strong level of ministerial support. Closing the Gap was an important policy strand for the Coalition Government and indeed was often credited to the Liberal Democratic partners in the coalition, David Laws (Minister for Schools) in particular.

As it was phrased in the original tender document:

> The Secretary of State recently approved plans for the Closing the Gap: Test and Learn scheme to provide opportunities for schools to undertake rigorous research so that:
>
> 1   successful approaches to supporting the most disadvantaged children to achieve academic success are identified and spread between schools and across the teaching profession;
> 2   stronger links between the teaching profession and universities are built, helping to develop the academic standing of the teaching profession overall.
>
> The vision for this initiative is that it will begin to change the culture of education so that engagement in research is reinforced as an important part of teachers' practice and they are supported and enabled to inform their own practice and that of others within their school through the use of robust evidence, with a direct impact on educational outcomes for their

pupils. The scheme should make a genuine and significant positive impact on practice by producing outputs appropriate for and accessible to practitioners, disseminating these in an engaging and effective way. Through the support given to teachers to robustly test interventions, the scheme should also complement work supported by the Education Endowment Foundation and wider efforts to develop an evidence-informed teaching profession.

(NCTL, 2013: 3)

The stated goals of helping disadvantaged children to achieve academic success and forging greater research links between the teaching profession and universities were laudable and ambitious aims. However, it could also be argued that there was recognition here of the difficulties involved in changing school-based approaches to evidence-informed teaching. This was encapsulated in the tender document in the desire to 'change the culture of education so that engagement in research is reinforced as an important part of teachers' practice'. The implication was that robust evidence would not only change practice and improve educational outcomes for disadvantaged learners, but that this would involve an educational cultural change. A further implication was that this robust research evidence would provide teachers with the opportunity to test the effectiveness of interventions and to disseminate the findings to other schools.

RCTs in education

So if closing the educational attainment gap for disadvantaged children was to be the 'substantive' focus, why was it that the project should be designed along the lines of a Randomised Controlled Trial (RCT)? Presumably it would have been possible to conceive of a large-scale project that was based on other research methodologies, including, for example, a range of case studies (Yin, 2014) or mixed method approaches (Johnson & Onwuegbuzie, 2004). However, as discussed in Chapter 1, it had become clear, under the influence of the Coalition Government, that RCT models were particularly favoured. The two key manifestations of this emphasis were the rolling out of the Education Endowment Foundation (EEF) as a major player and the commissioning of the medical journalist and researcher Ben Goldacre to write a report for Michael Gove.

The EEF had been established in 2011 using funds provided by the DfE and channelled through the Sutton Trust. As presented on its website, the aims of the EEF are as follows:

Our focus is on supporting projects that show promising evidence of having a measurable impact on attainment or a directly related outcome. We are interested in testing projects' effectiveness through robust independent evaluations, where appropriate as randomised controlled trials. If they are shown to have an impact, they should be able to be replicated and scaled up to improve outcomes for other disadvantaged pupils.

(23/06/15: https://educationendowmentfoundation. org.uk/apply-for-funding/)

Ben Goldacre had become a well-known name through his books and publications in the media on the topic of 'bad science'. Although he is clearly from a medical research background, Michael Gove arranged for the DfE to commission him to write a paper about educational research (Goldacre, 2013). This was launched in March 2013 at an event held at Bethnal Green Academy, when Mr Gove publicly committed himself to prioritising educational research – much better to use research than to rely on the ideas of politicians, he self-deprecatingly suggested. Goldacre's paper was a curious document, which relied almost entirely on medical research to argue the case for suggesting that there should be an overriding – if not total – reliance on RCTs in education. At the time, some qualms were expressed by some members of the educational research community (James, 2013; Menter, 2013), although critics were careful to agree that RCTs have an important contribution to make. The concern was more about the apparent disparagement of other forms of educational research, including small-scale teacher research, and the possibility that RCTs would become the sole vehicle that might attract major funding.

The other big issue underlying the whole project was the idea of a large-scale, school-based but coordinated scheme of this sort being carried out within a 'school-led system'. How could it be that a geographically wide-ranging and very variegated group of schools could take part in one project when they were each encouraged to be making their own decisions? To what extent was this a contradiction? It certainly presented a significant challenge for the civil servants at the NCTL who were tasked with delivering a very large-scale scheme. Schools Minister David Laws had originally suggested that 1,000 schools should be involved, but that the scheme should not be 'imposed' by the college as it was all to be part of the move towards a self-improving school-led system. As one of us has suggested elsewhere (Menter, 2014), it is hard to envisage a system that has 23,000 leaders nationally. Indeed, the notion of a 'school-led system' might be seen as something of an oxymoron. However, the NCTL officials were determined to encourage schools to be as active as possible in determining the nature of the work, but at the same time were very anxious to ensure that the taxpayers' money – £4 million in all – would be well used and not wasted. This was indubitably an immensely challenging scenario for everyone concerned and was one of the reasons that the National College was much more involved in the operation of the scheme than it would have been on most other projects that have been contracted out.

The original invitation to tender for this project referred back to the 2010 White Paper, *The Importance of Teaching* (DfE, 2010), as follows:

The White Paper sets out the Government's plans to raise standards and improve the quality of teachers and school leadership through school-to-school support and peer-to-peer learning. It refers to a 'self-improving system' or what the Secretary of State describes as a 'decentralised culture of self-improvement in schools' and sets out plans for a new national network of Teaching Schools. Modelled on teaching hospitals, the approach gives outstanding schools (as judged by OFSTED) the role of leading the training and professional development of teachers, headteachers and contributing to the raising of standards through school-to-school support.

(NCTL, 2013: 2)

So, from the outset it was intended that schools themselves would play a leading role in the development and implementation of the whole project, challenging though this was likely to be given the large numbers and variety of schools to be involved.

Additionally, the multi-partner nature of the project team was another quite unusual and potentially challenging feature. While it is not uncommon for consortia to bid for and to undertake research projects of various kinds, each partner bringing particular expertise to the table, this project consortium had four partners. The team was led by a major educational consultancy, CfBT (which has subsequently changed its name to the Education Development Trust), working with two universities (Durham and Oxford) and an educational knowledge brokering and training organisation, CUREE (the Centre for the Use of Research and Evidence in Education). And, as mentioned above, the commissioning body itself, NCTL, remained closely involved throughout the project. Furthermore, there were the seven organisations that were the proprietors of the respective interventions, ranging from Oxford University Press to Portsmouth University, through AfA to CUREE itself. Finally, there was also GL Assessment, the company whose tests were selected for the pre- and post-tests. Therefore a total of 12 separate organisations were involved in some formal way in the project, in addition to the 623 schools in total that participated in trials (387 schools in year one and 286 in year two).

The appropriateness of RCTs

So if there were very significant organisational and managerial challenges in the project, for some participants there were also some concerns about ethical questions arising from the adoption of RCTs in educational research and about the difficulties of identifying causal relations through RCTs. In other words, RCTs might well demonstrate the relationship between interventions and outcomes (correlations) – that is, they might identify 'what works' and 'what doesn't work' – but they could not readily provide explanations of *why* a particular approach does or does not work. The ethical questions around

RCTs in education are brought to the fore by Brooks et al. (2014), who suggest that as well as the traditional concerns about the ethics of maintaining current practice with the control group while testing the purported 'better' practice on the intervention group, there must be ethical concerns about the disparagement of other forms of educational research. They refer to Delandshere (2004) who they report 'has argued that the shift in government funding in the USA, to privilege RCTs, had the effect of marginalizing those who are engaged in other forms of research'. Moreover, they say she contends 'that within this particular paradigm . . . teachers and teacher educators become positioned very much as consumers of research products rather than actors engaged in the intellectual work of teaching and learning' (Brooks et al., 2014: 71). If Delandshere is correct, the adoption of an RCT approach would seem, at least to some extent, to negate the project's (and Goldacre's) ambition to ensure that the schools and the teachers therein were active agents in the construction of the project.

This overriding commitment by politicians and educational policy makers in England to RCTs, in spite of such challenges and difficulties, seems to be based on a desperate quest for certainty. In the light of this prioritisation of RCTs, it is very surprising that many of the educational research textbooks of the twentieth century – at least those published in the UK – often say little or actually nothing about RCTs. Indeed, one of the most popular educational research methods texts, by Cohen, Manion and Morrison, even in their sixth edition from 2007, suggest: 'Randomized controlled trials belong to a discredited view of science as positivism' (p. 278). This seems quite an extraordinarily dogmatic statement, but nevertheless does reflect much twentieth-century educational research thinking! No doubt part of the problem lies in the fact that many such methods texts are aimed at 'solo' researchers, perhaps undertaking masters or doctoral work where a large-scale sample is not easy to arrange. Some other such texts, however, do talk of experimental or quasi-experimental designs which may share some RCT features (for example, see Thomas, 2009). Of course, there is also a substantial literature that argues for the appropriateness of RCT design to answer particular research questions about what might work best in educational contexts (e.g. Styles, 2009; Torgerson and Torgerson, 2008). The question remains whether RCTs are always the appropriate research method to answer questions that look at complexity and variety in educational contexts.

The philosopher of education Richard Pring recognised the growing attraction of RCTs (and for him the T stands for Tests not Trials) when he wrote in 2000:

> Research based on randomized controlled groups is, of course, well established in medical sciences. Thus, if one wants to know the impact of a particular drug, then one randomly selects two groups of patients, and then, keeping all other variables constant, observes carefully the effect on

one group of this particular drug. The groups have to be large to play down the significance of 'rogue factors' or particular exceptions to the general case.

(Pring, 2000: 36)

Pring writes in defence of ethnographic, illuminative, qualitative research and expresses considerable scepticism about the value of RCTs, even if he does not go as far as Cohen et al. Gert Biesta (2010), writing more recently, also develops a philosophical critique of RCTs in education and argues forcefully that education is a very different human process from medicine and that the analogy may be a very misleading one.

Cartwright and Hardie (2012), while not focussing in particular on educational research, nevertheless offer a careful analysis of some of the common misuses and abuses of RCT methods in social and medical sciences. In particular they suggest that the importance of context is often ignored and can lead to the simplistic adoption of a 'what works' approach to policy making.

Nevertheless, it was clear from our interviews with stakeholders in the policy community that, from the outset in this project, the underlying methodological paradigm would have to be that of an RCT, simply because that was what at that time reflected the mindset of the politicians. There was also awareness from a design perspective of the challenges of 'getting positive results from a policy perspective and actually finding out whether something works or not from the school's perspective'. As this stakeholder pointed out, there is little point 'demonstrating that doing trials works at a policy level if the answers aren't useful at a practice level'.

The 'RCTness' of Closing the Gap

Turning now to consider how this particular project was designed, we first consider how CtG matches up to some of the classic features or conventions of RCTs. These include:

- the comparison of results for an intervention group and a control group;
- both sample groups to be identified through the application of randomising;
- the application of the same pre- and post- test at the same time (or at least over the same time period);
- the calculation of an effect size based on the comparison of results from the control and intervention groups.

Through our own involvement in the project and through our many discussions with our project partners and many of the teachers involved, we have identified some of the challenges to the RCT conventions that arose in this project. We certainly acknowledge that most of these challenges derive from the great ambition behind the scheme, but each of the nine challenges we set out here are matters from which we suggest we may be able to learn for the future.

1. One RCT or seven? The design of the whole project as implemented incorporated seven different classroom or school interventions, and so in one sense this could be seen as seven parallel RCTs, rather than as one. What the seven interventions had in common within the design was a claim that their adoption could lead to a reduction in the attainment gap, especially as it affected more disadvantaged children. The fact that the interventions ranged in focus from specific numeracy interventions to aspects of literacy, as well as whole school or school management policy interventions, makes comparison between the effects of the interventions difficult to assess. As one stakeholder put it, there was a danger inherent in the project of drawing inferences from 'the aggregation of seven lots of data'. In addition, schools were asked at an early stage to indicate a preference for the intervention/s which they would like to administer. Some schools, post allocation, were allowed to trade with other schools within their alliance for their preferred intervention. Whilst this suggests a potential greater commitment to the implementation of the intervention, it also suggests that the process of selection was less than random. In other words, the selection of interventions was not random (and was not intended to be), even if the selection of the test and control groups within schools was.

2. Were the tests fit for purpose? Participants in the study (i.e., school students identified as intervention or control group members) were each administered with one of two tests. For the two interventions that were primarily about numeracy (*Numicon* and *First Class at Number*), a numeracy test was administered. For the remaining five interventions the test used was a literacy test. Both tests had been very systematically developed and trialled by their proprietors, GL Assessment. It emerged during the project that the tests were popular within many of the schools because of their diagnostic element. They helped teachers to recognise the detailed strengths and weaknesses of pupils in their numeracy and literacy development, respectively. However, they had indeed been pre-designed to assess respectively only aspects of numeracy and literacy. The seven project interventions in fact each had their own specific aims and desired outcomes, some of which would be difficult to measure quantitatively. While all the interventions had been selected for this project because they in some sense sought to improve the achievement of underperforming students, their success was nevertheless being assessed through generic numeracy and literacy tests. Indeed, it is important to point out that within the project, 'achievement' and 'underachievement' are implicitly being taken to be synonymous with success or lack of success in either numeracy or literacy. Although there was some recognition that complementary qualitative data would need to be collected for some of the interventions, most notably AfA and Growth Mindsets, this proved to be very difficult to do in a systematic way despite the introduction of some tools for qualitative data collection in the training phase. As one stakeholder put it towards the end of the project, the 'worry being that all kinds of really useful evidence simply won't be available because we didn't design it into the system in the first place'.

So the project as a whole could be seen as an attempt to assess whether these interventions led to improvements on the scores on these numeracy and literacy tests as opposed to being an assessment of whether the unique goals of each of the seven interventions were being achieved. This was particularly apparent where some of the interventions measured by the literacy tests were concerned with addressing whole school issues of aspirations or attitudes to learning.

Furthermore, some of the interventions may actually take some years to affect students' progress and so would be difficult to measure within the timescale of the project. The assumption within the design is that if interventions were to have a positive effect it would be more or less immediately detectable through these assessment tests.

So, to summarise, the original intention to carry out research to address the achievement gap led to an emphasis on measures of literacy and numeracy development which, while of considerable interest, were not necessarily very closely aligned to the interventions that were being implemented in the project. Indeed, this might well be one explanation of why so few of the interventions had a very marked positive effect size (see Chapter 2).

3. The wide range of settings. There were several other factors that might be seen as 'complicating' the design compared with that of a conventional RCT in education. Involvement in the project was to be available to many different age groups, from pre-school through to secondary, and also was to be available in special school settings as well as mainstream schools. So it was that in order to be sensitive to different effects in different settings, considerable care would be needed to draw any general, let alone universal, conclusions from the study. Of course, none of this invalidates the study because the whole essence of 'control' is that it does facilitate comparison of unlike participants because of the randomisation that is part of the design. However, it does mean that the interpretation of the results in this very diverse range of settings needs to be done with considerable caution.

4. The seven interventions: other research. Several of the seven interventions have other studies associated with them. For example, AfA has on ongoing programme of evaluation and analysis (see afaeducation.org), the outcomes of which are the basis of promotion for the whole scheme. AfA is was also being evaluated by an EEF-funded RCT project seeking to assess measures of wellbeing, resilience and engagement of vulnerable learners. Growth Mindsets, as developed by the University of Portsmouth, based on the ideas of Carol Dweck, has also been the subject of much other research, including studies by the EEF (see https://educationendowmentfoundation. org.uk/). Research Lesson Study, an approach sometimes based on practices in Japan, has been something of a focus for a group of researchers in the UK who have been very excited by its apparent impact on professional learning as well as on students' learning (see Dudley, 2012). So one may reasonably ask how this CtG project was expected to complement or supplement what was already known about the success of these interventions. It seems that there may have been a missed opportunity for the kind of cumulation of research evidence, the lack of which has been one of the criticisms of educational research in England (Tooley and Darby, 1998).

5. The seven interventions: commercial interests. All seven of the interventions have a proprietary basis, at least in the form in which they were involved in CtG. This has meant that there are very clear commercial sensitivities in becoming involved in this project and in the outcomes of research in the reporting stage. As a representative of the commissioning body said, this was not anticipated in their initial conception of the project, and so it is fascinating to consider how this was the pattern that emerged and to think about the influence of commercial interests on the rollout of the scheme. However, as we see state education in England increasingly becoming a 'mixed economy' with a significant coalescence of private and public interests (Ball, 2007), such commercial interests are much more common than in the past. For the proprietors of these interventions, involvement in the CtG project must have been considered as posing a risk, perhaps a considerable risk, especially to the reputation of the 'products' that each of them was promoting.

6. Data collection. One of the great strengths of the project was the trust placed in schools to both implement the interventions and to carry out the pre- and post-tests. However, this proved also to be a weakness as the NCTL reported considerable problems in getting data returns from schools and, in particular, in the identification of students who matched the criteria for being disadvantaged. The design also meant that the management of data collection was delegated and information had to go through several stages from the NCTL to the Teaching School Alliances through a designated trial co-ordinator, then through the management structures of partner schools before it got to the classroom teachers who were responsible for the pre- and post-testing of both control and intervention groups. Many trial co-ordinators were able to attend the pre-intervention training but many others did not. Subsequent changes in trial co-ordinator and classroom teachers who were administering the intervention also affected data collection. In addition, the secondary qualitative data was not systematically collected in most schools. This is not surprising given the large scale of the project and the difficulties of quantitative data collection, and it may be that some alliances will have used their own significant contextual data that will have helped them to interpret the national results when they were published.

7. Validity of the RCT. The large scale of this two-year project raised questions about validity within the design. Interviews revealed different interpretations amongst the major stakeholders involved in the design and implementation of CtG. One organisation pointed out that there was a time pressure on both the NCTL and the DfE to produce results. Instead of taking a year to design the project, as initially envisaged by one of the university stakeholders, the project was up and running in just over one school term. For this stakeholder, time pressures meant that that the design led to tensions 'in both the feasibility but also the outcomes that different stakeholders wanted'. Another stakeholder argued that 'pragmatic' delivery arrangements in schools 'seriously threaten(ed) the validity of the exercise of a randomised controlled trial'. This organisation believed that the methodology over the two years of the project had 'deteriorated to the point where you could not demonstrate success or otherwise'. They maintained that whilst the first year's results maintained a distinction between the control and treatment groups, this was not the same in the second year of the project where there was more freedom in delivery of the interventions. They argued that randomisation within schools at the level of individual pupils meant that 'there are circumstances where you cannot prevent pollution of the control group by the intervention group'. This suggests the possibility that results in the second year may be contaminated as the distinction between control and intervention in some schools was blurred.

There may be some doubt therefore about both 'measurement validity' and about 'content validity'. Punch (2009) defines the first of these as 'the extent to which an instrument measures what it is claimed to measure' (p. 246). Content validity, in Punch's terms, 'focuses on whether the full content of a conceptual definition is represented in the measure' (ibid.).

Another stakeholder argued that in this type of design external validity (generalisability) is more important than internal validity (internal logic and consistency) because the possibility for change across the project was high. Giving teachers freedom in delivery meant that there were inherently lower levels of internal validity as the interventions were not, nor could be, laboratory controlled. This was less the case in small-scale trials conducted by 'early adopter' schools (see). However, the 'real-world' nature of the large-scale RCT meant that schools bought into the project both intellectually and also in terms of using their devolved grant to buy in training for the interventions. This stakeholder argued that 'it's got very high levels of mundane realism and therefore more external validity in terms of saying "if you buy this for this amount of money then this is what's going to happen"'. Finally, a fourth stakeholder concluded that CtG revealed that whilst the smaller trials have shown that some schools and many teachers hold a sophisticated understanding of research methodologies and implementation, and this knowledge and expertise was used particularly well in the smaller school-based trials, there is still much to do to develop the infrastructure needed to deliver large-scale RCTs.

In terms of the collaborative effort in order to run larger scale trials I don't think we're there yet. There's a lot more work to be done in terms of explaining exactly how important it is for certain activities to be carried out at exactly the right moment and how rigorous you need to be making sure you have your control group and your intervention group separate and that there's no accidental use of the intervention strategies with the control groups, the timings of the tests and all that kind of stuff which will affect the results. It could be done but I think it needs to be done in a slightly more systematic way.

(Stakeholder 4)

8. Mixing methods. One increasingly common means by which educational research has sought to address the potential shortcomings of RCT-based approaches is through combining quantitative and qualitative methods. This is frequently described as mixed-methods research. As Punch (2009) suggests, 'we can learn more about our research topic if we can combine the strengths of qualitative research with the strengths of quantitative research while compensating at the same time for the weaknesses of each method' (p. 290). Johnson and Onwuegbuzie (2004) argue that researchers who use mixed methods have potential to answer complex research questions without rigid adherence to quantitative or qualitative paradigms. In the early stages of the CtG scheme, members of the project team discussed how qualitative methods might be incorporated into the approach taken. In many of the training rounds, school colleagues were encouraged to complement their engagement in the quasi-experimental approaches of the interventions and the associated testing with qualitative enquiry into their own experiences related to the interventions. It did emerge in the project when teachers were talking about their work that many of them had complemented the obligatory activities for the national project with their own small-scale data gathering, through interviews and observations of pupil responses to the interventions, for example. In terms of the project design, however, there is clearly a difficulty in associating such localised and idiographic insights with the quantitative patterns emerging from the national project. There was therefore some considerable 'unevenness' between the quantitative and the qualitative aspects of data collection. For example, pre- and post-testing was seen as compulsory by both intervention and control schools, but qualitative data collection was not. Therefore, the project as a whole could not reasonably be described as 'mixed methods', even though it may well be that some teachers and groups of teachers at a local level may have experienced it in some ways as combining approaches. As one of the stakeholders commented, teachers in the early adopted trials often borrowed some of the experimental methods for RCTs after undergoing research methods training, but they were less confident with the methods and validity of qualitative methods. For this stakeholder, this suggests that there is 'real scope for training teachers to do research methods well'.

9. Fidelity of implementation. Given the large numbers of schools and individual teachers involved in the trials, fidelity of implementation in such an ambitious project was always going to be challenging. As discussed in Chapter

1, the initial training events introduced the key tools and protocols that were designed to establish fidelity and further extensive support was available during the duration of the project. However, the Teaching Schools were responsible for managing the fidelity of the trials. This was particularly challenging in the year 2 replication trials where the schools had to manage separation between a control and intervention group in the same school. Fidelity may have also been affected by personnel changes of trial co-ordinators or teachers implementing the trials in individual schools.

Innovation in the CtG project

In spite of the nine difficulties or challenges discussed above, it seems to us that there are two key distinctive features that do mark this out as a very innovative project that is possibly unique in research within the UK. The first is the scale of the project. We can no doubt think of major cross-sectional cohort studies that are often longitudinal in nature. These are studies that enable and facilitate broad sociological, and some educational, insights to be gained (such as the Youth Cohort Studies – see https://www.gov.uk/government/collections/statistics-youth-cohort-study). But this project, in being based on some specific classroom interventions, was the first large-scale, quasi-experimental study that aimed to be able to relate particular pedagogical innovations to student outcomes on a large scale. The fact that the attrition rate was low (around 10–15 per cent) across the two rounds of the project marks the project out as a significant success in terms of schools' and teachers' participation in a major research project.

However, the second aspect that makes the project distinctive was the aim to develop research skills and research capacity among the professional staff working in the schools (the effectiveness of this is discussed in Chapter 7). Through the design of the programme with its training rounds and networking events, the overall intention was to build an enduring legacy of research disposition and expertise that would enable teachers to continue with their own research projects into the future, whether within single schools, within alliances or in broader networks. In this respect, CtG was quite different from much of the early EEF work. However, it should be noted that more recent EEF initiatives, such as Research Use in Schools, do seek to stimulate just this kind of development (https://educationendowmentfoundation.org.uk/news/eef-launches-1.5-million-fund-to-improve-use-of-research-in-schools/). Colleagues from both NCTL and CfBT reported that they were pleasantly surprised to come across many teachers with a psychology background who understand both experimental design in general and the specifics of RCTS, as well as many teachers who understood the mathematics of effect sizes within RCTs. Indeed, many alliances took the ideas from the RCTs and used these to develop their own experimental small-scale RCT-like research designs. Some 50 of these received further research funding to develop these interventions.

The NCTL acknowledged the need for a more rigorous understanding of the importance of implementing interventions and tests at the right time, as well as ensuring the separation of control and intervention groups to avoid cross-contamination of results. Nevertheless, the fact that many teachers and alliances became involved in collaborative experimental research suggests that the project has had a potentially significant impact on the research capacity within schools, and in conjunction with universities as well, on schools' ability to engage with other research from their own contexts and circumstances. Indeed, the schools with the most advanced understanding of experimental methods also developed the most sophisticated contextual qualitative methods for a closer understanding of the reasons for positive or negative effect sizes.

Conclusion

The project as a whole was very significant in its ambition and in the influence it had on many teachers and schools across England. It was the most serious and sustained project of its type – multi-sited, large-scale, quasi-experimental research with many characteristics of an RCT and with the aim of supporting the learning of the most disadvantaged children in the Teaching Schools that took part. As we have seen, the very ambition of the project led to a number of significant challenges which would need to be addressed in any future scheme on a similar scale. By comparison, the work of the EEF, although when added together may be seen to be using a resource considerably larger than CtG, has nevertheless been largely carried out on a much smaller scale in more localised settings. However, it too makes claims of adopting RCT methods. Indeed it may well be that the EEF work can claim greater 'purity' of 'RCTness' simply because of the smaller scale of each of its many projects and the inherently less complex design. This does not reduce the wider value of the CtG project, although it does suggest that in educational research in multiple sites with multiple interventions the scale does not necessarily lead to an improvement in overall research quality. In medical research, on the other hand, it is generally the case that the larger a trial the more dependable the results are judged to be.

Any future work of this kind might valuably be based in part on considerations of the challenges that emerged here. For example, might it be better to limit the number of different interventions? Might it be advisable to build in some qualitative elements from the outset, rather than adding them in on a rather *ad hoc* basis as the work progresses? Should the pre- and post-test assessment instruments be more directly linked to the nature of the interventions that are being carried out?

The idea of a reformulation of teachers' professionalism and identity is being mooted in many contexts at present. For example, we have seen the emergence of the Chartered College of Teaching, the promotion of teachers' research engagement by the Teacher Development Trust (TDT, 2015), the emergence of the teachers' network ResearchED and the publication of the BERA-RSA report in 2014 calling for research-rich schools and for the development of research literacy among all teachers (BERA-RSA, 2014). All of these are consistent with this move to develop teachers' research literacy in England and elsewhere. And within this project the way in which a university-based team worked in very active partnership with the other team members has brought a particular set of expertise into the mix which has not necessarily been present in some of the other schemes. Nevertheless, as we saw earlier, it has also been suggested that RCT approaches to educational research – at least as conceived conventionally – may not be the most obvious way of bringing teachers themselves into research activity. RCTs may actually tend to position teachers as consumers of research rather than as active participants. Of course the very design of this project sought to overcome this likelihood by actively engaging the teachers, rather than seeing them as the 'tools' of an externally devised RCT (see Churches, 2016). It is to be hoped that the extended mixed methods research capacity developed through CtG means that evidence-based practice will in future mean engagement and involvement in both large-scale and locally contextualised research.

References

Ball, S. (2007) *Education plc: Understanding Private Sector Participation in Public Sector Education.* London: Routledge.

BERA-RSA (2014) *Research and the Teaching Profession – Building the Capacity for a Self-improving Education System (Final Report of the BERA-RSA Inquiry into the Role of Research in Teacher Education).* London: BERA.

Biesta, G. (2010) *Good Education in an Age of Measurement.* Colorado: Paradigm.

Brooks, R., te Riele, K. and Maguire, M. (2014) *Ethics and Education Research.* London: Sage.

Cartwright, N. and Hardie, J. (2012) *Evidence-Based Policy.* Oxford: University Press.

Churches, R. (2016) *Teacher-Led Research.* Carmarthen: Crown House.

Cohen, L., Manion, L. and Morrison, K. (2007) *Research Methods in Education.* Sixth edn. London: Routledge.

Delandshere, G. (2004) The moral, social and political responsibility of educational researchers: resisting the current quest for certainty. *International Journal of Educational Research,* 41(3), 237–256.

Department for Education (DfE) (2010) *The Importance of Teaching.* London: DfE.

Dudley, P. (2012) Lesson study in England: from school networks to national policy. *International Journal for Lesson and Learning Studies,* 1(1), 85–100.

Glover, T., Hannan, S. and Warburton, K. (2014) *Sustainable Business Models for Teaching Schools.* Nottingham: National College for Teaching and Leadership.

Goldacre, B. (2013) Building evidence into education. Available online: http://media. education.gov.uk/assets/files/pdf/b/ben%20goldacre%20paper.pdf (accessed on 19th August 2015).

Greany, T. (2015) *The Self-Improving System in England: A Review of Evidence and Thinking.* ASCL.

Greany, T. and Brown, C. (2015) *Partnerships between Teaching Schools and Universities: A Research Report*. London: UCL, Institute of Education.

Gu, Q., Rea, S., Hill, R., Smethem, L. and Dunford, J. (2014) *Teaching Schools Evaluation: Emerging Issues from the Early Development of Case Study Teaching School Alliances*. Nottingham: NCTL.

James, M. (2013) New (or not new) directions in evidence-based practice in education. Available online: https://www.bera.ac.uk/wp-content/uploads/2014/02/Mary-james-New-or-not-new-directions-in-evidence-based-policy.-Response-to-Ben-Goldacre.pdf?noredirect=1

Johnson, R. B. and Onwuegbuzie, A. J. (2004) Mixed methods research: a research paradigm whose time has come. *Educational Researcher*, 33(7), 14–26.

Menter, I. (2013) From interesting times to critical times? Teacher education and educational research in England. *Research in Teacher Education*, 3(1), 38–40.

Menter, I. (2014) Presidential address: educational research – What's to be done? *British Educational Research Journal*, 40(2), 213–226.

National College for Teaching and Leadership (NCTL) (2013) *Commercial Template: Further Competition (Closing the Gap: Test and Learn Capability)*. Nottingham: NCTL.

Pring, R. (2000) *Philosophy of Educational Research*. London: Continuum.

Punch, K. (2009) *Introduction to Research Methods in Education*. London: Sage.

Styles, B.J. (2009) The future is random – why the RCT should often be the method of evaluation. In: St. Clair, R. (Ed.) *Education Science: Critical Perspectives*. First edn. Rotterdam: Sense Publishers.

Teacher Development Trust (TDT) (2015) *Developing Great Teaching*. Available online: http://tdtrust.org/wp-content/uploads/2015/06/Developing-Great-Teaching-Summary.pdf

Thomas, G. (2009) *How To Do Your Research Project*. London: Sage.

Tooley, J. and Darby, D. (1998) *Educational Research: A Critique*. London: Office for Standards in Education.

Torgerson, D. and Torgerson, C. (2008) *Designing Randomised Trials in Health, Education and the Social Sciences*. Basingstoke: Palgrave Macmillan.

Yin, R.K. (2014) *Case Study Research: Design and Methods*. Fifth edn. London: Sage.

Chapter 4

Closing the Gap and professional learning

Two targets for a national project

Philippa Cordingley, Paul Crisp and Bart Crisp

Introduction

This was a unique project in the context of education research in the UK with many exciting challenges. The brief for phase 1 – consultation and design – contractors, lead by CUREE, was to apply the disciplines and protocols of the randomised controlled trial (RCT) to a programme for developing interventions, teachers and skills focussed on closing gaps for vulnerable learners collaboratively with leaders in the education sector. The rationale for the focus on trials methodology was to produce stronger causal evidence and to control for allocation bias with randomisation. This design was to be handed on to a phase 2 implementation contractor (only selected part way through the design process) who in turn had to run the trials without conventional (centralised) trial co-ordination but instead working through a network of Teaching School based local trial co-ordinators. This was expected to be controversial in both research and practitioner communities, each with their own concerns about this hybrid model. The whole consultation and design exercise had to be completed in a single term (plus summer holiday) instead of the normal year-long planning and preparation process for a single trial. This was not a single trial; it was expected to be the largest multi-strand, experimentally-evaluated intervention in school settings anywhere, ever. There were many policy, funding, research design and management uncertainties at the start of the exercise which had to be resolved during the design process and many strands of activity with competing requirements to be balanced.

Researchers will argue, with some justification, that trials that produce no positive outcomes are as valuable a contribution to science as major breakthroughs. Whatever the conceptual merits of that stance, this programme had other policy and educational imperatives. Its focus was explicitly on the morally and politically charged objective of closing the achievement gap for vulnerable pupils. It was going to be large and relatively expensive and there was a substantial critical audience who disagreed with the strong RCT emphasis in the design. Trial specialists were equally critical of what they saw as a lack of purity in the conception and rigour of the implementation. Though a large number of Teaching Schools had volunteered to participate in the trials, they had done so more or less blind to the detail of the funding and management arrangements, the intervention alternatives on offer and the logistical and practical challenges of participating. These large and small factors would all influence the actual participation of schools and the success or failure of the programme in closing gaps for vulnerable learners and developing CPD and R&D capacity in the system.

In addition to the issues around strategies for 'closing the gap' and controversies about research design, was the whole question of the role of continuing professional development and learning (CPDL) and school improvement strategies. It was the hypothesis of the CUREE and Durham development team – tested separately and together in published research and in previous collaborations – that the principal vehicle for school improvement was CPDL. It followed, therefore, that the interventions themselves had to incorporate well-designed CPDL in their delivery strategies if they were to be successful. This issue is explored in greater depth below.

In reality, many things were being trialled in this programme in addition to the CPD: the individual interventions themselves and their effectiveness in closing the gap; the approaches to involving school leaders and practitioners in the focus and design of the programme; the whole programme of large-scale RCTs; and the distributed trial management model. And it was all being done at breakneck speed.

What follows is an account of the way the processes of designing the programme delivery model and methodologies and of engaging the users in the programme content, focus and design intersected with and influenced the programme's core aims and the CPDL.

Objectives

The funds for this programme were earmarked to close the gap for vulnerable learners through support for Continuing Professional Development and Learning (CPDL). As other chapters explain, the decision was taken to host this within a randomised controlled trial (RCT)-like initiative in order to enable facilitation and to build capacity for research and evidence-informed practice using designs with strong causal inference. A need for the CPDL to be supported through relatively structured interventions that were capable of being researched in this way thus became an essential prerequisite so as to reduce the variability in the use of the approach. In 2013, at the time the scheme was initiated, neither trials nor interventions were widely understood concepts in schools, so building the ownership and enthusiasm to recruit schools at the scale and in the very short timescale required needed to start from the inception of the work. So the first steps for the team from the Centre for the Use of Research and Evidence in Education (CUREE), with support from Professors Rob Coe and Steve Higgins from the University of Durham, were to establish a series of mechanisms for consultation and awareness building. The aim was to work, wherever possible, from the growing network of Teaching Schools, especially those with an active focus on research and development (R&D) and CPDL.

CUREE's proposal to NCTL and its work during the design phase started from an interpretation of the evidence about both Closing the Gap for vulnerable pupils, which drew heavily on CUREE's own work for NCTL on *Leadership for Closing the Gap* (Cordingley, Temperley and Buckler, 2010), and on Professor Higgins' lead role in the development of the Sutton Trust-Education Endowment Foundation *Teaching and Learning Toolkit* (Higgins et al., 2013), which was in turn based on systematic technical reviews and meta-analyses of research evidence about the effectiveness of different educational approaches.

Although CPDL proved to be a major strand in the programme at several different levels, it was positioned at the start as the means through which interventions to close gaps for vulnerable pupils were supported rather than as an intervention in itself. The first-order goals were to close the gaps for vulnerable learners and promote evidence-informed practice. But improving outcomes for learners requires good teaching and teachers (Coe, Aloisi, Higgins and Major, 2014), which in turn requires well-designed CPDL (Cordingley et al., 2015). This was borne out in this project as all but one of the long list of interventions (and all of those eventually selected) that had good evidence to suggest they would be successful in closing gaps for vulnerable learners also had extensive CPDL as the principal means of implementing the intervention.

The evidence about effective CPDL and the interventions

The project took as its starting point the evidence from systematic reviews of the evidence about CPD, drawing in particular on the Evidence for Policy and Practice Information (EPPI) centre-endorsed review 'What do specialists do in CPD programmes for which there is evidence of positive outcomes for pupils and teachers?' and Timperley, Wilson, Barrar and Fung's (2007) *Best Evidence Synthesis*. This meant that we were looking for interventions with built-in, sustained support for CPDL that included:

- support for specialists in both the nature of the intervention and in designing effective CPD activities;
- extensive peer support and reciprocal risk taking;
- arrangements for developing practice and understanding of underpinning principles side by side;
- clarity from the outset about goals for pupils and the links between these and the CPD;
- embedding the use of evidence about how pupils respond to the changes arising from the CPD within the learning process and professional learning conversations to help teachers refine their approaches.

Whilst this rich array of aligned professional development experiences had not been a characteristic of many CPD programmes per se, at the time that the Closing the Gap: Test and Learn programme was being planned, it was possible to identify a number of specific teaching and learning interventions where such CPD had been wrapped around core approaches to pedagogy. But they were the exception rather than the rule and were very often only being offered in a limited number of locations or on a relatively small scale. The structure of the CPD was often not apparent from publicly available material, and so supplementary enquiries were made to ensure that the interventions chosen would be accompanied by CPD that was broadly consistent with the evidence about effective practices.

The focus of one intervention, Research Lesson Study (RLS), that was being put forward by a number of schools as a priority for testing was actually CPD itself. This was welcome in an initiative focussed on the use of CPD to close gaps for vulnerable learners. But although RLS is well known and has travelled quickly around the world on the basis of the enthusiasm of champions and enthusiastic users (Dudley, 2011), there is, as yet, relatively little evidence from experiments about its efficacy for pupils. There was still less evidence about its effectiveness for vulnerable pupils at the time because a core tenet of RLS is that the participating teachers choose three pupils as focus pupils for each lesson cycle, and it was very difficult to collect consistent evidence about the characteristics of the focus pupils chosen. An analysis of the structure of Research Lesson Study against the characteristics of effective CPD set out above suggests that there can also be a structural vulnerability inherent within the programme. If the teacher trios lack pedagogic content expertise and knowledge it may well be that the programme as a whole lacks access to essential specialist knowledge.

Despite these challenges, the quantity and range of enthusiasm for RLS was so extensive that the team identified the support needed and circumstances under which RLS might become an included intervention to enable the advisory group, which was responsible for final decision-making around what would be implemented in the trial programme, to consider it on a par with other interventions. We concluded that:

- a sustained training programme would have to be developed;
- there should be a focus within RLS on literacy;
- we should provide tools to scaffold the selection of approaches to try to ensure access to research materials about effective literacy interventions to help the trios select approaches likely to work for vulnerable focus pupils; and
- insisting upon a literacy leadership champion to support the work of the trios would create the circumstances in which RLS would be providing schools and teachers with similar levels of support to the other short-listed interventions.

The size of the trial (both in terms of number of participating students and number of interventions being trialled) posed a number of logistical challenges for the successful operation of the CPDL component because the training for each intervention needed to be lined up with the lifetime of the project overall and in particular with the testing windows. Bearing in mind that, as outlined in *Developing Great Teaching* (Cordingley et al., 2015), to be effective CPDL needed to be conducted over an extended period of time with multiple opportunities for reviewing progress and planning for the future. This meant that there was a significant point of potential failure if the training could not be aligned correctly. The design team, in particular colleagues from CUREE and CfBT, therefore worked hard to assemble a comprehensive picture of the necessary timeline for trialling of all of the interventions and co-ordinated with training providers and GL Assessment to agree a plan which would a) allow for the parallel controlled-trialling of all seven interventions, and b) enable genuinely effective CPD to take place across the lifetime of the project. This plan necessarily required some deviations from standard operating procedure for several of the participating training providers, but ultimately these were justified by the successful execution of the trial.

Identifying and selecting interventions as ownership building: What was an 'intervention'?

There are many activities, stratagems, techniques and resources which purport to enhance learner outcomes, and it was necessary to define what could be considered an 'intervention' for the purpose of this programme. We took as the starting point the characteristics defined in the programme specification that interventions should:

- show 'significant promise' for *closing the gap*; but
- may not have an existing secure evidence base;
- be capable of being conducted under RCT-like conditions; and
- complement, not replicate, work of the Education Endowment Foundation (EEF).

We derived a more elaborated working definition of 'intervention':

1 A set of specified and designed pupil-facing activities likely (as shown by existing evidence or a plausible extrapolation) to achieve positive outcomes for a given:

- population of pupils for whom the system faces CtG challenges;
- subject or topic where it is hard to CtG; or
- population of schools where there are particular challenged in CtG.

2   A process supported by a set of protocols, tools and activities for teachers and school leaders for effective implementation and contextualisation of the strategies and activities for classroom use with pupils.

3   Knowing that the programme's objectives included operating at scale, the selected interventions had to address issues and problems of real significance to school leaders and teachers if they were to secure buy-in. So we added to the core characteristics some other desirable ones. The selected interventions should, if possible:

- go beyond core subjects and into curriculum-related concepts that represent enduring 'wicked' issues – e.g., algebra or fractions in mathematics;
- focus on key pedagogic strategies that have been proven to work but which are challenging for teachers to use – particularly in the UK – and which may also be harder to use in some subjects than others (e.g., enquiry in MFL);
- focus on interventions of promise but which require support, e.g., AfL or coaching linked to subject experiences;
- include interventions or approaches that are popular but where there is little or no evidence of positive impact – exploring the possibility of improving them;
- explore the transfer of interventions from one context to another.

4   There needed to be a rationale for the interventions chosen, as clear and compelling as possible, but also capable of securing buy-in for interventions that:

- had a good chance of succeeding;
- were implementable at scale with input support; and
- were researchable.

5   This led to a more elaborated set of criteria. The intervention had to have:

- evidence that interventions had promise but were not proven;
- a likelihood of fidelity/quality implementation;
- likelihood of take-up by schools which would select:

  - things that were 'wicked' challenges for schools;
  - things that were popular in schools;
  - relevance to things that schools would have to attend to for policy or practice demands, e.g., new national curriculum (policy), changing demographics (practice);

- potential for expanding the current knowledge base;
- fit with ethos of the Teaching Schools programme.

The criterion that the intervention had to be supported by protocols and techniques for effective implementation had important consequences for the selection exercise as there were many generic 'approaches' which were insufficiently well specified to be trial-able. Some of these (for instance assessment for learning, problem-based learning) were popular and would have met the fourth criterion above. In different circumstances, or in a different programme, we might have encouraged some development work and piloting, but neither programme specification nor timetable permitted this.

Consultation on needs and potential responses

Within four weeks of starting the work, the team had mobilised a range of networks of schools focussed on CPDL and research and development (R&D) and initiated a consultation process designed to explore the views of school leaders and teachers about both the priorities for vulnerable pupils that were creating gaps and barriers to learning and the kinds of interventions and CPDL activities that they would like to see supported but also tested in this way. This consultation took the form of online surveys and focus groups with both partner Teaching Schools supporting the design process and schools who had expressed an interest in contributing. The survey and focus groups asked participants about:

- the issues that CtG: Test and Learn should target, such as:
  - which groups of pupils would benefit most from interventions; and
  - which aspects of learning and outcomes the Test and Learn project would impact most;
- what they thought about a "starter" list of possible interventions; and
- other interventions which schools thought would also be worth considering.

A total of 233 responses were received to the survey and 19 teachers were involved in four focus group discussions. The National College also, more formally, asked school leaders to nominate interventions that could be trialled, and 24 additional suggestions were put forward by this route. The survey and focus group data together offered a long list of over 60 potential interventions.

The team from CUREE and Durham designed and carried out a process which would reduce this to a long list of between 12 and 20 interventions to be presented to a steering group of Teaching School Alliance R&D leads who would then provide additional guidance on which should be trialled. The process which the team created aimed systematically to select interventions most suitable for trialling. We started by gathering information on the 'interventions' which would enable us to identify:

- what the intervention was intended to achieve;
- a description of its features;

- the phase(s) it targeted;
- subject focus (if any) and scope;
- if, and to what extent, the intervention was supported (by resources, protocols, training);
- its approximate cost; and
- to what extent it was assessable.

A substantial fraction of the suggestions made (particularly via the online survey) were eliminated at this first stage because we were not provided with (and could not find) sufficient information about the proposal to take it further – for instance, it was a general approach or idea (for instance, 'learning walks'); it existed in multiple forms (like data tracking); we could not find any previous evaluation; or it was not in widespread use.

The remaining interventions were then scored on a scale of ten for each of three major criteria which the team judged to be key to determining the likelihood of success in the trial process. These criteria were:

- the accessibility of the intervention's planned outcomes, its suitability for RCT-like methods and the likelihood of the CPDL achieving its goals in the light of the evidence from systematic research reviews about effective CPDL;
- the manageability of the intervention within the Test and Learn timescales and resource levels and the likely demands on participating schools; and
- the extent to which the intervention matched the criteria identified by schools in the consultation process and, hence, the likelihood of take-up by them.

From this process emerged potential interventions that:

- were sufficiently close in their design to findings about effective CPDL to have a reasonable chance of having a positive effect in closing the gap;
- were capable of being evaluated through an RCT-like experimental design;
- would be, just about, manageable within the initiative's extremely demanding timescales and very tight resource constraints; and
- met the criteria about gaps to be closed and types of approaches that emerged from the consultation.

The technical/research factors evaluated were:

- How researchable/assessable is the intervention?
- What is the target population?
- Why should it work (e.g., the logic model)?
- What is the existing supporting evidence of impact?

- Why should it be tested (including the benefits to a 'closing the gap' project)?
- What are the main (primary) quantifiable outcomes?
- Were there other relevant outcomes?
- How could the main outcomes be tested, e.g., were test materials readily available?

The following chart, Figure 4.1, illustrates the outcomes of that scoring exercise.

Twelve approaches or interventions from the long list emerged as feasible from the technical analysis and were then presented to the Teaching Schools' Research and Development Advisory Group. A further intervention, Lego Therapy, was added to the shortlist (taking the total to 13) as it was considered very innovative and a good fit with the school-driven desirability criteria even though it had not scored enough in the technical analysis to get in to the top group.

The R&D Advisory Group carried out a ranking exercise for the long list of interventions, focussing in particular on the likely buy-in and take-up by schools and the practical manageability of the interventions from an expert school leadership perspective. This generated extensive discussion by the group drawing also on the technical scores for accessibility/suitability for RCT identified by the team from CUREE and Durham.

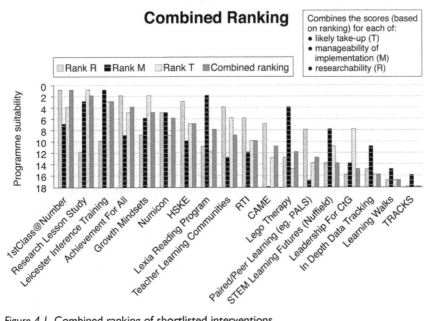

Figure 4.1 Combined ranking of shortlisted interventions

Two other features of the process also generated considerable discussion and some expressions of concern:

a   the ethics of trialling in the education context; and
b   the dominance in the shortlist of 'commercial' interventions.

The ethics discussion itself resolved into two sub-issues:

1   the now traditional viewpoint that it was unethical to withhold a benefit from a pupil in the interests of science; and
2   a more legalistic issue around data protection and whether schools would be in breach of their duties in sharing data about pupils with the researchers (and potentially the Teaching School 'trial managers').

On the former, the design team pointed out that one of the inclusion specifications focussed on this ethical point; an intervention should be considered for trialling only if a) there was reason to believe it was efficacious, but b) there was not conclusive causal evidence that it was. The other key clarification was that those pupils not receiving the intervention would be expected to be taught in the existing (presumably best practice) way and would benefit, albeit a little later, from the intervention if the trial was successful. The design team and the National College/DfE project managers were also able to assure Advisory Group members that the data management protocols fell within the existing usage provisions and any performance data about pupils would be anonymised for analytical purposes. Though the ethical discussion did not reveal widespread concern, we did build into the guidance being passed to the implementation contractors the recommendation that the ethical issues should be explicitly aired in the introductory training (which it was – though, in practice, there was very little worry about the ethical issues expressed by the schools participating in the trials).

The relative dominance of fully worked-up interventions with a clear methodology, protocols, resources and training was a consequence of the speed and scale of the programme overall. Interventions could not be trialled without these features and, in their absence, they would have to be created at a cost of time and money. In practice, one approach was of great interest to the user community representatives – Research Lesson Study – and was in widespread use but in multiple different forms and not particularly focussed on the needs of vulnerable pupils. In this one instance, the programme agreed to support a pilot/development phase before moving to full trial.

It was a misconception, but one which persisted long into the implementation phase, that the other interventions were 'commercial'. All were 'owned' by either a public sector organisation (e.g., local authority, a university, the Crown) or a charity, some of which were set up explicitly to develop, promote and support the intervention (e.g., Achievement for All).

However, most also had to charge for their services in order to be sustainable in the longer term.

The final list of interventions selected was:

- 1stClass@Number – an intervention which uses teaching assistants to deliver a mathematics intervention which aims to give learners additional metacognitive control over their maths learning to bring about improvements in attainment.
- Achievement for All – a whole-school intervention designed to aid leadership and classroom practitioners in providing targeted, evidence-based improvement strategies to learners.
- Growth Mindsets – a specific incarnation of the various interventions based on Carol Dweck's research developed by Portsmouth University, which had already been involved in smaller-scale trialling.
- Inference Training – an intervention designed to help weak readers build their ability to grasp the full meaning of text as they read it by equipping them with a range of techniques for improving their inference abilities.
- Numicon – a multi-disciplinary, multi-sensory approach to mathematics learning which helps children understand number relationships, see patterns and make generalisations, and which has had particular success in the past with children with short-term learning problems such as those with Down's syndrome.
- Research Lesson Study – a version of the Lesson Study approach originally developed in Japan, in this instance based on the work done by Peter Dudley, which was adapted for testing by CUREE through the introduction of a specific, focussed literacy component.
- Response to Intervention – adapted from its original use in the United States for implementation in the UK by CUREE, this intervention uses close-case analysis of individual learners to target specific, small-scale literacy interventions to their needs at whole-class, small-scale and one-to-one levels, depending on which is most appropriate
- An additional intervention – using computer mediated learning for literacy development – was originally proposed for trialling, but the provider withdrew citing concerns about the demanding timescale and the problems of providing training at scale and at speed.

The allocation process

The overall goal was to end up with seven pools of schools allocated to interventions, each of roughly similar size. The exception to this was Achievement for All (AfA). Due to the more stringent requirements and higher cost (see below), the final pool for AfA was designed to be slightly smaller than the others.

In the last couple of weeks of term, the participating Teaching Schools (and their nominated Alliance Schools) were sent details of the seven interventions and were asked to rank them in their preference order (and to identify any which they specifically did **not** want to trial). The research team started the allocation process by working with the known preferences expressed by the participating schools. The team then allocated the remaining places in the pools for each of the interventions to participating Teaching School Alliances, taking into account the number of schools who did not complete the preferences survey. The aim was to enable alliances to then make choices about interventions between participating schools. The process is described in detail below.

Phase one: Reference-based allocation

1   The overarching aim was to achieve seven roughly equal-sized pools of schools to enable the test and learn trials to have an equal chance of demonstrating impact (the size of the pool of schools affects the effect size).

2   Interventions were allocated to schools who had expressed a preference within the timescale on the basis of the first preference of the school, wherever possible, or failing that on the basis of its second preference. Allocation was to a group which was then to be randomised to intervention or control.

3   Achievement for All was allocated first because it required a high level of commitment and was very demanding of resources and attention.

4   Beyond AfA, the initial spread of the first choices was analysed to identify interventions where the pools were under-represented (e.g., RTI, which was new and relatively unknown in this country).

5   Phase-specific interventions (Numicon and 1stClass@Number) were allocated next. All primary schools that selected these interventions as their first choice were allocated to the relevant pools. Schools were also allocated to these interventions based on their second choice if their first choice was not AfA, RTI or the other of the phase-specific interventions.

6   Finally, Inference Training, RLS and Growth Mindsets were allocated to intervention pools on the basis of first choices.

7   As a result of completing this process, all schools that expressed their preferences were allocated to an intervention group for randomisation of their first or (less often) their second choice. Fifteen schools completed the survey without expressing any specific preferences. The research team contacted each of these schools individually asking them to clarify their position. Once these schools replied they were allocated in accordance with their first choices.

8   We identified ten of the RLS schools to act as year 1 pilots to carry out R&D on tailoring RLS to Closing the Gap. We chose Teaching Schools that had chosen RLS to be part of this pilot group.

Phase two: Random allocation

9   After completing the allocation for all schools that expressed preferences, we randomly allocated pools of interventions to alliances so that choices could be made on the ground whilst maintaining the overall size of the intervention pools. First, we merged the databases sent to us by NCTL to create a single list of participating schools.

10 The list was checked for duplicate entries. All of these were: 1) copied into a separate tab for record; 2) dealt with individually and checked on Edubase. In the instances when there was an obvious duplication of the same record, resulting, e.g., from a special school being present in both primary and secondary original spreadsheets, one of the entries was removed. Where the two schools with the same name were different (i.e., had different URNs and were in different locations) both such entries were kept intact in the list of the participating schools.

11 We then removed from the list all those which had completed the survey and had therefore already been allocated to an intervention during phase one.

12 We established what our target numbers of schools allocated per intervention were and subtracted the number of schools thus far allocated to each intervention, in order to determine how many schools were still needed for each intervention.

13 We then used the randomise function within the spreadsheets to make a notionally random allocation of interventions to the remaining schools. This was specifically to enable us to make sure the numbers worked and notional in the sense that the allocation would ultimately be made to an alliance in general for local allocation.

14 Numicon and 1stClass@Number as phase-specific interventions were given priority and allocated first. We first filtered the list to include only primary schools and then randomly allocated the required number of schools.

15 One of the few remaining AfA places was allocated to a teaching school allied to a large number of schools to increase the likelihood of the choice being a positive one.

Once the process was complete we created a table indicating which interventions were randomly allocated to which schools within an alliance and removed the individual school indicator but without naming any specific school to allow for some choices with alliances. All unallocated schools (who had expressed preferences) were allocated to the other six interventions – aiming to have a broad spread of schools across all six – using the criteria in the following order:

1   first or second choice preferences;
2   interventions with low numbers of first or second preferences;

3   phase-specific interventions (Numicon and 1stClass@Number);
4   all the remaining interventions and schools. All primary schools that selec-
     ted these interventions as their first choice were allocated to the relevant
     pools. Schools were also allocated to these interventions based on their
     second choice if their first choice was not AfA, RTI or the other of the
     phase-specific interventions.

Randomised assignment

In order to maintain the methodological integrity of the trial, it was necessary
to ensure a minimum pool size for each intervention so that the resulting sample
size was large enough to produce potentially statistically significant results. Once
the pool of potential triallists was established for each intervention, schools were
randomly assigned (through a process operated by the National College project
manager) to an intervention (treatment) or control (non-treatment) group.
Schools in the intervention group were then sent details of the process, invited
to training sessions and so on, but this was all communicated through the trial
co-ordinator in the Teaching School which nominated the participating
schools.

Systems, processes and guides

The final element of the first phase of the project was to help establish the
conditions for its successful implementation by the Closing the Gap team at
NCTL and the phase 2 capability contractors (CfBT supported by Oxford
University, CUREE and Durham). This involved:

1   establishing with the intervention providers the detail of their provision
     and any adjustments that need to be made;
2   producing broad descriptions of each of the interventions to enable the
     schools to make informed choices about the CPD and intervention they
     would engage with;
3   devising the protocols for managing the interventions and the CPD to
     provide an effective environment for intervention and CPD support whilst
     also creating a robust environment for conducting RCTs in the context
     of the programme's distributed leadership;
4   providing advice and guidance to the College's Closing the Gap team on
     other features of the programme; and
5   documenting the whole process and creating guides and other resources
     for programme managers and school research leads.

Recommendations made by the initial development team were designed
to help balance the requirements of the interventions for closing the gap, the

requirements of the CPD and the constraints arising from the decision to evaluate this through robust experimental methods. Once the design of the logistical support came into play, many of these recommendations were over-taken by events. But it is useful to consider how the balances between the CPD, the aim of closing the gap and the robustness of the evaluation were struck at the end of the first phase of the project as this sets the context for both the subsequent work to close gaps and for evaluating this in a trial-like context.

Managing the groups

A delayed intervention for control groups or 'wait-list control' approach was agreed for all seven selected interventions as the most likely to help close gaps for most pupils and to enhance CPD overall. It was also thought to be the most appropriate approach from the research design point of view and most achievable given the complexity and size of the programme. This meant that those schools that were control in year 1 would have an opportunity to carry out an intervention in year 2 of the programme. It was also recommended that control schools would be able to choose their intervention in year two as the priority for closing the gap might well have changed as schools would then be working with new year groups and, as the evidence about CPD showed, ensuring that CPD is focussed on the needs of specific pupils is key to success. In order to achieve sufficient trial power, the minimum size of each pool needed to be 40 schools.

Sustaining commitment

As with any CPD programme and indeed any research project, particularly if it is delivered at scale, there was always a risk of schools dropping out of the programme. The extensive attention given to consulting schools about the gaps and interventions and giving them choices about the interventions and CPD they were accessing were thought to be key to reducing these risks and, in the first year at least, drop out was remarkably low.

This risk of drop out was particularly high for control schools. To address this we had, in our correspondence to schools, highlighted the benefits of being a control school including the opportunity to select an intervention in the light of direct evidence emerging in their own and neighbouring alliances about the successes and challenges of the interventions in schools. Schools also received reassurance that should they be allocated to control, there would be sufficient resource for them to deliver an intervention in year 2.

A key intersection between the design of the programme as a whole, its efficacy in closing the gap and the CPD was the pivotal role of Teaching Schools and their research leads in managing communications, recruitment, testing and securing and maintaining co-operation of control schools. These

Teaching Schools had their own goals with regards to CPD, closing the gap and R&D. We believed that if a Teaching School had all its participating schools allocated to control groups, the risk of it leaving the programme would be very high. It was therefore crucial that the randomisation process be carried out so that it achieved a balance between the numbers of schools in any alliance that were control or intervention groups (see separate notes above on randomisation).

Intensity of participation

Primary schools were asked to choose one class for the trial; secondary schools to choose two classes. This enabled schools to focus on specific gaps that mattered to them, to focus their efforts and manage the amount of time out of class for CPD that schools, often quite vulnerable schools, had to cope with. It took into account the financial constraints involved with testing the entire classes with the target pupils for both the treatment and control groups twice. It also helped to make the process manageable for the schools because the trial-like approach required that testing was completed before allocating schools to the intervention or the control group, something that meant schools and teachers had to cope with an unusual degree of uncertainty in contemplating and planning for CPD.

Selecting focus pupils

For all of the CPD interventions except Growth Mindsets, the CPD involved teachers, at the very least in the early phase of their CPD, working with a focus group of pupils. This was also important for the evaluation. Schools were encouraged to select focus pupils using two broad criteria: 1) vulnerability (FSM, Looked after, SEN) and 2) low achievement (in a particular area, i.e., literacy or numeracy). Tools and protocols were developed in phase one to help schools use evidence about focus pupils' background characteristics and the outcomes of the standardised assessments. The process of selecting focus pupils by the teachers was sometimes important in the design of the CPD, but selection of focus pupils by the research team would have led to greater robustness in the evaluation. On the other hand, the selection of the focus pupils by the schools made a contribution to the ecological validity of the evaluation because in 'real life' schools would be selecting the pupils themselves, without relying on external researchers and standardised assessment data.

In the end the pupils were selected by the schools after the testing, frequently during the CPD programmes themselves. Also, for a range of practical and logistical reasons and the loss of lots of the forms recording the selection of the focus pupils, the evaluation moved from a planned analysis and comparison of the learning of focus pupils and the rest of the class, to a simpler comparison of the progress of FSM and non FSM pupils.

Research Lesson Study

Research Lesson Study was in a significantly different position to all the other interventions as it had to run as a pre-/post-test pilot in the first year for a rather smaller group of just 20 schools. Schools were allocated to RLS RCT at the beginning of the programme alongside the other interventions. This meant that at least 100 schools needed to be allocated to RLS (20 to the pilot and 80 for the RCT phase in year 2). The tools and materials developed for the pilot were then refined at the conclusion of the pilot phase, following feedback from participating schools.

There are specific challenges in balancing the requirements of the CPD, the rhythm of the school year and the requirements of the evaluation for RLS in the second year because both the trial and the implementation for the wait group had to be accommodated in one academic year. This resulted in a particularly truncated period of training and implementation.

The role of standardised tests and other evidence in the CPD and the programme

Standardised tests in literacy and numeracy were selected for the programme, and in several interventions extensive use was made of the evidence from the baseline tests because the interventions and the CPD both involved in-depth diagnostic analysis of pupils' starting points. In most interventions, the test focus (literacy or numeracy) was straightforward and was directly relevant to the intervention, i.e., Numicon and 1stClass@Number – maths; Inference Training and RTI – English. But for the three remaining interventions (AfA, RLS and Growth Mindsets) the focus was not necessarily upon a particular curriculum area. It was not possible to fund both literacy and numeracy tests for these interventions, so it was recommended that a literacy test be used for AfA and RLS and that the possibility of using a numeracy test for Growth Mindsets be explored.

Innovations and learning within the formal training programme

In addition to CPD to support the intervention, the programme offered a series of CPD events and tools to support the learning of Teaching School research leads. The content and process for these events had to wrestle with numerous contending needs. The early CPD and induction sessions had to take place with very little notice. All the CPD sessions had to take into account that there would be a diverse group in attendance, with a wide variety of levels of experience, both in general and specifically in relation to RCTs. Later CPD sessions involved significant numbers of people who had not been involved in the project from the beginning. Each session and each component of the CPD was trying to achieve multiple goals: building commitment to the project among participants; giving local leaders an overview of the CPD and the interventions so they could support schools in their alliance as they worked though the CPD and the interventions; informing participants about the format of the trial program; and, during the second and third CPD sessions in particular, providing participants with a greater degree of interest in and experience of research with information about how to carry out their own mini-RCTs. Embedded in all these sessions were a number of tools (Spillane, 2005; Robinson, Hohepa and Lloyd, 2009) specifically designed to scaffold the early stages of development and increase coherence and consistency.

Here is an illustration of the structure and content of the first round of CPD for Teaching School research leads who would be acting in effect as local trial co-ordinators for the duration of the project, providing them with the necessary information to fulfil this role:

- the first full CPD session comprised an introductory session, helping participants to reconnect with the Test and Learn project aims and explore the different reasons schools in their networks had for taking part and their different levels of capacity for engaging with trial methodologies;
- a recap session to enhance and extend participants' understanding of the nature and source of the interventions and allocations and programme goals;
- an exploratory session to develop an understanding of the connections between the interventions and how the work reinforces existing R&D capacity-building activity across the alliances;
- an explanatory session to develop participants' understanding of (and, hopefully, enthusiasm for) RCT-like R&D, and to introduce the role of qualitative evidence in conducting and making use of trials;
- a session to develop participants' understanding of the tools and protocols developed to support fidelity in trial implementation, and to enable read-across qualitative work within and between schools and alliances;
- a session to help participants explore the nature of the assessment protocols established for the project;
- a practical session exploring the timelines and practical requirements of the interventions which participants would be mediating across their alliances;
- a Q&A review and summary session.

Before the team settled on a structure for the second CPD event, colleagues from the CUREE planning team conducted phone interviews with R&D leads at alliances who had been involved in conducting the interventions to get some insight into what the driving issues for R&D leads were likely to be. In the light of this evidence, the second CPD session encompassed:

- a collaborative session to enable participants to share their progress and experiences so far, and identify goals for continued improvement/development;

- a planning session in which participants were asked to consider one of two hypothetical scenarios related to helping schools make decisions on the back of RCT results and make suggestions for how to respond to the challenges these scenarios presented;
- an analytical session in which participants developed their own research skills/understanding through focussing in depth on identifying good research questions and related methods;
- a learning session in which participants were introduced to and given a chance to familiarise themselves with a variety of methods of research dissemination;
- a reflective plenary session in which participants reviewed the connections between the content of the training and both action planning and evaluation.

The CPD sessions also took place in the second year of the Test and Learn project, and so included a diverse range of participants, some of whom would have been involved in the trials for over a year and some of whom would be completely new to it. The design team therefore decided to construct a 'three track', differentiated offer – one which supported old hands, people in the midst of the process, and people who were completely new to it. The CPD session involved:

- an introductory session in which participants took stock of their current situation and where they needed to go next;
- a session in which participants were given both time and structure in which to consider what involvement in the Test and Learn project as a whole would need to include in order to be a success for them, their schools and their pupils;
- a series of parallel sessions:
  - a session based on those used in previous training rounds, aimed at relative beginners, which introduced them to and provided them with some experience of analysing and making use of the programme's research methods, concepts and tools;
  - a session for participants in the midst of supporting interventions, intended to extend the previous session's activities in conceptualising/ visualising success and how it can be achieved, particularly through making use of the progress of their peers to generate new ideas;
  - a session for participants who had completed the interventions through Test and Learn and were looking to plan further R&D activity for the future and potentially conduct further, smaller-scale trials. This session was intended to provide some structure which could and would sustain the momentum already generated by these participants through their involvement in the Test and Learn project.

- a debriefing session in which participants could analyse and explore the outcomes of the previous session they had been involved in;
- a critiquing session for participants to think about and experience concrete examples of what makes for good (and poor) research dissemination;
- an action planning session to give participants an opportunity to use what they had learned from the day in the future.

Conclusions

Although the *impact* of the interventions on closing the gap was evaluated very thoroughly, this was through only one quantitative, methodological lens. The CPD itself was provided by facilitators operating co-operatively within the constraints of the programme but independently of it. Very little evidence was collected centrally about the CPD or about its impact upon the teachers. The main mechanism for doing this was a survey to teachers and school leaders where the focus was predominantly on the impact of the CPD on intervention and the fidelity of implementation. But the systematic research reviews of CPD highlight the difficulties in use of perception data for evaluating CPD (Timperley et al., 2007). Colleagues who have made great progress or who start from a very sophisticated starting point tend significantly to underestimate how much progress they have made because they can see how much more is possible. Colleagues who are relative novices or still in the early stages of integrating a new approach into their practice tend to significantly overestimate progress because their attention is still focussed on surface features and have not yet had an opportunity to explore the underpinning principles and the way that these affect responses to different pupils.

So it is not possible to draw firm conclusions about how far the investment in CPD capacity and its development through a co-construction model with sector leaders made a difference. Nor is it possible to provide much textured evidence about the similarities and differences between the CPD implementations as they took place on the ground; the written design plans were strikingly similar, with the exception of the much larger, whole-school focussed AfA. But anecdotally, at the time of writing, there is a positive story to tell. For example, over a period of just four weeks CUREE was working with or approached by four schools and Teaching Schools who either participated in CPD as part of the Closing the Gap: Test and Learn or whose new leaders had been research leads in other participating schools. In each case they wanted to extend and/or build on the capacity developed during the programme. As an aside it would be interesting to learn about the career progression of the R&D leads and intervention champions. What was particularly striking was the use of tools and protocols from RTI and the CTG RLS model such as the questioning framework for coaches, the progress monitoring tool and the close case analysis tool we saw being used more broadly. Over a longer timescale we have heard, for example, that RLS is still alive and well and being actively used across the Sawston Teaching School Alliance, and the evidence submitted to the DfE Expert Group on CPD from the South West region included an extensive description of the continuing use of Closing the Gap interventions, especially RLS in the CPD work of Teaching Schools in that region.

CPD was only one strand in a complex intervention. Closing the gap is a complex challenge. Working to do so at scale adds another layer of complexity, and evaluating the enterprise through a highly distributed, RCT-like evaluation framework was innovative in the extreme. The balances that had to be achieved were only possible because of the shared, strong moral purpose and the curiosity and interest of R&D leads in Teaching Schools who had hitherto lacked attention and focus to the same degree as their peers working on, for example, Initial Teacher Education or leadership development. The speed and intensity of response and sustained buy-in in the first year of the programme is a testimony to the contributions of a very large group of people. Many colleagues thought the timescale breathtaking. But in the event we are now reflecting on whether the pace of development might actually have contributed to securing initial buy-in, and whether it acted as a prism that focussed and concentrated efforts and enabled colleagues from different fields of expertise and different ideological stances to secure commitments to working in new ways.

The speed and scale of the programme, taken with the commitment to a trial-type evaluation approach, imposed significant constraints on the type of intervention included. It was evident in the early exploratory phase that some stakeholders – particularly school leaders and practitioners – hoped to see broad, weakly detailed strategies and approaches (such as 'learning walks' or 'assessment for learning') included. Others put forward their favourite packaged solutions but unfortunately many (and it would be invidious to name them here) lacked any significant evidence of impact – there was no discernible correlation between popularity and efficacy. The design team, under different conditions, would have liked to include some of these, particularly those in widespread use. To do this we would have needed the time and resources to establish the logic model, a standardised set of procedures and protocols, and to pilot the approach – before launching a full-scale trial. In most instances those interventions with a track record and a fully worked-up set of procedures and a means of implementing them at school level (in most instances this meant training) came at a cost.

Many, particularly those in the research community, doubted that the programme could be successfully launched, let alone delivered, because of the speed, scale and lack of centralised control systems normally associated with clinical-style trials. In practice none of these conditions was life threatening and, as noted above, the speed may have added a sense of urgency and priority which enabled the interventions to get some purchase in the quotidian reality of school life.

References

Coe, R., Aloisi, C., Higgins, S. and Major, L. E. (2014) *What Makes Great Teaching? Review of the Underpinning Research*. London: Sutton Trust.

Cordingley, P., Bell, M., Isham, C., Evans, D. and Firth, A. (2007) 'What do specialists do in CPD programmes for which there is evidence of positive outcomes for pupils and teachers?' Report. In: *Research Evidence in Education Library*. London: EPPI-Centre, Social Science Research Unit, Institute of Education, University of London.

Cordingley, P., Temperley, J. and Buckler, N. (2010) *Leadership for Closing the Gap*. Available online: http://webarchive.nationalarchives.gov.uk/20140719134807/http://www.nationalcollege.org.uk/download?id=142921&filename=leadership-for-closing-the-gap-full-report.pdf

Cordingley, P., Higgins, S., Greany, T., Buckler, N., Coles-Jordan, D., Crisp, B., Saunders, L. and Coe, R. (2015) *Developing Great Teaching: Lessons from the International Reviews into Effective Professional Development*. London: Teacher Development Trust.

Dudley, P. (2011) 'Lesson study development in England: from school networks to national policy', *International Journal for Lesson and Learning Studies*, 1(1), pp. 85–100. doi: 10.1108/20468251211179722

Higgins, S., Katsipataki, M., Kokotsaki, D., Coleman, R., Major, L. E. and Coe, R. (2013) *Teaching and Learning Toolkit*. London: Education Endowment Foundation. Available online: https://educationendowmentfoundation.org.uk/resources/teaching-learning-toolkit

Robinson, V., Hohepa, M. and Lloyd, C. (2009) *School Leadership and Student Outcomes: Identifying What Works and Why [BES], Iterative Best Evidence Synthesis Programme*. New Zealand: Ministry of Education. Available online: http://www.peersupport.edu.au/wp-content/uploads/2014/08/Student-leadership.pdf

Spillane, J. P. (2005) 'Distributed leadership', *The Educational Forum*, 69, pp. 141–150. doi: 10.1007/978-1-4020-9737-9.

Timperley, H., Wilson, A., Barrar, H. and Fung, I. (2007) *Teacher Professional Learning and Development: Best Evidence Synthesis Iteration [BES]*. Wellington, New Zealand: Ministry of Education. Available online: https://www.educationcounts.govt.nz/publications/series/2515/60169/60170

Part 2

Teachers and research methods

Some wider issues

Chapter 5

Room in the toolbox?

The place of randomised controlled trials in educational research

Steve Higgins

Introduction

This chapter considers the role of randomised trials in education as a necessary but not sufficient research design for drawing conclusions about effective educational practice. Using a toolbox metaphor, it identifies what kinds of questions are appropriate for different RCT designs in terms of supporting causal inference as part of a wider set of tools for educational inquiry. Trials have one key feature, randomisation, which uniquely addresses some aspects of potential bias in evaluative educational research. A review of the designs of the trials used in the Closing the Gap project helps to identify some strengths and weaknesses of randomisation, particularly in relation to the internal and external validity of the findings. A contrast will then be drawn between the large-scale and micro-scale designs in Closing the Gap: Test and Learn in response to Biesta's (2007) challenges about the democratic deficit in notions of 'what works', which he claims restricts opportunities for participation in educational decision making. By contrast it is argued that causal evidence is necessary, but not sufficient, for the normative professional judgements of teachers, and that teachers can be closely involved in the development and use of randomised trials.

Biesta (2007) critiques the idea of evidence-based practice and in particular the ways in which it has been promoted and implemented in education. He draws attention to a number of issues, in particular focusing on the dynamics between scientific and democratic control over educational practice and research and identifying the 'scientific' with a 'technological model of professional action'. This is not a necessary connection however, and I argue the dichotomy is a false one. It is possible to hold a 'scientific' view of causation at the same time as seeing education as a process of symbolically mediated interaction. Of course, the interpretation of the meaning of the findings of 'scientific' trials in terms of the impact of an intervention may be different as a result of this interpretation. A synthesis of these viewpoints puts greater emphasis on the internal validity of the trial findings in terms of answering the question, 'Was the intervention effective *there*, in terms of the outcomes measured in the trial?' The subsequent question of, 'And will it be effective in *my* school, for *my* pupils?' (in terms of external validity) requires, in my view, either extensive replication to understand the range of contexts where it can be successful or professional judgement and interpretation based on the limited inference from a single trial. This perspective is supported by a more rigorous understanding of what an 'average treatment effect' means in scientific terms (Deaton & Cartwright, 2016), what can be inferred from the findings, in terms of the average impact in relation to the schools, teachers and pupils in the trial, and how similar these pupils, teachers and schools are to the context under consideration for application in terms of 'evidence-use'.

Biesta (2007) examines three key assumptions of evidence-based education: first, the extent to which educational practice can be compared to the practice of medicine; second, the role of knowledge in professional action, particularly in terms of what kind of knowledge assumptions are appropriate for and relevant to professional practices that can be informed by research outcomes; and third, the expectations about the practical role of research implicit in the idea of evidence-based education. Perhaps unsurprisingly, I disagree with Biesta in some important respects on each of these issues, but most importantly his view that scientific knowledge diminishes democratic control over education and the decision making of practitioners. By contrast, I argue that access to and engagement with 'scientific' knowledge is an essential condition for the democratic participation of teachers in making judgements about educational practice.

Biesta draws the conclusion that the notion of evidence-based practice is a limiting concept which not only restricts the scope of decision making to questions about effectiveness, but also that it restricts the opportunities for participation in educational decision making. He argues that we must expand our views about the interrelations among research, policy, and practice to keep in view education as a thoroughly moral and political practice that requires continuous democratic contestation and deliberation. On this point we agree, though I would go further and argue that the role of evidence is more crucial for practice here than for policy. Or rather that the role of evidence-based policy should be to support evidence-based (or more precisely evidence-informed) practice due to the variation in findings across educational trials and the challenge of interpreting average treatment effects from both single trials, as well as the pooled averages from research syntheses such as those found in meta-analysis.

These are serious claims against the use of rigorous inquiry and evidence in education that require further analysis in terms of whether these consequences are necessary and inevitable, or, if not, what can be done to mitigate the challenges of democratic participation in research by teachers and whether the sacrifice of causal inference could therefore be justified. The importance of causal claims is what I turn to in the next section.

Evaluation of impact in education

Impact evaluation in education usually means assessing the effects of policies and initiatives or other approaches to bring about intentional change in terms of valued educational outcomes for learners.[1] The aim of such research is to identify the impact so as to provide a retrospective assessment of whether the policy, intervention, or approach was actually responsible for any changes in outcomes for learners (Higgins, 2017). The aims of the initiative will therefore determine the main questions for the evaluation (Rossi, Lipsey & Freeman, 2003). These are usually causal questions as policy makers, practitioners, and researchers want to know whether the initiative has actually been responsible for any improvement.

Impact evaluation therefore tends to be summative rather than formative, in that the aim is to identify the effects of what has happened, rather than improve the effectiveness of a policy or intervention for the future. A key concept in any assessment of effectiveness or evaluation of impact is therefore understanding the nature of any comparison being made, or the 'counterfactual' condition. We would ideally like to know what would have happened to pupils' learning both with and without the initiative taking place. This is not possible, of course, as a single student cannot both experience and not experience an initiative. We can't run a parallel worlds experiment in real life. So, different kinds of comparisons provide evidence for a stronger or weaker argument about the robustness of any causal claim in terms of whether an initiative has had an effect or not. The nature of the particular counterfactual or comparison in an impact evaluation affects what is a plausible explanation and a reasonable interpretation of the findings. More specifically, it affects the internal validity of the evaluation claims: what is the evidence that it has actually *worked*? Each of the approaches to impact evaluation in Table 5.1 (below, adapted from Higgins, 2017) seek to understand whether an initiative has achieved its aims or not. The strength of the claim weakens as the comparison is less capable of providing evidence that the change being evaluated is the actual cause of any improvement. The counterfactual comparison becomes less convincing the greater the threats to internal validity.

Randomisation aims to take account of both known and unknown factors which may account for differences in groups, as opposed to matching, which controls for known factors (such as age, gender, socio-economic background, special educational attendance). Randomisation therefore aims to take account of aspects of the complexity of a context which may not be known in advance. Experimentation is a deliberate inquiry which makes intentional change and aims to identify the effects of that change. A further goal may be to identify and test a specific causal model or to validate *how* the change has been effective or which students benefited most. Approaches such as theory-based evaluation seek to do this by having a clear conceptualisation or logic model which attempts to explain how the policy or intervention produces the desired effects (Fitz-Gibbon & Morris, 1996). In this approach, factors or features of the

Table 5.1 Counterfactual comparisons and threats to internal validity in evaluative research designs

	Design	Counterfactual	Internal validity
Experimental	Randomised controlled trial (RCT)	Comparison of average outcomes from random allocated groups of students who are equivalent and either do or do not experience the change.	Provides a counterfactual which can infer causation. Controls for selection or allocation bias, regression to the mean and temporal effects; controls for both known and unknown characteristics which may influence learning outcomes (the majority of the time with a sufficient sized sample), except for the play of chance. Can control for the effects of innovation or novelty with an appropriate design (e.g., three arm trial with 'business as usual' and 'placebo' comparison). Provides a population average treatment effect (when the sample is randomly sampled from the population of interest and is sufficiently large).
	Regression discontinuity design (RDD)	Statistical model of average outcomes just above the cut-off in relation to the outcomes from all students, where students can be randomised around the cut-off.	Controls for selection and maturation effects by modelling the pre–post relationship at the cut-off point. This cut-off point must not be manipulable (i.e., the cut-off is arbitrary on all but the cut-off scale). Does not control for effects of innovation or novelty. Assumes pre-post relationship can be accurately modelled. Provides a local average treatment effect (i.e., inference may be limited to those around the cut-off point).

	Quasi-experimental design (QED)	Comparison of average outcomes from allocated groups of students who are non-equivalent and either do or or do not experience the change.	Provides a limited counterfactual which can infer limited causation. Does not control for selection or allocation bias, regression to the mean effects and temporal effects; does not control for any unknown characteristics which may influence learning outcomes. Does not control for effects of innovation (unless more than one intervention condition is included). Provides a sample average treatment effect.
Observational	Natural experiments Matched comparison groups Difference in difference (regression)	Outcomes from similar students who do not experience the change.	Does not control for selection or allocation bias that is related to unobserved or unmatched characteristics. Groups must be sufficiently similar for analysis (matching). Does not control for effects of innovation.
	Time-series (e.g., single group design)	Outcomes from the same students a number of times before and after a change (usually a minimum of three occasions).	Does not control for selection or allocation, other external change, or maturation and growth. Can provide limited causal inference if input and output variables correlate strongly (e.g., use of a particular approach in some time periods but not others).

theoretical model are included in the evaluation design so that any association can also be explored. This might include aspects of fidelity (tracking how faithfully those involved adopted the changes in practice) or measures which might indicate changes in participants' behaviours or the processes of the new practices being evaluated which are consistent with the theory and which would therefore be expected to be clearly correlated with successful outcomes. If 'evidence' is taken here to mean 'causal evidence of impact', then it seems clear that such evidence is necessary for decision making in education. We need to know whether some things have been successful or not: whether they 'worked' as intended. In education, there are many factors which make this difficult to assess. I argue that this makes such designs to test causal claims more important, not less; though it is also important to understand the limit of the warrant of these claims. In the next section I turn to why it is particularly important in education to attempt to identify cause and effect.

Understanding what is happening in classrooms

One of the challenges in identifying and understanding learning classrooms is the complexity involved in the interactions between learners and the teacher (and other adults) in relation to intended educational aims and outcomes. Doyle (1977) characterised this in terms of 'multidimensionality, simultaneity, and unpredictability' (p. 52). He also described a range of strategies which teachers use to deal with this complexity in terms of:

1   Chunking (the ability to group discrete events into larger units);
2   Differentiation (the ability to discriminate among units in terms of their immediate and long-term significance);
3   Overlap (the ability to handle two or more events at once);
4   Timing (the ability to monitor and control the duration of events); and
5   Rapid judgement (the ability to interpret events with a minimum of delay).

These strategies are all necessary to manage and cope with the complexity and hecticness of classrooms, but make it difficult to determine some aspects of cause and effect. This is because, as they are inducted into the profession, the ecological nature of teachers' learning (or their 'coping strategies'; Pollard, 1982) means that their observations and experiences are filtered and interpreted often at an unconscious level or in relation to the immediate needs at hand. A novice teacher often struggles with behaviour and classroom control, and order can become an end in itself, rather than a means to an end (such as better learning). This makes teaching susceptible to a number of human biases in terms of interpreting and managing this complexity and highlights the challenge of validly and accurately identifying cause and effect. These inevitable and understandable biases also map onto aspects of research design and the approaches we can take to critically examine our understanding of cause and effect in class-rooms. Whether we like it or not, we all form 'personal theories' (Cole, 1990) about how teaching relates to learning. They are one of the main reasons that I argue that studies with strong causal warrant are sometimes necessary, but never sufficient, in educational research. It is all too easy to interpret practices and processes which reinforce our existing beliefs about cause and effect in the classroom and which bolster our personal theories without sometimes checking that they are actually achieving what we believe.

A number of natural biases make it difficult for any individual to judge the accuracy of their perceptions when identifying cause and effect in classrooms. Many of these can be dealt with through systematic data collection and analysis, but some require further control for possible bias or misinterpretation (see Table 5.2).

A 'scientific' approach attempts to control for other possible explanations for improvement. It aims to create a fair test of the claim that an intervention or approach is successful. Most potential biases can be addressed through rigorous and systematic data collection and analysis. Most require more than this. First, so as to provide a strong case for causal validity, an effective com-parison needs to be made (the 'counterfactual' condition, as discussed above). Second, the groups need to be equivalent in terms of both known and unknown factors which might explain any improvement. This can partly be achieved through matching pupils or creating equivalent groups that are as similar as possible in terms of the factors which might explain any differences in outcomes (e.g., current level of attainment, age, sex, free-school meal or special educational needs, and disability status). The advantage of randomisation is that, on average, it controls for both known and unknown differences. These measures do not, of course, guarantee that research adopting these principles will always be more accurate, but rather that, assuming that the imposition of the research design framework does not change the context in a way which alters the causal conditions, they will provide a more robust and accurate answer to a causal question.

The design of the macro-trials

The aim of the design of the large-scale school trials in Closing the Gap: Test and Learn was to conduct evaluative research of interest to schools which addressed just such causal questions, but to devolve much of the responsibility for the management of the trial to the schools themselves. Accordingly, the design team (see Chapter 4 for more details about the design and rationale for the macro-trials) identified a long-list of potential approaches then consulted school teachers and leaders about interventions and current gaps that were priorities for them through online surveys and focus groups. A shortlist of 17 interventions suitable for trialling was selected on the basis of:

Table 5.2 Some biases affecting causal claims

Natural bias	Description	Example	Design control
Anchoring bias	A tendency to rely on, or 'anchor', one piece of information in making decisions (often the first piece of information acquired on that subject).	Noticing particular pupils' response to an intervention (e.g., boys and technology) and attributing increased engagement and outcomes for some as evidence of success for all.	Systematic data collection of relevant data. Effective comparison group (or counterfactual comparison).
Confirmation bias	Likelihood of finding, remembering, or interpreting information so as to confirm existing beliefs or hypotheses, and/or finding less salience in alternative possibilities.	Seeing some pupils respond positively to a 'learning styles' intervention and interpreting this as evidence of the effectiveness of 'learning styles' rather than an increased range of teaching strategies being used, and/or with greater choice and responsibility for learning taken by pupils.	Systematic collection and analysis of relevant data.
Innovation bias	Tendency to favour change and see the positives (similar to confirmation bias).	Introduction of a digital technology which is successful, but which takes more teacher-time and is more expensive (i.e., is less efficient).	Systematic analysis of relevant data. Effective comparison group (or counterfactual comparison).
Maturation bias	Most pupils improve over time.	Pupils' reading improves after the introduction of reciprocal questioning, but hard to determine the extent to which the new approach was responsible.	Effective comparison group (or counterfactual comparison).
Selection bias	Pupils are chosen in relation to an expectation about how they are likely to perform.	Pupils are 'triaged' by schools according to how close they are to the C/D grade or Level 3 to 4 borderline, or more challenging pupils are rejected from a support programme.	Randomisation or independent allocation to control for known and unknown factors.

- the evidence of promise from research;
- the availability of suitable outcome measures and suitability for testing impact as a distinct or discrete approach;
- the manageability within the project's timescales and resource levels and likely demands on participating schools; and
- the appeal to schools based on criteria identified by them (to increase likelihood of take-up and relevance of findings).

At this stage the aim was to end up with seven pools of schools of roughly similar size allocated to these interventions as groups for randomisation. A smaller pool was identified in terms of sample size for one intervention because of the higher cost and the greater demands made on schools and because of the intention to test this approach over two years.

Participating Teaching Schools and their partner schools were sent details of the seven interventions and asked to rank them according to their preferences and to identify any which did not meet their current needs or which were not suitable for their context. This was so that the approaches were not tested in conditions which were not appropriate or where they would not be selected by schools. The key aim was to identify a match of schools to possible interventions for subsequent randomisation, which in turn aimed to minimise selection bias as far as possible within the constraints of the project so as to make the comparison a fair test.

The final design phase aimed to help establish the conditions for successful implementation for research and involved:

1   establishing (sometimes, negotiating) with the intervention providers the detail of their provision so that the intervention was replicable;
2   producing broad descriptions of each intervention;
3   devising protocols for managing the interventions for schools to use and to improve the comparability of implementation;
4   providing advice and guidance to the College's Closing the Gap team on other features of the programme, particularly the selection, design, and logistics of testing and the management of randomisation; and
5   documenting the process and creating guide resources for programme managers.

This step was to ensure that what was tested in each context was replicable, both across the schools in the project, but also for subsequent adoption (should the approaches be shown to be successful). A wait-list design was used so that schools allocated to control groups in the first year could carry out the intervention in the second year (should it be successful). This was for ethical reasons and for equity in terms of the resources and support offered to the schools involved. A minimum of 40 schools was needed in each group to ensure adequate power for analysis so as to increase the likelihood of a conclusive result (whether positive or negative), together with the use of the same assessments which met the requirements for validity and reliability across the interventions.

A number of strategies were put in place to reduce the risk of drop-out and attrition, including providing schools with opportunities to make their own choices about the intervention groups they were allocated to and particular target groups of pupils (within the overall design and randomisation constraints) as well as making the benefits of and commitments to being a control school clear. Pupil groups were selected according to a protocol based on vulnerability (such as FSM, Looked after, Special Educational Needs and Disability) and low achievement in specific areas (such as literacy or mathematics). Within this framework schools could select target pupils themselves, so the team developed a Pupil Identification Tool to structure the process and base it on criteria from the analysis of appropriate test and descriptive data to ensure common processes across schools and to reduce the risk of re-introducing selection bias. The research design therefore tested use of the approach in schools. This is an effectiveness question in that it aimed to answer the question: is this approach effective in schools in typical conditions? An alternative would have been to try to answer an efficacy question: is this an effective intervention? However, this would have meant more rather strictly controlling the protocols for use to ensure consistent processes (see Table 5.3 below).

One of the interventions, Research Lesson Study, was distinctive as it required development to enable trialling for Closing the Gap. It was therefore offered as a pre-/post-test pilot with a group of 20 schools in the first year, and, subject to a successful pilot, as a full trial in the second year.

It is important to be clear about what kind of question a trial is answering as this affects the design and interpretation of the findings. The model the Education Endowment Foundation (2016) uses is shown in Table 5.3.

For most interventions, standardised tests for either literacy or numeracy were appropriate progress measures as these mapped directly onto the curriculum and were the focus of the intervention. Where interventions were cross-curricular, the team recommended literacy and numeracy tests. It was, however, recognised that some interventions would have additional outcomes, and that schools and researchers would need to collect other evidence about complementary outcomes. This aimed to acknowledge the importance of a wider range of outcomes from education, but also the constraints under which schools work and the value of success in the current assessment system for individual pupils.

The team recommended that each series of pre-tests in all intervention and control schools for a particular intervention needed to be completed within a four-week window and that pre-testing should occur before randomisation, target pupil identification, and any training as the first stage of the interventions, so as to avoid allocation bias. Post-testing was recommended at the end of the academic year as it would make the interventions easier to compare, would

Table 5.3 Trial stage

Trial stage	Description	Inference
Pilot study	Conducted in a limited range of schools (e.g. three or more) where an intervention is at an early or exploratory stage of development. More fine-grained data used to develop and refine the approach and test its feasibility in schools. Initial indicative data collected to assess its potential to improve outcomes.	Is/is not feasible and has/does not have indications of promise
Efficacy trial	Aims to see whether an intervention can work under ideal or developer-led conditions across a range of settings (e.g. ten or more) schools. Has an impact evaluation to identify effect on attainment and a process evaluation to identify the elements of effective practice.	Has been effective/has not been effective under ideal conditions.
Effectiveness trial	To test whether an intervention can work at scale in a large number (e.g. 40 or more) schools, where the developers are no longer the only deliverers. Has an impact evaluation to assess the effect on attainment and a process evaluation to identify the challenges and solutions to roll-out. The cost of the intervention at scale will also be calculated.	Has been effective/has not been effective under typical conditions at scale.

allow a focus on sustained or longer-term benefits, and be easier to manage logistically. It was also recommended that pre- and post-testing should be conducted on the trial participants who were in the control/wait-list groups (and not just the 'intervention groups') to provide an effective comparison group or counterfactual.

These measures were all put in place to provide as fair a test as possible of interventions and approaches that schools would be likely to adopt and to let them run as closely as possible to the way schools would manage them were they not in a trial, so as to see if there was any overall average benefit for these interventions compared with what schools normally did (the counterfactual).

The design of the micro-trials

One of the goals of the Closing the Gap: Test and Learn project was the development of understanding of educational research methods among the research leads from the 206 participating lead schools. A key strand in this was the 'Early Adopter of Teacher-Led RCTs' programme (or 'Early Adopter' programme: see). This involved inviting proposals for small-scale experimental research studies (teacher-led randomised controlled trials or quasi-experimental 'micro-trials'). Additional training and support was provided to schools that were successful, and there were no requirements regarding the focus and content of the studies or the nature of the measures used other than they had to be of professional interest to the proposer and amenable to experimental inquiry.

The teachers were all encouraged to choose an area of their practice which they wanted to improve based on a hunch or hypothesis about what might be successful and then to design a study to test whether or not it improved outcomes for pupils as rigorously as was practical in a school setting. Most of the teachers were familiar with some contemporary approaches which aim to provide quantitative estimates of effect, such as Hattie's (2008) *Visible Learning* or the Sutton Trust–Education Endowment Foundation's *Teaching and Learning Toolkit* (EEF, 2017). The teachers designed the experiments, undertook them, usually collecting pre- and post-test data, and analysed the data (with help from the CfBT Education Trust team (now Education Development Trust): see). Support included identifying the advantages and disadvantages of between-subject versus within-subject designs, choosing and designing tests to ensure validity and reliability, and the benefits of pre- and post-test designs and when to use them. They also wrote up their research studies in a poster format and presented findings at a conference, echoing Stenhouse's (1981) notion of 'systematic and sustained inquiry, planned and self-critical, which is subjected to public criticism and to empirical tests where these are appropriate' (p. 113), but differing from more usual action research-based approaches (which many of the schools were already involved in: see Chapter 1) by using small-scale experimental trials which sought to control for possible allocation and maturation bias (see Table 5.2 above), as well as other possible threats to internal validity.

The range of areas of inquiry and approaches to evaluate these varied considerably across the micro-trials (see for more details), but the research design was tailored to the inquiry question so as to produce as robust an answer to the question (usually an impact question) given the constraints of one or two teachers pursing the investigation within their own professional context. There is a long history of classroom investigations and teacher self-study (see, for example, Loughran, 2004) though rarely including small-scale trials with randomisation (for some exceptions see Coe, Fitz-Gibbon, & Tymms, 2000 and Gorard, Siddiqui, & See, 2016). In health, such approaches are now advocated to help researchers and practitioners understand whether interventions are having intended effects, when and for whom they are effective, and what factors moderate an intervention's effect, so as to develop more effective 'just-in-time' adaptive interventions (Klasnja et al., 2015). Similar potential has been recognised in educational settings.

'Scientific' knowledge and the democratic deficit

The Closing the Gap: Test and Learn project shows that experimental trials with randomisation which involve schools and teachers in selecting the focus for experimental inquiry and in managing and conducting the process of the trials themselves are both feasible and acceptable in schools in England. This in itself is sufficient to counter Biesta's (2007) claim that 'scientific' approaches *necessarily* create a democratic deficit in educational research. As Churches, Hall, and Brookes argue in Chapter 2, the programme overall has shown that schools and teachers have the capacity to engage in research through both large-scale, multi-arm trials and small-scale, experimental studies: both macro- and micro-trials. This involvement appears to have increased interest in and discussion of research and research findings. Contrary to some of the beliefs expressed at the start of the programme, schools were not resistant to the use of control groups, or to the use of quantitative approaches and statistical analysis, or to the use of randomisation as a method to improve the internal validity of research in schools. Importantly, the project has also shown that teachers and schools can take a more active role in the delivery of randomised controlled trials, as the Education Endowment Foundation has also discovered with their 'aggregated trials' model (e.g., Siddiqui, Gorard & See, 2015; Gorard et al., 2016).

However, it must also be acknowledged that this approach is not a panacea for education research. Testing approaches using trials methodology requires a well-formulated question of the form 'on average, does intervention or approach X improve Y outcomes for pupils, when compared with Z (usually either "business as usual" or an active comparison of an alternative intervention or approach)?' The design and analysis of trials is not without its challenges (Xiao, Kasim & Higgins, 2016). Whilst these kinds of questions are undoubtedly important for the profession (and for policy decisions), not all important educational questions can be formulated in this way, or are amenable to causal experimental inquiry of this kind. I see the different types of educational research methods as a toolbox which needs to be matched to a particular educational inquiry question. Randomised experimental trials have a particular function and are best suited to questions of causal impact – was approach X responsible for effect Y? They are like a chisel which has been designed and developed for working wood, but, as a tool with a particular function, chisels are not useful for hammering nails, sawing wood to size, or bolting or fixing items with screws. Similarly, randomised experimental trials are not sufficient to identify or understand the complex causal processes which lie behind effects. They help with identifying the 'what' in causal investigations but not the 'how' or the 'why'. However, to understand the 'how' and the 'why' also presupposes that the 'what' actually works, so I'd argue in all causal inquiries they have a role.

Evidence from trials cannot and should not determine what ought to be taught, but once the content of the curriculum is agreed and the broad pedagogical values of a school or system have some consensus, then evidence about the relative effectiveness of different approaches to achieve these goals are essential in informing the decisions educators need to make in the best interests of their pupils. Not all educational inquiries are causal or about effectiveness, however. Biesta is justified in his critique that education is also about values and that the aims of education and the nature of the curriculum are also essential areas for discussion, identification, and clarification, perhaps rather more than the current policy discourse allows. I would set the goals broader here too in terms of the range of tools we need in the educational research toolbox, drawing on other disciplines and research traditions in psychology, sociology, history, and economics, for example; for developmental studies, cohort studies, capturing the lived experiences of teachers and learners, these are all important traditions with methods matched to the focus of a specific research question.

'Scientific' knowledge about causes and effects in education is an essential tool for the professional educator, however. It is necessary, but not sufficient for professional decision making. Not to be open to evidence from research with strong causal inference is problematic as it implies professionals are limited to opinion and judgement, with only limited knowledge about the effectiveness of what they do in relation to specific ends (e.g., reading or proficiency in aspects of mathematics). If teachers are to understand the effects of what they do, then engaging in and with educational research with strong causal inference is a necessary part of developing as an effective teacher. The benefits outweigh the costs. In terms of Biesta's (2007) 'democratic deficit', I am perhaps more concerned at the issues of power which lie behind control over aspects of the education system, in terms of pedagogy, curriculum, and assessment. If researchers and practitioners collaborate to develop understanding of cause and effect in education, both at the level of classrooms and at the level of schools, this may help redress the political balance of power between policy and practice. The issue for me is therefore not whether randomised experimental trials are possible or desirable in education, but rather when this particular research tool provides the best answer to an educational question and then where and how to use the technique to best effect.

Note

1 Impact evaluation may, of course, also include the effects of change on educational systems or on the perceptions of those involved, rather than outcomes for learners.

References

Biesta, G. (2007). Why 'what works' won't work: Evidence-based practice and the democratic deficit in educational research. *Educational Theory*, 57(1), 1–22.

Coe, R. Fitz-Gibbon, C., & Tymms, P (2000). *Promoting Evidence-Based Education: The Role of Practitioners*. Round table presented at the British Educational Research Association Conference, Cardiff University, 7–10 September 2000. Available online: http://www.leeds.ac.uk/educol/documents/00001592.htm

Cole, A. L. (1990). Personal theories of teaching: Development in the formative years. *Alberta Journal of Educational Research*, 36(3), 203–222.

Deaton, A., & Cartwright, N. (2016). Understanding and misunderstanding randomized controlled trials (Working paper no. 22595). Cambridge, M.A.: National Bureau of Economic Research.

Doyle, W. (1977). Learning the classroom environment: An ecological analysis. *Journal of Teacher Education*, 28(6), 51–55.

Education Endowment Foundation (2016). *EEF Evaluation: A Cumulative Approach*. London: EEF. Available online: https://v1.educationendowmentfoundation.org.uk/uploads/pdf/EEF_evaluation_approach_for_website.pdf

Education Endowment Foundation (2017). *The Sutton Trust–Education Endowment Foundation Teaching and Learning Toolkit*. London: EEF. Available online: https://educationendowmentfoundation.org.uk/resources/teaching-learning-toolkit

Fitz-Gibbon, C. T., & Morris, L. L. (1996). Theory-based evaluation. *Evaluation Practice*, 17(2), 177–184.

Gorard, S., Siddiqui, N., & See, B. H. (2016). An evaluation of Fresh Start as a catch-up intervention: A trial conducted by teachers. *Educational Studies*, 42(1), 98–113.

Hattie, J. (2008). *Visible Learning: A Synthesis of over 800 Meta-analyses Relating to Achievement*. London: Routledge.

Higgins, S. (2017). Impact evaluation: A case study of the introduction of interactive whiteboards in schools in the UK. In R. Coe, J. Arthur, M. Waring & L. V. Hedges (Eds). *Research Methods and Methodologies in Education* (2nd Edition). London: Sage.

Klasnja, P., Hekler, E. B., Shiffman, S., Boruvka, A., Almirall, D., Tewari, A., & Murphy, S. A. (2015). Micro-randomized trials: An experimental design for developing just-in-time adaptive interventions. *Health Psychology*, 34(S), 1220.

Loughran, J. J. (2004). A history and context of self-study of teaching and teacher education practices. In J. J. Loughran, M. L. Hamilton, V. K. LaBoskey & T. Russell

(Eds). *International Handbook of Self-study of Teaching and Teacher Education Practices* (Volume 12) (pp. 3–7). Dordrecht: Kluwer.

Pollard, A. (1982). A Model of Classroom Coping Strategies. *British Journal of Sociology of Education*, 3(1), 19–37.

Rossi, P. H., Lipsey, M. W., & Freeman, H. E. (2003). *Evaluation: A Systematic Approach.* Thousand Oaks, CA: Sage.

Siddiqui, N., Gorard, S., & See, B. H. (2015). Accelerated Reader as a literacy catch-up intervention during primary to secondary school transition phase. *Educational Review*, 68(2), 139–154.

Stenhouse, L. (1981). What counts as research? *British Journal of Educational Studies*, 29(2), 103–114.

Xiao Z., Kasim, A., & Higgins, S. E. (2016). Same difference? Understanding variation in the estimation of effect sizes from educational trials. *International Journal of Educational Research*, 77: 1–14.

Chapter 6

The potential of teacher-led randomised controlled trials in education research

Richard Churches, Robin Hall and Steve Higgins

Introduction

Teachers involved in Closing the Gap: Test and Learn were given training to conduct teacher-led randomised controlled trials and other forms of experimental research. This chapter reports findings from three studies. Firstly, qualitative evidence from focus groups with the teachers who completed studies is discussed (Study A). This is followed by a retrospective case-controlled study using the Evidence-Based Practice Questionnaire (Study B) which sought to compare the evidence-based practice of teachers who had undertaken research with a control group who had not. Finally, the outcomes of the teachers' research is reported (Study C). This includes a presentation and discussion of the levels of significance and effect sizes that the teacher-researchers reported. Implications of the approach and the findings are then discussed.

Background

For over a decade, the case for developing randomised controlled trials (RCTs) to provide stronger causal evidence in education (Torgerson & Torgenson, 2001) and the wider public sector (Haynes et al., 2012) has occupied a central space in policy debates. After such a long period of discussion and investment in initiatives such as the Education Endowment Foundation (EEF), it seems likely that such developments will continue and expand. Indeed, a recent extensive review of the literature (Connolly, 2015) indicates that there are about 800 identifiable randomised trials in educational settings, about two-thirds have been commissioned in the last ten years, with about half from North America, and about a quarter focusing on academic or cognitive outcomes. Since 2011, EEF have commissioned over 130 randomised trials investigating impact on academic outcomes, involving about three-quarters of a million pupils and one in four schools in England (EEF, 2016). At the same time the usefulness of effect size calculation by teachers in a school improvement context and within education research in general has emerged as an important theme (Coe, 2002), fuelled in part by the commercial success of Hattie's meta-analyses (Hattie,

2009) and the Sutton Trust–EEF *Teaching and Learning Toolkit*. However, taking the long view, and learning lessons from medicine and health care, the transformation of the global education profession into an evidence-based or evidence-informed profession will require far more than the mere accumulation of evidence, important though this is. There will also need to be levels of engagement with experimental research methods and in terms of quality and inference to enable teachers to read, understand and critique the education literature that applies a quantitative scientific method. Specifically, and as Churches and Dommett (2016) argue, it seems likely that the development of teachers' scientific literacy will emerge as a key theme for government focus and teacher training both in England and internationally. By extension, the development of scientific literacy and an understanding of the strengths and weaknesses of experimental research methods could in turn enable a more critical appreciation of areas such as the application of neuroscience knowledge to education and commercial products in general (Devonshire and Dommett, 2010).

The National College for Teaching and Leadership (NCTL) set up the Closing the Gap: Test and Learn programme (CtG) with two parallel purposes. Both of these related to the Teaching Schools initiative in England and the desire for this initiative to parallel the role of Teaching Hospitals (training teachers, conducting research and leading improvements in schools within wider alliances with the Teaching School). The primary purpose of CtG was the delivery and reporting of large-scale collaborative randomised controlled trials (discussed in Chapter 2 especially), in which greater responsibility for delivery and implementation was placed upon schools in order to evaluate the ability of a school-led system to take on such trials. A second purpose was the further development of research methods understanding (both qualitative and quantitative) among research leads from the 206 Teaching Schools that participated. Several strands of activity took place as part of the Regional Training and Research Development and Networking Events offered to the schools to support this (see Chapter 2). The 'Early Adopter of Teacher-Led RCTs' programme (or Early Adopter programme) was the name given to a research grant award embedded in the second year of the programme. This involved putting out a call for experimental research study proposals (teacher-led randomised controlled trials or quasi-experimental studies) and providing additional training and support to schools that submitted a successful proposal. There were no requirements regarding the content of the studies or the nature of the measures used.

The Early Adopter programme developed from the four half-day training modules delivered at the Research Development Networking Events over the course of the programme. Although these sessions were initially only intended as a means of developing teachers' understanding of experimental research (including RCTs), the significance of the events rapidly became clear. Almost immediately after the first few events, Teaching Schools began to use the materials and to try out experimental forms of research design. In turn, interest in the practical use of the materials increased considerably during the first year of the programme resulting in requests for funding from some schools (see Churches, 2016; Churches and Dommett, 2016).

In response to the growing interest, NCTL allocated a fund sufficient to cover fifty £2,000 grants. In total, the programme received 66 high-quality applications. Application forms included the requirement to produce a research protocol following the standard sections expected for an experimental study. This required a clear description of the research design, statement of hypotheses and proposed methods (participants/randomisation, procedures, and materials and apparatus). Teaching Schools could submit more than one proposal and proposals were evaluated anonymously. NCTL and Education Development Trust (formerly CfBT Education Trust) awarded grants to the highest-scoring proposals and several Teaching Schools received more than one grant. To support the successful applicants, an Early Adopter launch event took place on 15th December 2014. This included a series of sessions to help teachers plan further to deliver their designs and build a network of contacts. Successful recipients for the research grants were required to complete their data analysis before the end of the summer term and to prepare a conference poster for presentation at a national dissemination event, held at the National College's building in Nottingham on 21st October 2015. In total 48 teachers completed studies and were able to present their findings in a conference poster format at a national dissemination event at the National College in December 2015. Two incomplete studies were the result of personal circumstances or change of staffing in the school. One teacher study did not reach a conclusion, but the teacher presentation delivered a 'lessons learned' poster at the dissemination event.

The four RDNEs, as well as providing the opportunity for participating Teaching Schools to network and learn from one another's experience, were designed to provide a comprehensive programme of learning that enabled schools to design and deliver their own small-scale RCTs. Thus, in turn, they sought to develop teachers' scientific literacy within the context of the programme. The content, embedded within the four events, covered the following:

- Designing an RCT and exploring different research designs. For example, the advantages and disadvantages of between-subject versus within-subject designs, choosing and designing tests to ensure validity and reliability and pre- and post-test designs and when to use them. Teachers were also taught about quasi-experimental designs and the testing of more than one intervention at once.
- Implementation, sampling, sample size and randomisation (using Excel). This included managing a trial to avoid confounding variables that might arise as a result of delivery.

- Statistical analysis and interpretation of findings. This included how to conduct preliminary assumption testing, calculating effect sizes, selecting the right test and reporting levels of significance.
- Writing up quantitative research and understanding the conventions that apply to this style of research. This session also sought to develop schools' capacity to critique such research and included the use of poster design, building on the extremely well-received training delivered by Oxford University colleagues at Training Event 2.

To ensure that the teachers used the right inferential test following preliminary assumption testing, Richard Churches, Jan Lawrance and Mick Blaylock (Education Development Trust, formerly CfBT Education Trust) developed a series of simple-to-apply Excel spreadsheet programmes. These allowed teachers to quickly check normality (both via histograms and inferential testing), homogeneity of variances and to check for outliers. The spreadsheets also not only produced both one- and two-tailed p-values but also the correct effect sizes, depending on the distribution of the data and the usually expected test statistics according to American Psychological Association (2012) guidelines. As well as including independent and paired samples t-testing, the Mann-Whitney U and Wilcoxon-Signed Ranks tests, the sheets were extended to accommodate more complex designs allowing for the use of ANCOVA (parametric and non-parametric forms) and ANOVA and repeated measures ANOVA with planned comparisons. Examples of the types of research and analyses that the teachers were able to conduct can be found in Churches and McAleavy (2015), Churches (2016), Churches and Dommett (2016) and NCTL (2016).

Parallel to National College for Teaching and Leadership work, CfBT Education Trust (now Education Development Trust) included experimental research design training to 25 maths teachers as part of the National Support Programme in Wales, international teachers in an open access course in Dubai and other training to school teachers and education professionals. This parallel strand of work has yielded a wide range of other experimental studies, nine of which are reported in a conference poster format in Churches and McAleavy (2015) alongside three Closing the Gap: Test and Learn conference posters covering Early Adopter grant studies associated with Kyra Teaching School Alliance (which is part of the CfBT Schools Trust).

This paper reports on three studies that focused on the 46 quantitative experimental studies that were completed by teachers who were part of the Closing the Gap: Test and Learn programme. The three studies had four interrelated aims.

- To report on teacher perceptions with regard to their engagement with experimental research training and study completion (Study A).

- To assess the self-reported evidence-based behaviours, beliefs and skills of the teachers who completed experimental or quasi-experimental research projects (Study B).
- To record and discuss the types of design and range of topics chosen for investigation by the teachers (Study C).
- To present and discuss the levels of significance found within the studies together with a meta-analysis of effect sizes that were detected and discuss the implications of these (Study C).

Study A presents for a second time the focus group evidence that is included in the National College for Teaching and Leadership final research report (Churches, 2016). Study B uses an adapted version of the Evidence-Based Practice Questionnaire (Upton and Upton, 2006; Upton, Upton and Scurlock-Evans, 2014) within a retrospective case-controlled analysis. Study C summarised qualitative and quantitative data to describe the characteristics and outcomes of the 46 completed quantitative studies. The conclusion to this chapter summarises the implications and findings from this strand of delivery and looks at the wider implications for teacher practice, the development of scientific literacy amongst teachers, for education research more generally and for the development of evidence-based and evidence-informed practice.

Study A: Findings from focus groups undertaken as part of the research dissemination day that was attended by teachers who completed experimental research studies

Approach

In total, 57 participants associated with the 48 completed conference posters attended the national dissemination event. The event was structured to have an introduction and plenary session, two conference poster sessions and the oral presentation of research from three studies that were selected in advance of the event (paralleling the type of structures found in post-graduate research conferences). In the middle of the day the participants were divided into five focus groups which were positioned in different locations of the same room. Each focus group was led by a facilitator who took the participants through a series of pre-prepared questions. All three of the present study authors were facilitators alongside two others. Each of these questions was explored in the following way. Firstly, the facilitator introduced the question, there was then a group discussion and finally each participant was given time to reflect on the discussion and record their thoughts in response to this on a participant log. Because all of the focus groups needed to take place in the same room there was no opportunity to record the sessions or produce transcripts. Therefore, the analysis which follows is based upon the participant logs and flipcharts created by the facilitators (which aimed to capture the big ideas emerging from each group). We would like to acknowledge Paul Gutherson's role in carrying out the initial content analysis.

The findings below also appear in Churches (2016) within a wider discussion of the dissemination event and its context.[1] Three question areas were presented to the focus groups for discussion and individual reflection:

- What have you learnt from being part of the Early Adopter programme?
- Has engagement with experimental research changed your perception of evidence-based practice in education (if so, how?) and what next steps could you (or will you) take?
- What do you see as the potential application for teacher-led research of this sort in the future?

Findings

Question Area 1: What have you learnt from being part of the Early Adopter programme?

Being part of the programme helped participants to develop specific research skills such as data analysis, report writing, controlling variables, impact measurement, proposal writing, research design and planning. It also helped participants develop knowledge in relation to research methodology. Some participants also reported that involvement had made them more reflective, broadened their minds and challenged their perceptions.

Key learning identified by the focus groups included:

- the importance of critically engaging with research to improve practice;
- an increased understanding of research processes and the challenges and benefits of conducting research in schools;
- recognition of the limitations of research and of data;
- the empowering nature of research engagement for teachers and leaders;
- the benefits to teachers and learners of embedding a research culture in schools; and
- that process is a valuable outcome.

Question Area 2: Has engagement with experimental research changed your perception of evidence-based practice in education (if so, how?) and what next steps could you (or will you) take?

For some, engagement in the Early Adopter programme confirmed pre-existing attitudes towards the importance of evidence-based practice in education; for some it made them realise that small-scale enquiry was valuable and valid if it is well designed; for others it reinvigorated their interest in research and its relevance to the classroom. A small number of participants stated that they had previously been unaware of evidence-based practice and that involvement had 'opened their eyes'. As one participant put it:

I feel it's brought it back down to classroom level for me. I never used to read educational research as it seemed far too removed from what I was seeing on a daily basis – this has changed my perception.

Other participants spoke about how involvement in the Early Adopters programme had given them the tools to engage more effectively in research practice or how it would enable them to develop a research culture in their school.

A small number of focus group participants spoke about how involvement in the programme had influenced pedagogical debate within their schools.

Some of the next steps participants thought they would take included:

- developing existing studies further – for example, through lengthening the timescale of enquiry or increasing sample sizes;
- developing greater understanding of the methodological approach of RCTs and micro-enquiry;
- identifying new lines of enquiry;
- rolling out research and enquiry through their school;
- building capacity within and across groups of schools; and
- seeking funding, or setting aside budget, for more research projects in school.

Question Area 3: What do you see as the potential application for teacher-led research of this sort in the future?

Participants recognised the benefits of being involved in teacher-led micro-enquiry and suggested that the approach should be introduced during teacher training, in early career and new leader CPD programmes. They were keen to get more teachers involved and would make excellent advocates for the approach. Participants also noted that it was important to develop ways to easily and systematically share the findings of individual enquiries. The potential power of the approach was summed up by one participant, saying:

In ten years' time we won't be having a conversation about teacher-led research, it will be a defining characteristic of what a school does.

Focus group participants felt that teacher-led micro-enquiry has a range of future applications, including:

- testing new interventions and policy ideas before implementation;
- testing the impact of policy changes imposed from above;
- collaborative enquiries across different schools, alliances and contexts;
- replicating micro-studies in other contexts;
- building an evidence base of what does and what does not work;
- driving school improvement and linking to performance management; and
- as a central tool in CPD.

Conclusions of Study A

There was a considerable appetite to find effective ways to share the research from the programme and, beyond that, to build local and national networks of research-active teachers. Participants thanked the programme team and valued the time and opportunity to take part and to share their experience with others – in some cases it had triggered bigger conversations about research and evidence for schools and Teaching School Alliances.

A proposal to strengthen the evidence base arose during the focus groups: to establish a central 'expert' body that school-based researchers could feed the results of small-scale projects into and which, in turn, would then be 'packaged' into projects for other schools to replicate in order to collect more evidence of impact. Teachers also spoke about some of the problems associated with research in schools. They spoke of the difficulties of finding time to develop and conduct research where there is little or no budget; the difficulties of accessing research materials and support; and of issues around the dissemination of findings, especially in influencing decision-makers to take the findings of research seriously or of convincing others to apply the findings of research to their work.

Teachers appeared to have a considerable appetite for the use of experimental research methods alongside other research approaches within education and, in the case of the teachers who submitted a grant application, with appropriate training were able to tackle the more challenging aspects of this form of research including statistical analysis and the interpretation of findings.

Study B – Evidence-based practice and engagement in practitioner-led experimental research, a retrospective case-controlled study using the Evidence-Based Practice Questionnaire

Evidence-based practice has become a major theme in health care and medicine in recent years. Not surprisingly, bearing in mind the research traditions of these two fields, this interest has led to approaches to define evidence-based practice in a measureable way. One such approach, originally designed for use in nursing (Upton and Upton, 2005, 2006) but since then applied to a range of wider contexts (Upton et al., 2014), is the *Evidence-Based Practice Questionnaire* (EBPQ). In education, debates about the nature of evidence and practice have also emerged in recent years (for a review see McAleavy, 2016). Applying an adapted version of the EBPQ afforded the opportunity to measure the effect of learning about and then completing a teacher-led study on established areas that have been shown to be important within nursing, health care and social work.

Aims and hypotheses

The aim of Study B was to investigate retrospectively the effects of completing an experimental research study on the evidence-based behaviours, beliefs and skills of the research leads who had participated in the Closing the Gap: Test and Learn programme and who, in addition, had completed their own experimental study (either a randomised controlled trial, or a quasi-experiment). Based on the outcomes of this part of the programme, the quality of teacher studies that were completed and the focus group data (discussed below in Study C) we hypothesised that:

1   Completion of an experimental research study increases the frequency of self-reported evidence-based behaviours.
2   Completion of an experimental study enhances beliefs and attitudes about evidence-based practice and the extent to which teachers say they have changed their practice in response to evidence.
3   Completion of an experimental study leads to higher teacher perceptions of their skills in areas seen as important to evidence-based practice in the parallel field of health care.

Methods

Participants

Study B analysis used a sample of 108 participants who completed the EBPQ at the end of the Closing the Gap: Test and Learn programme. In total, 92 participant questionnaires were included in the analysis following case-matching, random sampling to reduce the number of control group participants where there was more than one control participant with tied characteristics and the removal of participants with incomplete questionnaires. There were 56 (61%) females and 36 (39%) males, 46^2 were in the intervention group and 46 in the control group. The median age of the participants was within the range 40–49.[3] The procedures subsection below describes in detail the process of sampling and case-matching that took place. The present study was introduced to the prospective participants as research into the effects of participant participation in the Closing the Gap: Test and Learn programme in which there would be some form of sub-group analysis to compare different groups of participants. Because we did not want to prime participant responses and risk the effect of demand characteristics that might have arisen if control participants were made aware that their self-reported practice was being compared to that of participants who had completed teacher-led studies (or vice versa), no hypotheses were shared with participants. In addition, participants were kept blind to the nature of the sub-group analysis and the aims of the study. Participation in the study was voluntary.

Design

The present research was a single blind retrospective case-controlled study. Participants previously exposed to additional training and development and the completion of a teacher–led experimental study as part of the programme described above were case-matched to a pool with an equal number of other research leads also taking part in the wider programme of large-scale randomised controlled trials. The **procedures** subsection below describes the sampling and matching criteria. We would like to thank Dr Penney Upton (Centre for Research and Action in Public Health University of Canberra) for her permission to use the EBPQ within this study (www.ebpq.co.uk).

Materials and apparatus

The *Evidence-Based Practice Questionnaire* (EBPQ) (Upton and Upton, 2006; Upton et al., 2014) is a 26-item self-report questionnaire. The questionnaire was designed to gather information and opinions about the use of evidence-based practice amongst health professionals and was given very minor adaptations to make it suitable for use within the present study (for example, replacing the word 'patient' with the word 'pupil'). The 26 items are grouped into three areas. These correspond to the frequency of self-reported evidence-based practice behaviours (Question 1, six items); beliefs about current ways of working and evidence-based practice, including an item which asks about whether practice is changed in response to new evidence (Question 2, four items); and the rating of skills associated with evidence-based practice (Question 3, 14 items). All items use a seven-point Likert scale, however, this is presented with a left and right dipolar sentence for the four items that make up Question 2. The EBPQ has shown strong internal consistency for the entire questionnaire and the practice and subscales. However, the attitude subscale has been associated with lower Cronbach's alpha, indicating that this may need refinement and should be considered less reliable than the other subscales. In relation to its construct validity, the EBPQ has demonstrated the ability to predict scores on other related measures (see Upton et al., 2014 for a discussion and review). The EBPQ was delivered via an online survey tool link which was emailed to the participants.

Procedure

All 206 research leads who had been involved in the Closing the Gap: Test and Learn programme were contacted after the Early Adopter programme dissemination event and were asked to complete the EBPQ with regard to the last year of their practice. This coincided with the period during which the teachers involved in the Early Adopter programme who received grants were undertaking their teacher–led experimental studies. Participants were informed that the results would be used to compare different groups who had taken part in the programme. However, in order to mitigate the risk of participant effects they were kept blind to the precise nature of that analysis and that the core purpose of the research was to compare the self-reported evidence-based practice of teachers who had completed experimental studies with those that simply acted as trial co-ordinators for the large scale randomised controlled trials.

A total of 46 of the teachers who received grants and completed experimental studies responded. In addition, 62 teachers eligible for the control group completed the questionnaire, of which 56 provided sufficient information for them to be case-matched to the 46 study completers. Case-matching controlled for: school phase (primary, secondary, special); number of years in teaching since qualifying; and gender. Where there was a larger pool of control matches than required, and/or there were tied possibilities for case-matching, random sampling and/or allocation was used to determine who would be the final case-matchee. Case-matching was conducted prior to analysis and prior to the downloading of the data set from the online survey programme.

To assess the extent to which random sampling out of participants with tied characteristics might have affected the results, the mean scores for Questions 1, 2 and 3 for the control group participants randomly removed from the study (n = 7) were compared with those who remained in the control group (n = 46). This showed that the mean scores for the seven removed participants (M = 4.07, 5.49 and 4.44, respectively) were similar to, but in all cases lower than the means for seven participants that were included in the analysis (M = 4.12, 6.00, 5.14, respectively). This indicates that if these seven participants had in fact been randomly selected instead of the seven that were left in the study as case-matchees, this would have amplified the effects found in relation to H1–H3 rather than attenuated them.

Statistical analysis

The appropriate statistical procedure for individual item Likert scale data with two levels to the independent variable is the Wilcoxon-Signed Ranks Test. As is the convention, we applied this irrespective of the distributions. However, with regard to testing the average of Likert scale scores within each of the three question areas assessed by the EBPQ, and noting the debates about whether amalgamated ordinal data can be considered interval (Jamieson, 2004; Carifio and Perla, 2008), where the data met the necessary assumptions (H2), a paired samples t-test was applied. To reduce the risk of family-wise error, as a result of conducting multiple tests within each of the three question areas of the EBPQ, a Bonferroni adjustment was carried out. Alpha (.05) was divided by the number of tests conducted within each question, thus establishing a more stringent threshold for significance. As all hypotheses were directional, a one-tailed p-value is reported.

Results

H1: Completion of an experimental research study increases the frequency of self-reported evidence-based behaviours.

Table 6.1 displays the mean values and standard deviation for the six items which make up Question 1 of the EBPQ alongside a summary of the results of inferential testing and effect sizes comparing the control group with the intervention group.

A Wilcoxon Signed-Ranks Test indicated that the average frequency of self-reported evidence-based practice behaviours for teachers who had completed experimental teacher led-studies was significantly higher ($Z = 4.53$, $p < .0005$) than those of teachers who had not completed their own experimental studies, with a large effect size difference between the two groups ($r = 0.67$).

After applying a Bonferroni correction for multiple comparisons (adjusted alpha = $.03/6 = .0083$) separate Wilcoxon-Signed Ranks Tests were performed on each of the individual items within Question 1 of the EBPQ. Research leads who completed an experimental study reported significantly higher levels of evidence-based behaviour with regard to the regular formulation of clear answerable questions at the beginning of a process towards filling a gap in practice, $Z = 3.40$, $p < .0005$, a large effect size ($r = 0.50$). This was also the case for the evaluation of the outcomes of practice, $Z = 4.35$, $p < .0005$ ($r = 0.64$). In addition, there was a moderate and significant positive effect ($r = 0.37$) with regard to critically appraising against set criteria, $Z = 2.50$, $p = .006$. Non-significant but moderate effect size differences were found for tracking down relevant research information once a question had been formulated, $Z = 2.39$, $p = .009$ ($r = 0.35$); the integration of evidence into practice, $Z = 2.26$, N-ties = 38, $p = .012$ ($r = 34$); and sharing information with colleagues, $Z = 1.93$, N-ties = 35, $p = .027$ ($r = 0.29$).

H2: Completion of an experimental study enhances beliefs and attitudes about evidence-based practice and the extent to which teachers say they have changed their practice in response to evidence.

Table 6.2 summarises descriptive statistics and inferential testing on control and intervention group scores related to the four items that make up Question 2 EBPQ.

A Wilcoxon Signed Ranks test on the average scores reported for the four items that make up Question 2 of the questionnaire indicated a non-significant difference in teachers' beliefs about evidence-based practice and the changing of behaviour as a result of completing an experimental study, $Z = 1.13$, $p = .127$ ($r = 0.17$). After applying a Bonferroni correction for multiple comparisons (adjusted alpha = $.03/4 = .0125$) again as for Hypothesis 1, separate Wilcoxon-Signed Ranks Tests were performed on each of the individual items.

There were small non-significant differences with regard to recognising the need to make time for new evidence, $Z = 1.14$, N-ties = 41, $p = .126$ ($r = 0.17$); welcoming questioning of practice, $Z = -0.263$, N-ties = 33, $p = .397$ ($r = -0.04$); seeing evidence-based practice as fundamental, $Z = 0.335$, N-ties = 32, $p = .36$ ($r = 0.05$). However, teachers who had completed an experimental research study were more likely to change their practice in response to evidence, $Z = 2.286$, $p = .011$, with a moderate effect size difference in their self-reported practice ($r = 0.34$).

Table 6.1 EBPQ Question 1 – Frequency of behaviour values for the control group and intervention group (research leads who completed an experimental research study)

	1 Control		2 Intervention		Z	p	r
	M	(SD)	M	(SD)			
Formulated a clearly answerable question as the beginning of the process towards filling this gap	3.93	(1.34)	4.91	(1.17)	3.40	< .0005[+]	0.50
Tracked down the relevant evidence once you have formulated the question	4.61	(1.67)	5.26	(1.16)	2.39	.009	0.39
Critically appraised, against set criteria, any literature you have discovered	3.83	(1.66)	5.28	(1.11)	2.50	.006[+]	0.37
Integrated the evidence you have found with your expertise	4.24	(1.66)	4.96	(1.25)	2.26	.012	0.34
Evaluated the outcomes of your practice	4.76	(1.57)	5.98	(1.00)	4.35	< .0005[+]	0.64
Shared this information with colleagues	4.67	(1.73)	5.35	(1.35)	1.93	.027	0.29

[+] = significant with alpha .0083

Table 6.2 EBPQ Question 2 – Relative agreement values for the control group and intervention group (research leads who completed an experimental research study)

Left dipole	Right dipole	1 Control		2 Intervention		Z	p	r
		M	(SD)	M	(SD)			
My workload is too great for me to keep up to date with all the new evidence	New evidence is so important that I make the time in my work schedule	4.04	(1.58)	4.41	(1.36)	1.14	.126	0.17
I resent having my teaching practice questioned	I welcome questions on my practice	6.02	(1.20)	5.91	(1.36)	−0.26	.397	−0.04
Evidence-based practice is a waste of time	Evidence-based practice is fundamental to professional practice	6.00	(1.14)	6.07	(1.06)	0.34	.369	0.05
I stick to tried and trusted methods rather than changing to anything new	My practice has changed because of evidence I have found	5.37	(1.29)	6.09	(1.05)	2.29	.011[+]	0.34

[+] = significant with alpha .0125

H3: Completion of an experimental study leads to higher teachers' perceptions of their skills in areas seen as important to evidence-based practice in the parallel field of health care.

Scores related to research leads' self-reported evidenced-based skills (EBPQ, Question 3) are presented in Table 6.3, alongside a summary of inferential testing results.

A paired samples t-test was used to evaluate the difference between the intervention group and control group overall mean rating for the skills components of the EBPQ (Question 3). There was a non-significant difference, $t(45) = 1.60$, $p = 0.059$ ($dz^4 = 0.06$), between the overall self-reported skills rating for the teachers who had completed experimental studies compared to those who had not.

After performing a Bonferroni correction for multiple comparison (adjusted alpha = $.05/14 = .0036$) a series of Wilcoxon-Signed Rank Tests was then used to evaluate the different skills areas within Question 3. Participants who had completed an experimental study reported significantly higher skills ratings compared to those that had not with regard to research skills, $Z = 2.98$, $p = .0001$, a moderately large effect size difference ($r = 0.44$). Similarly, completion of an experimental study appeared to have had a large positive effect ($r = 0.49$) on participants' ability to convert information needs into a research question, $Z = 3.29$, $p = .0005$) and to analyse critically evidence against set standards, $Z = 3.71$, $p < .0005$ ($r = 0.55$). Participants who had completed research studies also reported higher perception of their ability to disseminate new ideas about teaching to colleagues, $Z = 3.02$, $p = .002$ ($r = 0.46$) and review own practice, $Z = 3.78$, $p < .0005$ ($r = -0.56$).

All other skills-related areas showed a non-significant difference. IT skills, $Z = 0.69$, $p = .246$ ($r = 0.10$); monitoring and reviewing of practice skills, $Z = 0.81$, $p = .208$ ($r = 0.12$); awareness of major information types and sources, $Z = -0.48$, $p = .313$ ($r = -0.07$); ability to identify gaps in professional practice, $Z = -0.49$, $p = .311$ ($r = -0.07$); and knowledge of how to retrieve evidence, $Z = -0.381$, $p = .366$ ($r = -0.06$). There were also non-significant differences for ability to determine the validity, $Z = -0.05$, $p = 0.478$ ($r = 0.007$), and usefulness, $Z = -0.39$, $p = 0.347$ ($r = 0.06$), of materials, apply information to individual cases, $Z = -0.40$, N-ties = 30, $p = .347$ ($r = 0.06$), and share ideas and information with colleagues, $Z = -0.08$, $p = .469$ ($r = 0.01$).

Discussion

H1 was supported with regard to three out of six of the areas assessed by Question 1 of the EBPQ and in terms of the overall average score for these areas. Research leads who had completed an experimental research study that they had proposed, planned, implemented, analysed and written up were more likely to have formulated a clearly answerable question as the starting point to filling a gap in their practice and more likely to frequently appraise their practice

Table 6.3 EBPQ Question 3 – Self-reported skills values for the control group and intervention group (research leads who completed an experimental research study)

	1 Control		2 Intervention		Z	p	r
	M	(SD)	M	(SD)			
Research skills	4.63	(1.14)	5.37	(0.93)	2.98	.0001+	0.44
IT skills	5.15	(1.01)	5.28	(1.20)	0.69	.246	0.10
Monitoring and reviewing of practice skills	5.27	(1.14)	5.42	(0.89)	0.81	.208	0.12
Converting your information needs into a research question	4.54	(1.43)	5.59	(1.27)	3.29	<.0005+	0.49
Awareness of major information types and sources	4.93	(1.29)	4.85	(1.23)	-0.48	.313	-0.07
Ability to identify gaps in your professional practice	5.61	(0.91)	5.52	(0.91)			
Knowledge of how to retrieve evidence	5.11	(1.16)	5.02	(1.24)	-0.38	.366	-0.06
Ability to analyse critically evidence against set standards	5.11	(1.27)	5.54	(1.26)	3.71	<.0005+	0.55
Ability to determine how valid (close to the truth) the material is	4.89	(1.40)	4.89	(1.46)	-0.05	.478	0.007
Ability to determine how useful (applicable in the classroom) the material is	5.48	(1.09)	5.48	(1.11)	-0.39	.347	0.06
Ability to apply information to individual cases	5.43	(1.20)	5.35	(1.06)	-0.40	.347	0.06
Sharing of ideas and information with colleagues	5.78	(1.13)	5.74	(1.06)	-0.08	.469	0.01
Dissemination of new ideas about teaching to colleagues	5.20	(1.15)	5.91	(0.91)	3.02	.002	0.46
Ability to review your own practice	5.20	(1.24)	6.11	(0.80)	3.78	<.0005+	0.56

+ = significant with alpha .0036

critically in response to set criteria of any literature that they had found. In turn, they were more likely to evaluate the outcomes of their practice. Although half of the areas assessed by Question 1 were non-significant, all of the six question items yielded moderate or large positive effects on research leads' evidence-based behaviours where they had completed an experimental study. This suggests that in a replication with a larger sample size such activity might improve all areas of EBPQ Question 1. That completion of a study had the effects that it did on some of the areas assessed by Question 1 is perhaps not surprising, bearing in mind the strong emphasis in the training given to the teachers on areas such as identifying a gap in practice or the literature and defining a specific research question and testable hypothesis. Another aspect of the data that is worth noting is the change in the spread of scores as a result of completing a research study. In all cases, not only did teachers report more frequent evidence-based behaviours, but also the variation in frequency was reduced for the intervention group for all six item areas. Thus, it appears that completion of an experimental study not only increases evidence-based behaviour, but also reduces the variation in that behaviour.

With regard to the first three items of Question 2 (H2a) which assess teachers' beliefs and attitudes about the importance of evidence-based practice, there was no difference between the teachers who completed an experimental study and those who did not. This was also perhaps to be expected. There has been a strong discussion and emphasis within England on the need to develop an evidence-informed profession, and the teachers who participated in the programme, as a whole, were all from Teaching Schools which have found themselves at the forefront of such developments. Means for question items 2 and 3 were, for example, high for both the control and intervention groups. This said, teachers in both groups were less inclined to agree that that new evidence is so important that they make time for it in their work schedule. Despite this there was, however, a significant moderate positive effect (H2b) with regard to item 4 which assessed the extent that the research leads were likely to change their practice because of evidence that they had found compared to sticking to tried and trusted methods, a finding which echoes the results from Question 1.

Question 3 of the EBPQ (H3) lists 14 skills associated with evidence-based practice in nursing and health care. Teachers who had completed an experimental study reported significantly higher levels for research skills, converting information needs into a research question, critically evaluating evidence and the ability to review their own practice. Similarly, that these areas yielded significant differences, but other areas (such as IT skills) did not, could perhaps have been predicted from the nature of the content of the training programme – in combination with the demands of using these skills within an experimental study. Surprisingly, teachers who completed studies did not say that they were more able to assess the validity of evidence as a result of their learning. This may, however, have been because the majority of education research evidence that teachers encounter at present remains qualitative, with only a small amount of laboratory classroom-based experimental study accessible or relevant to teachers' daily practice.

Limitations and recommendations for the future

Retrospective cohort studies have a number of advantages. Because participants exposed to a condition are known to have been free from that condition at the beginning of the observation period, it may be more easily possible to indicate the temporal sequence between exposure and outcome, provided that participants can easily recall what they have been exposed to. Such designs are also useful in assessing rare exposures or situations in which it is not possible to randomise in advance. Selection bias can occur, however, particularly with regard to case-matching and the matching criteria that were used. In the case of the present study, although the researchers were able to easily identify the exposure group (those who received grants and completed studies), it was unclear to what extent those participants within the control group may have been influenced by the experimental research training that was offered more generally to all participants within the programme as a whole. A future study may wish to include a comparison of a control group with no exposure to research methods training like the training that was offered across the participating Teaching Schools within Closing the Gap: Test and Learn. If that future study were also to involve a case matching, it could be advantageous to additionally take into account prior research experience, a factor that was not assessed in the present study.

Study B conclusions

Firstly, Study B was fruitful in terms of demonstrating the ability of the EBPQ to be applied in the context of research leads associated with Teaching Schools in England. With regard to the findings from this application, overall it appears that the completion of an experimental study that has been designed by teachers themselves has a positive impact on teachers' evidence-based practices. Such activity also made a difference to some skills areas associated with evidence-based practice that have been defined in health care and nursing, although only on those skills areas that were directly included as part of the training programmes the teachers followed. However, there were no differences in research leads' beliefs about the importance of evidence-based practice. As the number of randomised controlled trials increases, it may be that (as in medicine and health care) including experimental research training and activity within degree courses and qualifications could be a way of ensuring that not only does teacher knowledge change but that teachers' adoption of evidence-based practices is encouraged.

Study C: Analysis of the outcome of the teacher-led experimental studies

Introduction

Study C begins with a descriptive analysis of the types of research designs chosen by the teachers and the range of content that was selected for investigation. It goes on to discuss the levels of significance found across the trials before then presenting a meta-analysis of the effect sizes.

The teachers were all encouraged to choose an area of their practice which they sought to improve and to design a study to test whether or not this improved outcomes for pupils. A total of 46 teachers completed their enquiries using an experimental approach. Whilst this, of course, has its limitations in terms of the evaluation of the impact of changes in complex classroom settings, the teachers were all keen to test their ideas robustly so as to identify any impact on their students' learning. Most of the teachers were familiar with some contemporary approaches which aim to provide quantitative estimates of effect (such as Hattie's (2009) *Visible Learning* or the Sutton Trust – Education Endowment Foundation *Teaching and Learning Toolkit*).

Type of design and topics chosen for investigation

Twenty-one studies took place in secondary schools or sixth forms, twenty-one in primary schools, two in nursery schools and two in special schools. The focus of the experimental research design training that teachers received was based on the principle that there is no correct form of randomised controlled trial (Churches and Dommett, 2016) if one takes the perspective on scientific method adopted in areas such as psychology. Participants were encouraged to think first about the gap in the research they intended to fill, define specific hypotheses and decide on a research design and randomisation approach that best fulfilled their research aim in the context of what was practical in their school context. The consequence of this was that a wide range of designs and approaches were adopted by the teachers in response to the real work challenges of implementing research protocols that in most cases focused on relatively short treatment windows (between one lesson and four months) compared to many larger-scale education trials.

The average sample size across the studies was 56.1 with the range of sample sizes from 8 to 231 ($SD = 52.2$, *Skew* = 2.13, *Kurtosis* = 4.66). In relation to the 46 studies that presented conference posters at the national conference event, the diversity of research designs chosen by the teachers was considerable (see Table 6.1, above): 60.9 % of the studies were between-participant (independent measures) randomised controlled trials, 21.7% within-participant (repeated measure trials) and 7% matched pair designs. The other studies include a mixture of quasi-experimental designs (mostly case-matched, non-randomised controlled trials), one parallel group design with gender as the independent variable and one 2 × 2 mixed factorial design; 97.8% of the studies used a pre- and post-test design and 2.2% a post-test only design.

With regard to the between-participant designs, a wide range of random- isation strategies were applied by the teachers (simple, pupil level (59.5%); simple cluster, classroom level (1.2%); and stratified (39.3%)). In terms of the addition of greater complexity within these designs, although 91.3% of the studies operationally defined the independent variable (IV) with two levels to the IV (i.e., they exposed the participants to two different conditions), 8.7% of the studies added a third level to the IV while 23.9% of the studies had more than one dependent variable and one study deployed a qualitative dependent variable.

In relation to the nature of the control conditions that were chosen by the teacher, in all but one case the control condition involved planning and delivering lessons and activities that were typical of current best practice in the schools. The exception was a study of the effects of giving support to parents to free their time to do reading with their children during the summer holiday compared to not giving that support.

Table 6.4 The topics chosen for investigation across the 46 completed studies

Teacher-designed approaches				Commercial products or externally designed/existing approaches	
Area of investigation	Number of studies	Area of investigation	Number of studies	Area of investigation	Number of studies
Classroom environment	2	Oral skills	1	Building learning power	1
Competition in pedagogy	1	Phase transition	1	Flipped learning	2
Engagement	3	Reading	1	Growth mindsets	2
Feedback and/or marking	7	Revision	1	Meditation	1
Homework	1	Self-esteem	1	Mind gym	1
iPad use	2	Spelling	4	NLP coaching	1
Mental maths	1	Support to parents	1	Oval Learning Cluster Number Masters	1
Mental toughness	2	Teaching assistants	1		
Metacognition	1	Writing skills	5		
Modelling	1				

Table 6.4 summarises the areas that the teachers chose to investigate using an experimental approach. The largest common area of interest was feedback and/or marking, a category which included a wide range of approaches including the use of IT to give children feedback. Writing skills, spelling approaches and engagement were the next three commonest areas that the teachers chose to investigate. Eight of the 46 studies chose to investigate commercial or external approaches, two of which (NLP coaching and mind gym – an approach previously referred to more frequently as brain gym) involved areas that have provoked a degree of controversy. Interestingly, the teacher studies both showed significant positive effects on growth mindset (as measured by the Implicit Theories of Intelligence Scale (Blackwell, Trzeniewski & Dweck, 2007)) and maths attainment, respectively. It was also the case that some interventions that teachers had expected to make a difference showed no significant difference compared to existing practice.

Levels of significance

As has already been mentioned, the training of the Early Adopter research leads focused on the wide range of experimental designs normally taught in psychology (see Churches and Dommett, 2016). In adopting this approach, the intention was not to stand in opposition to the usual style of randomised controlled trial that has been implemented in education. Typically, education randomised controlled trials have been larger-scale, five–six months or longer trials, with a standard two condition between-participant pre- and post-test design. The tradition in experimental psychology has been different with more laboratory-style short treatment window approaches, greater control of extraneous and potentially confounding variables and smaller sample sizes. As Churches and Dommett (2016) illustrate, however, there is 'no correct form of randomised controlled trial', and arguably education research has limited its current exploration of this form of research by not making use of variations in design (such as within-participant, or repeated measures design) or having more than two levels to the independent variable.

Rather, we would argue, the choice of design should be a question of the balance of external and internal validity that the researcher feels comfortable with in terms of ultimately being able to defend their conclusions. Large-scale trials over a longer period can often claim higher levels of external validity and the ability to generalise their findings, however the risk to the internal validity and reliability of the findings is greater since over a long period, and particularly in a school context, many extraneous variables can diffuse the results or even ultimately confound them. At the same time, in most cases, the unit of analysis from a teacher perspective is often the individual lesson, scheme of work or programme lasting between half a term and a term. A shorter trial period can also facilitate higher levels of mundane realism (the extent to which a study represents the usual daily practice of participants (Brewer, 2000)). It can also increase the potential to include single or double blind protocols into the study, as the period that any participants might have information withheld from them to reduce participant effects (such as demand characteristics) is much shorter and therefore can be considered more ethical as a full debrief can occur shortly after the period of necessary deception. In virtually all cases, most of the trials conducted by the teachers were over a relatively short treatment window, in some cases taking place over single or double lessons.

Taking a general overview of effect sizes and the levels of statistical significance that are often detected in the smaller-scale, tighter designs deployed in cognitive psychology and neuroscience, it was a reasonable prediction that similarly the teacher-led studies within Closing the Gap: Test and Learn would also produce such results. In total, 47% of the teacher studies produced results that were significant at the 95% threshold ($p < .05$), 34% at the 90% level ($p < .01$), 26% with a level of significance below $p < .001$, and 3.8% at $p < .0001$. 53% of the results were non-significant. In many cases, teachers' studies with non-significant results often yielded small, moderate or greater effect sizes. Non-significant results may be a function of sample size and the limitations of the scale of the experiment in identifying a positive effect (traditionally called a Type II error or false negative). These studies were not designed to be powered adequately in advance. It must also be noted that significance testing and null hypothesis experimental designs have limitations when applied to opportunity samples and only indicate the uncertaintly that might be typically expected where a sample is randomly selected from a specified larger population. However, we believe that this estimate of uncertainty is helpful in identifying the minimum uncertaintly associated with the effect, given the scale of the enquiry (for further discussion about significance testing see Wasserstein & Lazar, 2016).

Results and meta analysis of effect sizes across the quantitative studies

The majority of the findings across the 46 projects were positive (see Table 6.5) with only six negative effect sizes (and only one of these was statistically significant). The effect sizes ranged from –1.94 (p=0.074) to +1.71 (p<0.001). The weighted mean effect size of all of the 46 projects was 0.39 (N=2457). The unweighted mean effect was 0.42, with a median of 0.34, suggesting a small number of more extreme positive findings bias the unweighted mean upwards.

Study C conclusions

The Early Adopter programme has shown that there is both capacity and capability within some schools to roll out the strategy as a general approach to micro-enquiry and to develop a number of teachers' skills. More work is

Table 6.5 Effect sizes and confidence intervals for the completed teachers' research studies

Project title	n	d	CI from	CI to
Using an internet-based homework calendar that tracks submissions encourages a higher rate of homework completion	21	1.37	0.50	2.23
Talk Boost to develop the expressive language skills of children in Reception compared with practitioner-planned regular small talk groups	24	0.99	−0.02	2.00
The effect of a Mental Toughness Intervention Programme for Year 10 students	21	−0.41	−2.03	1.21
The impact of supported familiarisation in the transition between phases	88	0.43	0.21	0.66
A small group intervention, Pulling It Together, may be more effective at developing a child's phonic and word reading skills than small group additional 'phonics' lessons	8	0.33	−0.26	0.91
Flipped learning has a positive impact on attainment in MFL	18	0.21	−0.57	0.99
Aiming for speed: Will learning to play darts help to increase writing speed?	40	1.16	0.28	2.04
A preliminary pilot study indicating a positive effect for the use of iPads in the improvement of phonological attainment	22	1.23	0.12	2.34
Using the visualisation technique of bar modelling does not improve the choosing of an appropriate method to solve word problems in mathematics	46	0.03	−0.01	0.08
Peer feedback is equally effective in improving pupil progress in essay-writing at A-level as teacher feedback	28	0.12	−0.59	0.83
Increased involvement of teaching assistants in reviewing intervention programmes accelerates progress with SEN pupils to close the gap in maths	20	0.08	0.00	0.16
The effectiveness of two meditative techniques on the improvement on concentration in a SLD school	8	1.57	−0.62	3.76
There is little difference in the amount of time students spend revising if they are given time to produce their own revision materials during the lesson	231	0.26	0.01	0.51
The effect of the environment on pupils' level of engagement	29	0.77	0.20	1.34

continued . . .

Table 6.5 Continued

Project title	n	d	CI from	CI to
The effectiveness of playing games as a means of developing fluency in the automatic recall of times tables	44	0.27	−7.26	7.80
The use of kinaesthetic strategies for spelling in Year 2	38	−0.39	−0.81	0.04
Directive versus inductive approaches to teaching spelling: Which is the most effective in supporting effective learning and progress in spelling?	59	0.29	−0.50	1.08
The impact of domestic help to facilitate home reading			0.00	0.00
Peer reading improves the reading age of Pupil Premium children compared to only reading to adults	54	0.25	−0.16	0.66
Self-selected online gaming stimulus to improve boys' creative writing	118	0.38	−0.17	0.93
Effects of a weekly spelling test on pupils' progress in retaining spellings	88	0.80	0.23	1.37
The impact upon student engagement and attainment when directly responding to teacher's feedback	59	0.70	0.13	1.27
The effect of increased motivation and competition intervention in mathematics	61	0.11	−0.46	0.69
The impact of context-based learning on effort and achievement within extended writing	29	0.02	0.04	−0.01
Does the use of digital games-based technology aid motivation, engagement and attitude to learning in the classroom with a Year 9 mixed ability class?	22	1.71	0.55	2.88
Changing a classroom's teaching environment can raise attainment in English and mathematics	116	0.24	−1.34	1.82
The impact of Growth Mindset interventions on students in different key stages	180	0.21	−0.57	0.99
'Look, Cover, Check, Write' improves attainment in Year 1 primary school lessons	88	0.39	0.09	0.69
Creative arts workshops and performance does improve the self-esteem and has no negative effect in speaking and listening skills of pupils with SEN	37	0.76	−0.07	1.59

continued . . .

Table 6.5 Continued

Project title	n	d	CI from	CI to
Pupils' progress does not increase if effort-related written feedback is used in addition to other regular feedback types	121	−0.16	−1.25	0.94
Meta cognition and maths attainment	29	0.56	0.09	1.03
The effect of mental toughness intervention to narrow the gap between Pupil Premium and non-Pupil Premium students	16	−1.94	−4.57	0.69
'In-lesson' feedback through OneNote may improve student progress	63	0.58	0.18	0.97
The use of iPads and applications in GCSE Spanish raises attainment in Listening and Reading examinations	56	1.67	0.61	2.72
An investigation into how effectively co-teaching closes the achievement gap for underachieving Pupil Premium students	20	0.05	−0.58	0.69
The effects of giving dedicated improvement and reflection time (DIRT) after feedback on written work has been provided	24	0.32	−0.10	0.74
Number skills video project: Supporting the Oval Cluster Number Master Programme	48	0.37	−11.07	11.81
Preliminary evidence from a small-scale pilot study regarding the use of an NLP-informed coaching programme to support Year 10 English teaching	59	0.58	0.00	1.17
Verbal and visual-digital feedback on creative writing in rural primary schools improves progress rates compared to written feedback – a preliminary study	231	0.45	0.12	0.78
Learning from a test that we failed to complete (qualitative study)	N/A			
The effect of personal-interest-based learning on progress in Early Years classrooms	24	−0.48	−1.15	0.19
The attainment of students when taught using a flipped classroom method in comparison to those given a traditional lecture-style lesson	48	1.07	0.28	1.86
The effect of physical activity on academic performance of pupils in maths	60	0.66	0.06	1.27
The effect of specialist art teaching on improving handwriting	28	0.34	−0.30	0.97
The effect of mindset training on low and high ability learners – preliminary evidence from a case-matched quasi-experimental study	33	−0.02	−0.26	0.22
Total	2457	0.39	Weighted mean	

required to build and develop capacity, and there is a need for different variants of micro-enquiry combined with larger-scale enquiry if we are to achieve a stronger teacher-led, school-led system of improvement. Micro-enquiry has a bright future – through micro-enquiry teachers can take control and take responsibility; it empowers them to make more complex and sophisticated professional decisions within their own professional lives.

Several implications emerge from the findings described above. The approach has potential as a means to develop teachers' research literacy so that they can more easily engage in and develop an understanding of this type of evidence as the number of RCTs increases. This is far from a theoretical point. Indeed, as the recent review by Queen's University Belfast shows (Connolly, 2015), over 800 university-based education RCTs have taken place in the last ten years. In England alone the EEF has commissioned over 130 since 2011, involving one in four schools in England. If teachers are going to be able to engage with this research as part of an evidence-informed profession, then building experimental research understanding into teacher training is going to increasingly become a priority, as it is in the medical and healthcare professions. In turn, it would appear that this form of teacher research might be able to make an important contribution to the development of teacher-led research, resolving some of the challenges that a number of writers have pointed to (Bennett, 2016; Riggall and Singer, 2016). Secondly, the effectiveness of the research designs was almost certainly the result of the teachers using tighter, more controlled designs over a shorter period – designs which are more akin to laboratory psychological studies. In addition, the tests chosen (or developed) by the teachers were generally more closely related to the area of study and the manipulation of content within their experiments. In contrast, some larger-scale trials have deployed measures which are not directly related to the intervention in hand and as such could be termed 'surrogate measures'. A final reason for the nature of the results described above may relate to the nature of the activities the teachers carried out and the interventions that they designed and used. In most cases teachers chose things to test which were directly related to a specific school improvement challenge within their context and developed interventions which (based on the local knowledge and understanding) they believed to be likely to work. This focus on the interest of practioners could redress the balance of researcher-led concerns.

A second implication and potential of the approach becomes clear when one considers the strong role of context within the education evidence debate. Teacher-led RCTs have much potential as a means of mediating and exploring the effects of prior large-scale studies in the teacher's own context, so that external solutions can be appraised according to local circumstance and priorities for spending. By extension, such approaches could also become a powerful way for schools to pilot changes in pedagogy before they are rolled out across a whole school or TSA.

Finally, not only are teacher-led RCTs desirable professionally, they could also be very cost effective, particularly if teachers can collaborate across schools to build larger sample sizes (paralleling the concept of 'team science' that has grown up within the natural sciences in recent years). For example, one study led by Kyra TSA pooled eleven classes within ten primary schools, enabling a sample size of 231 pupils. It is not difficult to imagine how, with a small amount of central resources, even larger trials could be constructed in collaboration with teachers and at considerably less cost than many of the large-scale trials that have been delivered in recent years. Such an approach could then contribute to the generation of research evidence with this co-ordination and replication.

Notes

1 The authors would like to thank Paul Gutherson for his support with the initial data analysis.
2 That 46 teachers involved in the teacher-led studies completed the EBPQ and that there were 46 completed posters is purely coincidental.
3 The EBPQ requests participants' age range not exact age.
4 Morris and DeShon, equation 8 (2002).

References

American Psychological Associaton (2012). *Publication manual of the American Psychological Association* (6th Edition). Washington, DC: American Psychological Associaton.

Bennett, T. (2016). *The school research lead*. Reading: Education Development Trust.

Blackwell, L.S., Trzeniewski, K.H. & Dweck, C.S. (2007). Implicit theories of intelligence predict achievement across an adolescent transition: a longitudinal study and an intervention. *Child Development*, 78(1), 246–263.

Brewer, M.B. (2000). Research design and issues of validity, in: H.T. Reis & C. Judd (eds.), *Handbook of research methods in social psychology*, pp.3–16, New York: Cambridge University Press.

Carifio, L. & Perla, R. (2008). Resolving the 50 year debate around using and misusing Likert scales. *Medical Education*, 42(12), 1150–1152.

Churches, R. (2016). *Closing the gap: test and learn – research report*. National College for Teaching and Leadership/Department for Education (DFE-RR500b). Available online: https://www.gov.uk/government/publications/closing-the-gap-test-and-learn (accessed: 28th January 2016).

Churches, R. & McAleavy, T. (2015). *Evidence that counts: what happens when teachers apply scientific methods to their practice – twelve teaching-led randomised controlled trials and other forms of experimental research*. Reading: Education Development Trust.

Churches, R. & Dommett, E. (2016). *Teacher-led research: designing and implementing randomised controlled trials and other forms of experimental research*. Carmarthen: Crown House Publishing.

Coe, R. (2002). It's the effect size, stupid: what effect size is and why it is important. Paper presented at the Annual Conference of the British Educational Research Association, University of Exeter, England, 12–14 September 2002.

Connolly, P. (2015). *The trials of evidence-based practice in education*. Keynote Presentation, British Educational Research Association Conference, Belfast, September 2015. Available online: https://www.youtube.com/watch?v=svuMXlAsaCE.

Devonshire, I.M. & Dommett, E.J. (2010). Neuroscience: viable applications in education. *The Neuroscientist*, 16(4), 349–356.

Education Endowment Foundation (2016). *Annual report 2015–16*. London: Education Endowment Foundation. Available online: https://educationendowmentfoundation. org.uk/about/annual-reports/

Hattie, J.A.C. (2009). *Visible learning: a synthesis of over 800 meta-analyses relating to achievement*. London: Routledge

Haynes, L., Service, O., Goldacre, B. & Torgerson, D. (2012). *Test, learn, adapt: developing public policy with randomised controlled trials*. London: Cabinet Office.

Jamieson, S. (2004). Likert scales: how to (ab)use them. *Medical Education*, 38(12), 1217–1218.

McAleavy, T. (2016). *Teaching as a research-engaged profession: problems and possibilities*. Reading: Education Development Trust.

NCTL (2016). *Closing the gap: test and learn (teacher-led randomised controlled trials) – resilience*. Nottingham: National College for Teaching and Leadership. Available online: https://www.gov.uk/government/uploads/system/uploads/attachment_data/file/495939/Resilience_posters_FINAL.pdf (accessed 13th April 2016).

Riggall, A. & Singer R. (2016). *Research leads: current practice, future prospects*. Reading: Education Development Trust.

Torgerson, C. J. & Torgerson, D.J. (2001). The need for randomised controlled trials in educational research. *British Journal of Educational Studies*, 49(3), 316–328.

Upton, D. and Upton, P. (2005). Nurses' attitudes to evidence-based practice: impact of a national policy. *British Journal of Nursing*, 14(5): 284–288.

Upton, D. and Upton, P. (2006). Development of an evidence-based practice questionnaire for nurses. *Journal of Advanced Nursing*, 54, 454–458.

Upton D. Upton P. and Scurlock-Evans, L.(2014). The reach, transferability, and impact of the Evidence-Based Practice Questionnaire: a methodological and narrative literature review. *Worldviews on Evidence-Based Nursing*, 11(1): 46–54.

Wasserstein, R.L. & Lazar, N.A. (2016). The ASA's statement on p-values: context, process, and purpose. *The American Statistician*, 70(2), 129–133.

Chapter 7

Building research capacity and relationships in schools

The consequences of involvement in Closing the Gap

Ann Childs and Nigel Fancourt

Introduction

The aspiration in England for schools and teachers to engage *in* and *with* research (Everton et al. 2004; CUREE 2011) is not new, stretching at least as far back as 1950s, though other countries – including Scotland – have had a longer trajectory, stretching back to the late nineteenth century (Nisbet and Broadfoot 1980; Nisbet 2005). In the 1970s, Stenhouse's model of enquiry was a significant catalyst (Stenhouse 1975), underpinning the subsequent development of action research in England (Elliott 1991; Somekh 2010). It can also be seen in analysis of the impact of research on both policy and practice (CUREE 2011). Later a new strand argued for 'evidence-informed' practice, in the sense of adopting a tightly defined 'scientific' model of empirical research, and began to be advocated in the 1990s, for example by Reynolds (1991) and notably Hargreaves (1996). This position was reinvigorated by the Coalition government's adoption of Ben Goldacre as a policy advisor, who, drawing on his own background in medical research, largely rejected anything other than randomised controlled trials as the basis of a suitable evidence base in educational research (2013). Various other research organisations adopt a similar approach, notably NFER (Hutchison & Styles 2010), ResearchEd (2016) and Educational Endowment Fund and have all been firm advocates of the development of such research in schools. This approach has, however, been criticised by some, including Hammersley (1993) and Hattie (2015), who argue that research is a complex practice in itself which is inappropriate to expect schools to do and to do well. Furthermore, there had been a long-running criticism of much that was termed research in schools (e.g., Foster 1999), and allied to this were rival assumptions about teaching itself, with the critics wary of a view of teaching as the execution of scientifically informed effective procedures, preferring to conceive it a values-laden endeavour (Biesta 2015). In short, whilst many have long considered the involvement of schools with research to be important, there has been considerable disagreement as to what this means, especially what kinds of research matter in this context.

A significant motivation for initiating the Closing the Gap (CtG) project was to stimulate schools' involvement with and in a particular model of quantitative research (see Chapter 2) and was part of a wider Goldacre-inspired drive towards an evidence-informed profession (Goldacre 2013) that would not only use such research, but would also organise and conduct it. The then Coalition's policy vision compared schools with hospitals, organising and carrying out randomised controlled trials in order to find out 'what works', and was connected to a wider desire to encourage better use of data within schools (Brown 2013). This policy initiative was itself allied to a broader aim of encouraging schools to be independent of external advisors and controls, notably local authorities, through academisation, and independent of universities' involvement in initial teacher education through more school-led initial teacher education. However, the policy did not just envisage schools acting independently; it encouraged the lead school, designated a 'Teaching School', to form a robust network of schools – the 'Teaching School Alliance' – which would receive additional funds to support a range of initial teacher education (ITE) and continuing professional development (CPD) activities; the term 'teaching' in these titles might appear odd for a school, but was also drawn from a medical analogy with 'teaching hospitals' (see DfE 2014; National College for Teaching and Leadership 2015). These alliances would have to be engaged in ITE, CPD, school-to school support, and research and development.

The CtG project therefore went beyond developing an evidence-informed profession, towards an evidence-*generating* profession, but with a very tight definition of what should be considered 'evidence', which had implications for how the schools' involvement unfolded. In the first phase of the scheme, teachers were positioned more as research assistants implementing the interventions that had already been selected and conducting the RCTs, rather than deciding for themselves in which areas of their practice and with what kinds of evidence they wanted to engage.

However, later in the programme, through the 'Early Adopters' scheme, which supported 50 schools or alliances in conducting RCTs (see), schools designed their own RCTs that focused on their own concerns and so genuinely became a more evidence-generating profession. It was becoming apparent that schools' involvement in the project was both shaped by and shaping their attitudes to and capacity for research more generally – their 'organisational epistemology' (Toh et al. 2014). Moreover, the overall project was to be conducted by Teaching School Alliances since 'research and development' was one of the key six elements of teaching school status (DfE, 2014), which meant that the developing relationships within these alliances across different schools was inevitably part of the research process.

It seemed expedient to investigate these developments further, capturing some of the consequences of this unique experiment, even though this was not part of the initial principal design of the RCTs. More broadly, the CtG project can be viewed as an example of what Brown terms 'luxury' research, as it is it both an exemplar of the kind of research which is seen as valuable and also seen as politically prestigious, thus having both use and signifying value

(Brown 2015, p. 23). Researching its wider impact is therefore potentially help-ful when considering other innovations based upon luxury research. It is an idiosyncratic – although probably also comparable – case study.

Given this background, this chapter focuses on three key research questions:

- What was the engagement with research in the schools before they became involved in the CtG scheme, and how did research engagement develop in the schools as a result of the scheme? This investigates the initial patterns of research engagement and how they altered as a result of the CtG project.
- How did the schools and alliances conceptualise school-based research, and how did this change as they engaged with the scheme? This strand explores whether and how schools adopted the methodological norms which underlay the project, notably the significance of randomised controlled trials, particularly in contrast with other models of education research, notably action research.
- How did the professional research relationships develop within and between Teaching Schools, their Alliance Schools, and with other organisations as a result of the project? In particular, it looked at the ways that wider collaboration played a part in the development of research across schools.

In order to address these aims a questionnaire was sent out to all schools involved in the CtG scheme in June 2014, which included questions on the schools' approaches and attitudes to the project and research more generally. Second, ten school leaders with the responsibility for coordinating the research ('trial coordinators') in various Teaching School Alliances were purposively selected in June 2015 for interview, in order to explore the nature and structural position of research within these alliances.

Literature review: building research capacity in schools

Given the uniqueness of the CtG project (see Chapter 2), it is perhaps unsurprising that there is little research literature on the effect of involvement in external research on developing research capacity in schools (though see Cousins et al. 2006). Nevertheless, these issues obviously sit within the considerable literature on school engagement in/with research, but overlap both with a wider field on knowledge mobilisation across different sectors, including the academic research community's concerns with impact (e.g., Hemsley-Brown and Sharp 2003; Maynard 2007), as well as with much literature on teachers' professional development, school improvement and evidence-based policy-making (e.g., Brown 2015). As a result, terms such as 'research', 'knowledge', 'evidence', 'impact', 'enquiry' and 'data-use' are used in conflicting ways, as are such terms as 'exchange', 'mobilisation', 'transformation' and 'dissemination' (McKibbon et al. 2010), to add more confusion.

Valuable starting points for opening up these issues are four reviews of existing research: Hemsley-Brown and Sharp (2003) on the *use* of research to improve professional practice; CUREE (2011) on 'engagement in and/or with research' (p. 1) – the paper which introduced this valuable distinction – and includes a comparison with health and social care; Dagenais et al. (2012), a Canadian-based review of the 'use of research-based information and determinants of use' (p. 1); and Nelson and O'Beirne (2014) on 'using evidence in the classroom'. However, an indication of the complexities of the field, and the effects of different review criteria, is that there is very little overlap in the papers finally selected by the different reviewers; for instance, the only study in common between CUREE (2011) and Dagenais et al. (2012) was Hemsley-Brown and Sharp (2003) – itself a review.

Overall, the literature raises three particular issues for the CtG project.

In/with research. A consistent theme is that generally teachers do not engage with research – either existing research or internal data – let alone in research (Williams and Coles 2007) chiming with the policy-makers' perceptions at the start of the project. Teachers often held negative or cautious attitudes towards research (e.g., Shkedi 1998; Nicholson-Goodman and Garman 2007). Engaging in research was, however, an important catalyst for engagement with it – conducting one's own research often involved reading and critiquing other research (Nisbet 2005; Cousins et al. 2006; Lafleur 1995; Nelson and O'Beirne 2014).

External support for research was important in many studies, whatever the methodology, and alongside internal school support (e.g., Timperley and Alton-Lee 2008). This typically consists of support in research methodology and practical issues (e.g., Timperley and Alton-Lee 2008), often from universities or other research institutions and professional development providers. Throughout CtG, schools were offered various training events, both for the development of research capacity in schools (Network events), as well as the Early Adopter training sessions in running small-scale RCTs, and statistical analysis, including an online programme for analysing data (see Chapter 2).

CtG involved teachers in research as they had to carry out the testing and the interventions, but it did not itself require engagement with wider research literature. However, the main project itself was so large that there was the risk that individual teachers had little sense of the practice of research. Paradoxically, it could have been too gargantuan a project to enthuse teachers in research, as they had often minor technical roles in the overall project, especially in the early phase.

Teacher/School/Alliance. A critical factor in how teachers value research is the schools' institutional research culture (Dagenais et al. 2012), for instance, the extent to which it is open to organisational learning generally (e.g., Ratcliffe et al. 2005) and experimentation and initiatives in particular (e.g., Shkedi 1998); this is linked clearly to school leadership (Anderson et al. 2010). The CtG project demanded school leadership level involvement and indeed required schools to address the issue of being a control or intervention group only within the trials. Moreover, the project worked with Teaching School Alliances which could provide a more networked research culture as an example of joint practice development (Sebba et al. 2012; Judkins et al. 2014), but this also created an additional layer of complexity. For the CtG project, the wider changes in school entities, with academisation developing apace and different alliances and groupings emerging, offered new possibilities for the schools, though it also meant that the landscape was unsettled.

Generic/contextual. There is an important spectrum from the development of greater use of data by teachers and schools within their existing practice to inform decision-making and research as a formal practice, often aimed at external use. From a research perspective, this is the issue of generalisability, but from a school perspective, the value of research is seen in terms of 'relevance' (Miretzky 2007) and 'context' (e.g., Everton et al. 2000). Two of the review articles distinguished between different types of research. Dagenais et al. (2012) contrasted '*general* research-based information, which is the scientific evidence found in literature . . . and *local* research-based information, which is produced locally and intended for local use' (p. 286, original emphasis); CUREE (2011) made a similar comparison, though had two categories of teacher 'research/enquiry' (p. 26). The CtG project was very clearly at the 'general' end of this spectrum – though this might have implications for the particular local context of the schools involved and for how the different research traditions were understood within schools.

The research findings

This section takes the analysis of the interviews and questionnaires to address each of the key research questions for this chapter.

Tracking the changes in engagement with research as the CtG scheme unfolded

Over the course of the two-year scheme 'the programme worked with 206 teaching schools' (Churches 2016:17). In the first year of the scheme '387 trial site schools took part in the trials' and in the second year another 286 schools completed the trials (Churches 2016:17). The Teaching School Alliances were spread across the country and between urban and rural locations. However, as potential sites of research, the complexity of the structures of these alliances was note-worthy:

> The Empower Schools Alliance is a collaborative group of Primary and Secondary schools operating within the Stockport area. The Alliance

> works with a range of strategic partners including Oakridge Teaching School in Westley, Harely Local Authority and a range of Higher Education Institutions, including Cavereley University and Eastridge University. Hastley Primary School is the lead Teaching School, which provides the Alliance schools with a range of school improvement, CPD and wider developmental opportunities. (WL [these initials represent different respondents])

> We work with Cavereley University, work with a special school, we work with a number of other primary colleagues, we work with an early years nursery, so it's grown as the year's gone on. But also there are two teaching schools in Purton so we're trying work collectively with them so that we are meeting the reach between the two of us. (TC)

Alliances were working within and between different organisations, such as a number of schools, across different sectors, e.g., primary and secondary, independent and state, faith schools and non-faith schools, local authority controlled and academies and different practices, e.g., universities and local authorities.

In these alliances, before joining the CtG scheme, there was often research going on in different ways, and both engaging in and with research were already firmly embedded in the Teaching School Alliances, for example:

> Dakin primary school has been developing its evidence based practice over a number of years. The school development plan actions are conducted in teams, using evidence based research as a way of addressing school improvement priorities. This has served to develop a culture of enquiry across the school, with staff supporting each other within this model. (WL)

> Before Closing the Gap came along there was a lot of research already going on in the school and existing partnerships. (BH)

> I gathered the team of 12 people, two from . . . all six faculties. And we had a term when we would meet biweekly and we would systematically work through the literature review. (FG)

> We've . . . had to research before we've delivered anything. So we've always quoted from papers or books that are on a specific subject area. (PV)

Much of this existing research was maintained in parallel with schools' involvement in CtG.

However, involvement in CtG also seemed to catalyse changes in schools' engagement with and in research, as well as other changes, in a number of ways. Firstly, one trial coordinator perceived that involvement in the CtG scheme acted as a catalyst to enhance research engagement across her school and alliance. Before the scheme started, much of the responsibility for the action research fell on her shoulders, but involvement with the CtG scheme brought many more colleagues in her school and in her alliance into direct involvement in research and indeed, one of the trainee teachers in mathematics undertook a mini-RCT.

Secondly, trial coordinators reported developments in their expertise in research, for example:

> In our first year I feel like we have come a long, long, long way in terms of our understanding of research and development. And what we've managed to carry out and develop our expertise, has been a really steep learning curve for us. (TC)

Thirdly, involvement in CtG did seem to act as a direct catalyst for schools to develop their own research projects, particularly those schools involved in the early adopter scheme who conducted their own mini-RCTs, for example:

> Initially, all the thinking about RCTs greatly motivated myself, I knew that part of our school development and appraisals were about developing research methodologies, so each time I attended network meetings with CfBT I then returned and updated staff and we conducted 12 small RCTs across the school on a theme of staff choice. (WL)

For another school that was involved both in the main scheme and in the Early Adopter programme, respondents did perceive that the main scheme was 'a bit out of our hands', but they also perceived that their involvement in conducting their own mini-RCTs allowed them to develop their research skills in running RCTs. They perceived that over time their skills became 'more sophisticated' leading to, across the alliance, the development of research leads and significant links between the alliance and research publications. These issues will be explored more when we discuss the third question. In addition, in this school, RCTs became much more the norm over a previously strong tradition of action research. As the trial coordinator said:

> the action researchers have become RCT[er]s, I think they have become more significant. (MM)

Others involved in CtG, both in the main scheme and in the early adopter scheme, perceived that RCTs complemented other research methodologies, such as action research. For example, one trial coordinator involved in the main scheme commented:

> It was very interesting for me to see that methodology [RCT] come into teaching and I welcome it. I think it is an additional tool for schools to be able to decide what's likely to have the biggest impact. I have a strong background in Action Research and I think that ultimately all changes in schools, when you want teachers to change what they do, will boil down to them trying out things and evaluating it in a very qualitative way and I think RCTs will never replace the need for teachers to try out things and evaluate them for themselves. (JP)

Fourthly, more engagement with research seemed to catalyse one school's future engagement with research and the need to look at other research to inform their practice:

> For next year I've been thinking . . . is there any kind of research around [working with families] that could provide us with some evidence as to the impact? (TC)

Finally, involvement in CtG seemed to have other consequences beyond changing engagement with research such as developing a more sophisticated approach to the use of school-data in addressing issues:

> There hasn't been any other research that has grown from this . . . but being involved in Closing the Gap has made us develop the parental engagement element and to take a more holistic view, wider than our strengths in tracking and data. (RY)

However, not all were as confident or so committed. For example, one trial coordinator, even with training in conducting her own RCTs, did not feel able to conduct them:

> We have considered mini-RCTs and I and another colleague went to the first training session and, although I didn't feel I had the capacity to do a mini-RCT myself, I encouraged another colleague to do one, but she was really scared off by the maths. (HD)

In addition, one other Teaching School Alliance with a strong and vibrant research culture felt the scheme was badly organised and did not recognise the considerable engagement that the alliance already had with research, and so their participation dwindled.

Overall though, the evidence from the questionnaires and interviews suggest that CtG had been influential in these alliances, both at the most basic level of raising the question about conducting their own research as well as stimulating some to carry out their own projects.

Changing conceptualisations of research over the project

It seems that CtG stimulated an interest in research in schools and alliances in a number of ways outlined above, but how did they conceptualise this? Research is typically thought of as a university-based practice, but if it is school-based instead, it may be influenced by schools' priorities and practices. Firstly, for many respondents a concern with school improvement underpinned their conceptualisation about the purposes of research in school:

> Research is tied in with school priorities and particularly the impacts on teaching and learning. (WL)

> We wanted to be involved in something that was a national project, to see if we could learn any more, because we want to improve, because that's what we do all the time – can we improve? (TC)

Their approach was pragmatic, but it can also be seen as instrumental; research had to fulfil wider organisational priorities. This meant that it was closely associated with other organisational requirements:

> Well, we do research as part of our performance management targets . . . That's something that the headteacher at the school is very keen on. (RY)

Secondly, research also sat alongside performance management, school-to-school support or professional development. The choices within these were also pragmatic; one respondent described a plan for school-to-school support which was presented as a research project because:

> Schools that don't have a higher category come to the school that's outstanding and they look for faults rather than look for what they could do better. Because of the mindset of the people! "Oh they're not that brilliant because they were doing this that and the other!" (IF)

Further, schools' overriding concern with a range of issues seemed to inform their methodological choices for research, and in particular whether RCTs replaced or supplemented action research. The respondent continued:

> so it's kind of a research project. But it is set up slightly differently. It's not a random controlled trial, and it's kind of a joint professional development, a bit of CPD really. (IF)

The research element of this support was therefore a vehicle for other purposes – a way of allowing schools in different categories to work together so that support was not explicit or paternalistic. Moreover, the quotation also shows how respondents valued a variety of methodologies for achieving different aims, as another added:

> So we are kind of dipping our toes in, and, if it's a kind of buffet, we are trying to get all the different food for it! (TC)

This did not mean that the choice of methodology was arbitrary, as respondents considered that RCTs were a rigorous form of research.

> We've done quite a bit of work involving action research and enquiry-based practice and all staff leading their own CPD ... but nothing as structured and tighter. (WL)

This was considered important in informing policymakers:

> For education now, we need to be providing a bank of evidence-based research in order for what actually works to be done in schools, rather than on the whim of a minister. (IF)

Thirdly, as indicated above, RCTs were conceptualised as a more rigorous form of research, particularly in those schools involved in the Early Adopter programme, and these respondents described RCTs in language like 'rigorous', 'produce hard data', 'tighter and more structured', 'more focussed' and more 'methodical', resulting in evidence of 'what works'. For example, one trial coordinator, an early adopter, said in relation to the mini-RCTs in which his alliance was involved:

> We need to know what works ... So I suppose there's a general methodical approach to things and a rigour associated with what we are doing ... So we now have a relentless focus on those things the evidence suggest works best. (JB)

And he conceived of research involving RCTs as giving teachers more security in their actions:

> It has given staff a structure, a security blanket, to enable staff to collect some hard data to facilitate pupil progress reviews. (JB)

Furthermore, RCT research was conceptualised as being more responsive to the immediate context of the school and accessible to all teachers in comparison with published research:

> I mean one of the problems that we found around research is context-ualising it and translating you know a degree of theory into practice. (JB)

In this case the trial coordinator perceived that the nature of the mini-RCT research that they were conducting could only be very specific to their own context and it was valuable in giving them hard data on 'what works' in their context. Another felt that the mini-RCTs conducted as part of the Early Adopter programme in their school were more accessible for staff and had allowed teachers to see how useful research in their own school context could be to inform their practice.

Contrary though to the perception that RCTs made research more accessible to classroom teachers, others had different perceptions about the appropriate organisational place for conducting and using RCTs, with many considering that they were a more appropriate tool for senior leadership than individual teachers:

> Ultimately all changes in schools boil down to teachers trying things out and evaluating these qualitatively, so RCTs will never replace the need for teachers to try things out and evaluate them for themselves. But in terms of school leaders making decisions about whether to buy in one intervention or another, RCTs provide a large scale project that has been analysed statistically and had control groups which add validity. (HD)

Furthermore, one trial coordinator said that for senior leaders 'engagement with research and the research process' had allowed them 'to talk to each other more often and more purposefully'. This echoes the debate in the literature about generic and local research, in that individual local research is positioned alongside more generalisable studies. However, there was a twist here, in that schools and alliances had also to decide if generic research would be applicable to them. This was important because the CtG project might show that a particular intervention was generally ineffective, but they – in their professional judgement – considered that it was effective, and vice versa:

> When last week I met with the schools with whom we carried out the project, some of them, regardless of what the outcomes are going to be in terms of the data, said "Well, we really like this and are going to do it". And I've said "Well, are we going to wait until we see the impact in terms of the national data before we do anything else?" To which they've already made their minds up, and are doing it. (TC)

Given that any intervention might have been effective in some schools or alliances, this was not necessarily irrational. Another respondent used the notion of 'context' to explain school decision-making:

> And then we'll do a six-week trial of that, that's data driven, and then if it makes a difference in the six weeks then obviously it's working and we'll

continue with it. If it doesn't make a difference in those six weeks then we know it isn't working in our context. And it's not that the research is incorrect, it just doesn't work in our context. (IF)

Her own local data would be used to inform the school leadership and take priority over the generic findings within the school's overall educational aims. Thus, school or alliance priorities were the main determinants of research and informed its deployment and the weight given to it.

Overall, at the very least, RCTs were conceptualised as being a useful additional tool in the repertoire of research methods schools could draw on. For some, however, and these were mainly those in the early adopter programme, the use of RCTs were considered valuable in being able to provide many significant benefits and, for a few, became the principal mode of generating research evidence in their Teaching School Alliance.

Developments in professional research relationships

The third area concerns how professional research relationships developed within and between alliances and with other organisations, as a result of the project. Further, the distinction between different kinds of research for teachers and senior leadership, in the immediately previous section, would have implications for organisational structuring within schools:

> Classroom teachers very much want to see whether there were new things that would improve the quality of provision for children, and improve achievement for children. So they were looking specifically at their classes. So they were looking for a very child-led sort of focus, whereas I'm looking from their coordinator's point of view. (IF)

Nevertheless, all research needed institutional support.

> I've seen people try to do research projects in school when they are not supported by the school, or the senior leadership team, and it's very hard. So it really doesn't come from the top, but not top-down in a forced way. But it needs to have its input bottom-up, with the support of the top. If that makes sense. (IF)

This reflects the findings in the literature (e.g., Dagenais et al. 2012).

However, there were some really radical and substantial developments in research relationships and in collaborations within and between Teaching School Alliances reported as a result of the CtG scheme. Firstly, at a very basic level the project seems to have stimulated discussions between schools about research that would not have otherwise have taken place:

I mean what was nice about doing this research project was actually just the discussions you have with people from other schools, and you know what's currently going on in their provision. (PV)

However, in other Teaching School Alliances more formal research relationships developed, for example, one trial coordinator reported that CtG has resulted in the formation of research development teams:

Across the Alliance we now have research development teams to replace the cluster groups. RCTs now drive the whole process of improving teaching and learning. (WL)

This also resulted in alliance meetings regularly discussing the research taking place within the Teaching School Alliances. Another trial coordinator talked about how collaboration and sharing of research has developed across his alliance:

and it used to be an in-house thing, you know, it was just our school really. So I think maybe the project has brought us closer together because we've got these steering group meetings with the X teaching alliance, and now research and development is now a standard item on the agenda. (KG)

In addition, a network of 'research leads' were created who 'meet up once a half term to sort of share good practice about what we do about research'. In one Teaching School Alliance two professional learning communities already existed, but involvement previously in an EEF project and now in CtG was perceived to have:

widened our own research into what professional development looks like and the development of teacher learning communities. (JB)

In addition, in this alliance they have also trained up 'specialist leaders of education in professional learning communities, and actually how to deliver research and the RCT element is incorporated with that as well'. The role of 'research lead' had often emerged out of or, if it already existed, been galvanised by the CtG position of 'research coordinator' – indeed the fact that it was possible to identify such individuals to interview was significant in itself (see McAleavy 2016; Bennett 2016; Riggall and Singer 2016).

Second, these enhanced research relationships also resulted in much more sharing of research across the Teaching School Alliances through, as said above, alliance meetings and in school staff meetings, but also in organising dissemination conferences and in writing research reports and other publications.

Third, these developments and research relationships also involved other parties, such as local authorities, for some alliances:

Local authority conversations are becoming more significant. The LA has seen the enthusiasm for CtG within schools and wants to know more about what has been going on. (WL)

In addition, Higher Education Institutions (HEIs) were also seen to be important partners in research relationships for some Teaching School Alliances, particularly HEIs that they already had links with. As one trial coordinator said:

You know you can't miss out the higher institutions as well, and they should form part of what we're doing. (GE)

This Teaching School Alliance was organising a conference on research which included an invitation to HEIs as it was committed to having 'more of a collaborative approach' with HEIs. As a result, research coordinators and head teachers from the alliance met with representatives from higher education to facilitate collaboration more widely. Another trial coordinator saw previous relationships with local HEIs as a means to collaborate with them on publishing research. These links, though, very much suggest that Teaching School Alliances are seeking to become leaders in generating research, a role which has previously been the domain of HEIs.

This then raised a wider question about schools as leading educational research in their own right. A sense of empowerment was manifest in some responses and how it might develop:

We met with the 50 other schools that were part of those projects, and we were in that room and we were talking, we speed-dated about what we were going to be doing, that was such an empowering, and uplifting hour to spend just talking to people, amazing ideas and actually it was being driven by the profession. (TC)

Here is another respondent:

We might begin to think about research in schools – and again its borrowing from the medical field – as specialising in a particular area. So in the same way as you have . . . a hospital that focuses on specific areas, why don't we apply that to schools? So if you have a school where they are naturally gravitated towards something like growth mindsets, it might be an idea to, for schools and for government funding to create a sort of 'field hospital' in a particular area. And over a number of years they would specialise in an area, and then share that practice with other schools. (FG)

This would have implications for the inter-relationship between HEIs and schools in educational research; many pointed to strong links with universities, though usually in initial teacher education. Some also had research links, though in a range of methodologies and not just in RCTs. One had made connections with a US-based university, which had helped establish a research group and developed some joint research. However, what is interesting here is that some Teaching School Alliances were envisioning completely new structural arrangements for the educational research landscape, taking them well beyond their traditional role as research consumers. This is resonant with the policy agenda behind Teaching Schools, mentioned above, for, as part of their key responsibilities, they were charged to be leaders in the move to more school-led, school-based teacher education (both ITE and CPD). Here we see some evidence of Teaching Schools also seeing themselves as leaders in a reconfiguration of educational research. This in turn poses questions for HEIs about their own continuing role in teacher education and educational research (see Callahan and Martin 2007; Fancourt et al. 2015; Fancourt 2017), which is itself also situated within wider debates about the future role and function of HEIs in all types of professional education and related research.

Implications

The discussion presented here sheds valuable light on ways that CtG has acted as a catalyst on engagement in and with research in schools and presents some challenges for further development of research-informed schools. First, although the first phase of the main project principally cast Teaching School Alliance staff more as technicians in implementation of the interventions and then conducting the RCTs, there is evidence to suggest that, even at this level, the discussion of research was stimulated and, in one case at the very least, encouraged other staff in a school to become interested in research.

Secondly, whilst the complexity of alliance structures and links provided the economies of scale to support research leads, it also suggests a degree of fragility in the process. Different organisations and practices may have different motives and agendas, which may make research difficult to organise and support – especially without the support offered in the CtG project. Whilst there is a range of organisations promoting and supporting quasi-experimental type research, it is for the schools and alliances to approach these organisations. Furthermore, although the pragmatic positioning of research with school improvement provides a strong justification for research within school practices, it may dictate both what and how it is researched, alongside or within other aspects of schools' educational aims. Thus, the organisational epistemology of schools' research is located within wider organisational values, and current perceptions of the purity of research may not fit easily alongside these potential conflicting agendas.

Lastly, therefore, there are wider cultural and political issues as to how teaching and schools are conceived as much as how research is conceptualised across schools and alliances and across wider links with other organisations. This is about the conflicting perceptions of teaching as much as it is about the place of research in schools and the involvement of other organisations within this. At one level, this is only to be expected, as many areas of research have their own particular concatenations of methodology and institutional organisations, for example, the involvement of hospitals, universities and pharmaceutical companies in medical research, all with different motives and agendas. However, the particular issues in education here are compounded by the wider policy shifts relating to school structures, higher education and the research economy. Long term, school-led RCTs *may* flourish and develop as the most significant form of educational research, or more modestly become a valuable addition to a range of approaches and research organisations, in the light of these other factors. However, it is increasingly the case that schools and alliances are appointing a 'research lead', as the main lynch-pin for school-led projects – often our respondents in this small study – and it will be their endeavours which will determine the future shape of these forms of knowledge generation.

References

Anderson, S., Leithwood, K. & Strauss, T. 2010. Leading data use in schools: organizational conditions and practices at the school and district levels, *Leadership and Policy in Schools*, 9:3, 292–327.

Bennett, T. 2016. *The School Research Lead*. Reading: Education Development Trust.

Biesta, G. 2015. How does a competent teacher become a good one? On judgement, wisdom and virtuosity on teaching and teacher education. In R. Heilbronn and L. Foreman-Peck (eds.) *Philosophical Perspectives on Teacher Education*, 3–22. Chichester: Wiley Blackwell.

Brown, C. (ed.) 2013. *Leading the Use of Research and Evidence in Schools*. London: IOE Press.

Brown, C. 2015. *Evidence-informed Policy and Practice in Education: A Sociological Grounding*. London: Bloomsbury.

Callahan, J. & Martin, D. 2007. The spectrum of school–university partnerships: a typology of organizational learning systems, *Teaching and Teacher Education*, 23:2, 136–145.

Centre for the Use of Research & Evidence in Education (CUREE). 2011. *Report of Professional Practitioner Use of Research Review: Practitioner Engagement in and/or with Research*. Coventry: CUREE [online]. Available online: http://www.curee.co.uk/files/publication/[site-timestamp]/Practitioner%20Use%20of%20Research%20Review%20-%20FINAL%2011_02_11.pdf

Churches, R. 2016. *Closing the Gap: Test and Learn. Research report*. London: Department for Education/National College for Teaching and Leadership.

Cousins, J., Goh, S. & Clark, S. 2006. Data use leads to data valuing: evaluative inquiry for school decision making, *Leadership and Policy in Schools*, 5:2, 155–176.

Dagenais, C., Lysenko, L., Abrami, P., Bernard, R., Ramde, J. & Janosz, M. 2012. Use of research-based information by school practitioners and determinants of use: a review of empirical research, *Evidence & Policy*. 8:3, 285–309.

Department for Education (DfE). 2014. *Teaching Schools: A Guide to Potential Applicants.* Available online: https://www.gov.uk/guidance/teaching-schools-a-guide-for-potential-applicants

Elliott, J. 1991. *Action Research for Educational Change.* Milton Keynes: Open University Press.

Everton, T., Galton, M. & Pell, T. 2000. Teachers' perspectives on educational research: Knowledge and context, *Journal of Education for Teaching,* 26:2, 167–182.

Everton, T., Galton, M. & Pell, T. 2004. Educational research and the teacher, *Research Papers in Education,* 17:4, 373–401.

Fancourt, N. 2017. Creating a system of distributed expertise: the Oxford Education Deanery narrative. In A. Edwards (ed.) *Working Relationally in and Across Practices: A Cultural-Historical Approach to Collaboration.* Cambridge: Cambridge University Press, 172–190.

Fancourt, N., Edwards, A. & Menter, I. 2015. Reimagining a school–university partnership: the development of the Oxford Education Deanery narrative, *Education Inquiry,* 6:3.

Foster, P. 1999. 'Never mind the quality, feel the impact': a methodological assessment of teacher research, sponsored by the Teacher Training Agency, *British Journal of Educational Studies,* 47:4, 380–398.

Goldacre, B. 2013. *Building Evidence into Education.* Available online: [http://media.education.gov.uk/assets/files/pdf/b/ben%20goldacre%20paper.pdf] (Accessed 30th May 2014).

Hammersley, M. 1993. On the teacher as researcher, *Educational Action Research,* 1:3, 425–445.

Hargreaves, D. 1996. *Teaching as a Research-based Profession: Possibilities and Prospects. The Teacher Training Annual Lecture.* London: TTA.

Hattie, J. 2015. Leave research to the academics, John Hattie tells teachers. In *Times Education Supplement,* 24 April 2015. Available online: https://www.tes.com/news/school-news/breaking-news/leave-research-academics-john-hattie-tells-teachers (Accessed 24th August 2015).

Hemsley-Brown, J. & Sharp, C. 2003. The use of research to improve professional practice: a systematic review of the literature, *Oxford Review of Education,* 29:4, 449–471.

Hutchison, D. & Styles, B. 2010. *A Guide to Running Randomised Controlled Trials for Educational Researchers.* Slough: NFER.

Judkins, M., Stacey, O., McCrone, T. & Inniss, M. 2014. *Teachers' Use of Research Evidence: A Case Study of United Learning Schools.* Slough: NFER.

Lafleur, C. (1995) A participatory approach to district level program evaluation: the dynamics of internal evaluations. In J.B. Cousins and L.M. Earl (eds) *Participatory Evaluation in Education: Studies in Evaluation Use and Organizational Learning.* London and Washington, DC: Falmer Press, 33–54.

Maynard, A. 2007. Translating evidence into practice: why is it so difficult? *Public Money and Management,* 27:4, 251–256.

McAleavy, T. 2016. *Teaching as a Research-engaged Profession: Problems and Possibilities.* Reading: Education Development Trust.

McKibbon, K.A., Lokker, C., Wilczynski, N.L., Ciliska, D., Dobbins, M., Davis, D.A., Haynes, R.B. & Straus, S.E. 2010. A cross-sectional study of the number and frequency of terms used to refer to knowledge translation in a body of health literature in 2006: a Tower of Babel? *Implementation Science*, 5:1, 16.

Miretzky, D. 2007. A view of research from practice: Teachers talk about research. *Theory into Practice*, 46:4, 272–280.

National College for Teaching and Leadership. 2015. *Teaching Schools: The School Perspective*. Nottingham: National College for Teaching and Leadership.

Nelson, J. & O'Beirne, C. 2014. *Using Evidence in the Classroom. What Works and Why*. Slough: NFER

Nicholson-Goodman, J. and Garman, N.B. 2007. Mapping practitioner perceptions of 'it's research based': scientific discourse, speech acts and the use and abuse of research, *International Journal of Leadership in Education*, 10:3, 283–299.

Nisbet, J. 2005. What is educational research? Changing perspectives through the 20th century, *Research Papers in Education*. 20:1, 25–44.

Nisbet, J. & Broadfoot, P. 1980. *The Impact of Research on Policy and Practice in Education*. Aberdeen: Aberdeen University Press.

Ratcliffe, M., Bartholomew, H., Hames, V., Hind, A., Leach, J., Millar, R. & Osbourne, J. 2005. Evidence-based practice in science education: the researcher–user interface, *Research Papers in Education*, 20:2, 169–186.

ResearchEd. 2016. Our mission. https://researched.org.uk/about/our-mission/

Reynolds, D. 1991. Changing ineffective schools. In M. Ainscow (ed.) *Effective Schools for All*. London: David Fulton.

Riggall, A. & Singer, A. 2016. *Research Leads: Current Practice, Future Prospects*. Reading: Education Development Trust.

Sebba, J., Kent, P., & Tregenza, J. 2012. *Joint Practice Development: What Does the Evidence Suggest are Effective Approaches?* Nottingham: National College for School Leadership.

Shkedi, A. 1998. Teachers' attitudes towards research: a challenge for qualitative researchers, *International Journal of Qualitative Studies in Education*, 11:4, 559–577.

Somekh, B. 2010. The Collaborative Action Research Network: 30 years of agency in developing educational action research, *Educational Action Research*, 18:1, 103–121.

Stenhouse, L. 1975. *An Introduction to Curriculum Research and Development*. London: Heinemann.

Timperley, H. & Alton-Lee, A. 2008. Reframing teacher professional learning: an alternative policy approach to strengthening valued outcomes for diverse learners, *Review of Research in Education*, 32, 328–369.

Toh, K., Corbitt, B., & Beekhuyzen, J. 2014. A knowledge management model to improve the development of bushfire communication products, *Australasian Journal of Information Systems*, 18:3. doi: http://dx.doi.org/10.3127/ajis.v18i3.911

Williams, D. & Coles, L. 2007. Teachers' approaches to finding and using research evidence: an information literacy perspective, *Educational Research*, 49, 185–206. doi: 10.1080/00131880701369719

Chapter 8

Research ethics in Closing the Gap

Equipoise in randomised controlled trials in education

Nigel Fancourt

Introduction

This chapter considers various aspects of research ethics in randomised controlled trials in education. The ethical issues arose out of one large educational research project: Closing the Gap: Test and Learn. This project involved seven randomised controlled trials with randomisation at school level and four replications with randomisation within about 700 individual schools. First the chapter explores how research ethics were addressed in several policy documents that had argued for the use of randomised controlled trials in schools. Then there is an account of the ethical issues in the project and their pragmatic solutions. Five stages are identified: choice of interventions; the use of control groups; data collection; use of interim data; and subsequent research. The problems posed by two of these – choice of interventions and sharing of interim data – are then reviewed in detail in the light of the notion of equipoise, and particularly in identifying the appropriate expert community given the range of organisations involved, including schools themselves. The need for more attention to equipoise as a deliberative principle in educational research ethics is discussed, as well as some potential difficulties for school-led research.

The importance of addressing the ethical dimensions of any research involving humans hardly needs to be highlighted, and ethical conduct in educational research has long been seen as an essential element of current research practice (e.g., Burgess 1989; McNamee and Bridges 2002). Researchers have explained and reflected upon their ethical experiences and deliberations (Midgley et al. 2013), tackling issues such as: consent (e.g., Robinson-Pant and Singal 2013; Shamim and Qureshi 2013); anonymity (e.g., Walford 2005); children and young people (e.g., Parsons et al. 2015); and the use of images (Kaplan et al. 2011). This collective process of reflection has informed and been informed by the development of codes of practice, notably guidelines published by the British Educational Research Association (BERA 2011). In university-based research, there is usually a process of formal scrutiny across many disciplines, though some would argue that ethical reasoning has thereby become over-bureaucratised and researchers' deliberative judgements have been compromised or hidden, both in the social sciences (e.g., Haggerty 2004; Israel and Hay 2006; Hammersley 2010) and indeed in medicine (Chalmers 2011). The ethical issues surrounding research by teachers have also come under scrutiny (e.g., Zeni 2001; Brindley and Bowker 2013; Mockler 2014), as have the ethical issues of collaboration between universities and schools (e.g., Locke et al. 2013). There have therefore been recent pleas for 'greater opportunities for researchers to share their practices . . . so that creativity becomes a more transparent and, therefore, accepted part of the ethics landscape' (Parsons et al. 2015, p. 725). This chapter is intended to make a contribution to this openness.

With this in mind, some ethical challenges in the Closing the Gap (CtG) project are considered, but it is less a sharing of what the researchers practised and more a reflection on how it might have been improved. As the use of randomised controlled trials (RCTs) is growing (Connolly et al., 2017), this methodology is increasingly in the spotlight, and for instance Fives et al. (2015) recently reviewed some of the ethical issues arising from one educational RCT. Like Fives et al., this chapter will address some of the internal tensions in ethical deliberation. Unlike their article, however, it will not address the wider long-standing issue of whether RCTs are ethically permissible at all – in response to, for instance Morrison (2001) or Hammersley (2008). Furthermore, it will not consider the issues raised by the handling of ethical approval through bureaucratic processes; it focuses on the ethical principles to be applied, not who should apply them.

The CtG project was an unprecedentedly large-scale randomised controlled trial of seven different interventions, involving five research organisations and 700 schools across nearly 200 school alliances (see Chapter 1; also: Churches 2016b; Churches 2016a; and National College for Teaching and Leadership 2016a, 2016b, 2016c, 2016d, 2016e, 2016f, 2016g, 2016h). The organisational complexity and choice of methodology raised a range of epistemological and practical questions, as discussed elsewhere in this book. Furthermore, the project also presented several unusual issues for research ethics, some of which were identified and addressed in advance, whereas others emerged as the project unfolded. The official research report only gave a very brief account of these issues (Churches 2016b, pp. 38–39), so this chapter offers a retrospective review of the issues and how they were addressed, drawing on various internal documents as well as qualitative interviews with various stakeholders, as described in previous chapters (Chapters 1 and 3). After a review of research ethics in recent policy, the next section is chronological, identifying and commenting on the project's approach to ethical issues over the course of the research, followed by a review of how matters might have been improved and the implications of this for future research. It is certainly not intended to suggest that the best choices were made, but rather to illuminate the decision-making process and to inform future research design and ethical deliberation in randomised controlled trials in education.

The ethics of randomised controlled trials in recent education policy

The initial impetus for the CtG project was a desire within the Coalition government (between 2010 and 2015) to raise the attainment of pupils who faced educational disadvantages, and this has long been a concern of politicians of various shades. However, it also became a major part of the Coalition's drive to develop the use of RCTs modelled on medicine and the health sciences both in public policy generally (Haynes et al. 2012) and specifically in education (Goldacre 2013). There was however a reaction to the analogy with evidence-based practice in medicine, and some educational researchers argued that this methodological approach was neither new nor straightforward (e.g., James 2013; Taber 2013). Further, the policy aimed to enable schools to make research-informed decisions, so that time and money were not wasted on irrelevant or ineffective strategies – a 'what works' rationale. Put another way, the project was not simply an abstract investigation of interesting research topics; it was both grounded in political and professional concerns about under-achievement and educational equity and also a vehicle for developing research capacity in schools.

A striking feature of the documents by Haynes et al. and Goldacre was their framing of ethical concerns. In their argument for the use of RCTs in public policy, Haynes et al. (2012) hoped to dispel what they perceived to be the main criticisms of RCTs in a section entitled 'The case for RCTs – debunking some myths'. This covered issues of ethics as well as complexity, cost and need, and the term 'myth' is a surprisingly pejorative label for genuine methodological concerns. They explicitly focused on the ethics of using control groups:

> Sometimes people object to RCTs in public policy on the grounds that it is unethical to withhold a new intervention from people who could benefit from it. This is particularly the case where additional money is being spent on programmes which might improve the health, wealth, or educational attainment of one group.
>
> (Haynes et al. 2012, p. 16)

Although none were specifically cited, some educational researchers do indeed have these concerns (Morrison 2001; Hammersley 2008). In response to this argument, Haynes et al. (2012) argued from an analogy with medical research, holding that although it would be wrong to withhold an intervention if its benefits were definitively known, nevertheless 'we need to be clear about the limits of our knowledge and . . . we will not be certain of the effectiveness of an intervention until it is tested robustly' (p. 17). They then give examples of various standard practices across the public sector that had been considered appropriate until they were shown to be ineffective or even detrimental when tested in RCTs. One of the co-authors, Ben Goldacre, went on to address the educational issues specifically (Goldacre 2013), and unsurprisingly adopted the same language – 'myths about randomised trials' (p. 10) – addressing the related concern that 'people sometimes worry that it is unethical to randomly assign children to one educational intervention or another' (p. 11). He then narrowed this to a particular assumption: 'Often this is driven by an implicit belief that a new or expensive intervention is always necessarily better' (p. 11), and put forward a justification for RCTs on the basis of the need to tackle the claims of charismatic 'experts' with robust evidence.

Neither Haynes et al. (2012) nor Goldacre (2013) intended to provide a comprehensive guide to the ethical issues, but their approaches to ethical concerns raise some questions. First, they seem to assume that the main issue is that of reining in unsupported educational fads – in disproving current practice – but not developing innovative practice. Second, they simply counter an ethical objection to RCTs with an alternative claim, but do not provide any indication as to how one should balance these two claims, i.e., the potential benefits of a particular practice versus the uncertainty of its effectiveness. However, the ethical justification for conducting RCTs is not the same as ethical conduct in RCTs. It is a long established part of ethical reasoning that having the right to engage in an activity does not mean that the activity can be carried out in an unprincipled way. The ends do not justify the means, and Haynes et al. and Goldacre do the cause of RCTs in education a disservice by not addressing the ethical issues fully.

The ethical issues in Closing the Gap

The CtG project was in part the result of this new-found governmental admiration for RCTs, so it can be reviewed in the light of the preceding discussion, in order to consider how ethical issues were explicitly and implicitly considered, framed and played out over the course of the research. Much discussion of practice-based educational research has explored the ethical complexities of how schools work with external research organisations, typically universities, which may have differing approaches to the ethical issues at stake, particularly bureaucratic structures (Locke et al. 2013). A significant contextual factor in exploring these issues in CtG was the number of different organisations involved, including the government agencies (Department for Education and the National College for Teaching and Leadership), the two universities (Durham and Oxford) and two independent educational organisations (CfBT and CUREE), so who was responsible and how ethical considerations should be approached was unclear. Further, there were also 180 Teaching School Alliances and nearly 700 schools involved, who were also gathering and using some of the data from their own pupils – indeed one of the twin aims of the project was to promote research capacity for RCTs in schools. Clearly, there was a range of different professional responsibilities and ethical expectations at work that had to be reconciled, and it is fair to say – in retrospect – that this process could have been more nuanced.

Overall, there were five different stages which raised ethical issues: choice of interventions; the use of control groups; data collection; use of interim data; and subsequent research. These are discussed chronologically, to highlight how different issues arose over the course of the project. First, the initial planning stage involved choosing the different interventions to be in the project (see Chapter 4). This review was carried out by NCTL, Durham and CUREE, and included gathering a focus group of teachers for consultation, over 17 different meetings. The aim of this process was, according to the final report, to ensure that the interventions were a selection of those strategies 'which the current evidence supported as being effective in closing the attainment gap for lower-performing pupils, with a view to evaluating them using large-scale RCTs' (Churches 2016b, p. 19); however, the wording of the first clause is imprecise, especially the term 'evidence' in that, as another member of the team commented, 'we would not have proposed trials for things which were *known* to be effective for a specific context'. It would perhaps have been better to say that the interventions were a selection of those strategies which many practitioners considered were likely to be effective. The final selection included different types of strategy, from classroom-based activities, such as Numicon, to whole-school initiatives such as Achievement for All; however, they all satisfied the two requirements that whilst they were not definitively advantageous, they were also considered by the selection group to be unlikely to be detrimental in comparison to current practice.

The use of control groups was the focus of internal discussion, particularly as schools were thought to be likely to object to being involved on this basis. A member of the research team had a perception that there was 'a general tendency . . . to dismiss RCTs as . . . unethical', echoing the points raised in the policy documents (Haynes et al. 2012; Goldacre 2013). This was addressed in the early training rounds by drawing on a medical analogy, and particularly highlighting that the control group schools were not to be conceived as 'doing nothing', instead they were entitled and indeed encouraged to do as much as they could for their pupils, acting on their own professional judgement: the interventions needed to be better than whatever schools could provide themselves. In the event, a member of the research team reflected that 'we were surprised at the relatively low resistance to the concept of a RCT amongst the participants . . . by and large schools' concerns about randomised controlled trials have been almost entirely pragmatic ones, not the ethical ones': schools at least understood and accepted the ethical justification for RCTs.

Simultaneously, the process for giving consent needed attention. The most rigorous position would have been for explicit parental and individual consent for every pupil (e.g., Homan 2002). This would have been complex given the vast number of schools and pupils involved: the logistics of withdrawing different pupils from the research would be convoluted for classroom interventions such as FirstClass@Number, and harder again for whole-school projects such as Achievement for All. Further, requiring consent could exclude the very pupils whom the research was intended to benefit; as Shaw et al. (2015) suggested, lower attaining pupils tend not to be represented if active parental consent is required. On balance, headteachers' consent was considered appropriate for several reasons. First, under current legislation teachers have a legal responsibility for pupils' welfare (UK Government 1996), and are therefore deemed to be able to act in the interests of the child. Furthermore, they could also choose to adopt the interventions without parental consent; for example, a school would not need parental or pupils' permission to start using Numicon in lessons. Third, the lead research organisation was the Department for Education (through NCTL), and already had the right to collect attainment data on all pupils; neither pupils nor parents could withdraw from national analyses of school data, such as GCSE results. Thus, whilst law and ethics are not the same, it was considered appropriate to deem headteachers as the appropriate givers of consent, as there were no data on individual pupils.

A further concern was that the project was aimed at addressing the needs of educationally disadvantaged pupils, who could be seen as particularly vulnerable, and therefore requiring special considerations for consent. However, on balance, they were not deemed to require special treatment. They were in mainstream schooling, were not extremely vulnerable in the sense of being physically or emotionally at risk, the individual data on each of them was minimal and their data was often nested within whole-class or school data. Further, they were not singled out at the data collection stage, for instance by interviewing them apart from their classmates.

There is no evidence that schools or alliances withdrew on ethical grounds, nor that any parents objected to their child's involvement, though this point was not fully researched. Data were stored securely by the research team at the NCTL and CfBT, in accordance with the Data Protection Act. Durham University carried out some analysis of anonymised secondary data, which would not require formal internal ethical approval. At the analysis stage, no pupil, school or alliance was identified; however, as schools and alliances became involved in further projects, such as the 'early adopters' scheme (see), their involvement in the project became more visible, through ad hoc self-identification (Churches and McAleavy 2015; NCTL 2016c, 2016d, 2016e, 2016f, 2016g).

A new ethical issue arose at the end of the first year, once the interim data had been analysed. These data showed that the experimental groups for some of the interventions were not as successful as the control groups, particularly for the under-attaining pupils – RTI, FirstClass@Number and Inference Training (Churches 2016b, p. 47); under-attaining pupils in these trials made less progress than their peers in the control groups. The researchers had to decide whether to continue with these interventions at all, and/or whether to disclose the interim analysis to the schools. It might have been possible to halt the RCTs, but not disclose the data, though it would have implied some concerns, especially if some interventions were halted and not others. An alternative was to continue with the RCTs and to publish the interim data, in order to allow the schools to decide for themselves if they wished to continue their involvement. This could be seen as allowing the school leaders, as educational experts, to reconsider their consent on behalf of the pupils. The new information could inform their consent, and the decision to treat the head-teachers as suitable givers of consent would become more sharply focused. There was a complex interplay between consent and knowledge. One could argue that it was for the headteachers, as educational experts, to decide whether they still considered there to be uncertainty, given that they were effectively deciding on the pupils' behalf. If they were deemed to be able to act in the child's best interests by giving consent, then arguably they should have been given all the available evidence, if that might affect their decision-making.

The other concern was in terms of ethical obligations to the providers of the interventions and disclosure of the data. This type of relationship is not specifically identified in BERA's guidelines (2011), but is broadly covered by the discussion of the 'community of educational researchers' (p. 9), and includes not presenting a partial or distorted picture, for instance by releasing data or analysis, whether positive or negative, before the research was completed. In this case, the research had been planned as a two-year process, and one of the interventions (Achievement for All) was intended to take two years to effect, so it would have been premature to halt it beforehand. However, if this intervention were to continue it could then be considered unfair to halt other interventions which performed similarly, but were only planned to take a year, since they too might improve in the second year. In the event, only one of the interventions was halted – Inference Training. This showed a negative effect against a control group which made significant progress (Churches 2016b, p. 33), but there were also problems of instrument validity (see Chapter 3), in that the literacy tests measured pupils' comprehension, not ability to draw inferences; whilst pupils' ability to infer meaning might have a consequential effect on their comprehension, this would be indirect and potentially require a longer intervention.

This therefore was a new type of ethical decision within the project, involving balancing the new emerging findings about the effectiveness of the intervention against any ostensible benefits. Schools were not informed of any detailed results on the basis that the research was incomplete, and also that some of the data were missing before the start of the second academic year, though they were given a brief summary of the results of the trials. This decision was to some extent justified by some of the results after Year 2 in that some interventions which were relatively unsuccessful in Year 1 were no worse than existing practice in Year 2, for instance, Achievement for All and FirstClass@Number. However, other interventions deteriorated further in Year 2, notably Response to Intervention, which raises an ethical question about the process of deciding whether to continue.

Equipoise: debates in medical research

The preceding account of the ethical issues raised by the project raises some problems common to all educational research, such as consent or anonymity, but also two problems which are peculiar to RCTs: choice of interventions and the use of interim data. At their heart is a tension between, on the one hand, entirely ethical demands for beneficence and non-maleficence – to do good and not to do harm – and an epistemological question about the certainty of knowledge. This can be framed in classical utilitarian terms as a process of reconciling remoteness, certainty and extent (Bentham 1996; Frankfort-Nachmias and Nachmias 1992); when selecting the interventions, it was not certain whether any of the interventions were effective, but it was also considered by the reviewing panels of teachers that they would not be harmful, and indeed might be beneficial to their pupils.

In retrospect, it would have been valuable to have looked more closely at the considerable discussion in medical research about the ethics of RCTs. Medical researchers have to ask similar questions when deciding whether to test out a new drug or procedure and also when they are confronted by interim data halfway through a clinical trial. In these situations they often make use of the principle of equipoise, which some have urged should also apply in the social sciences and education (Gorard 2013; Fives et al. 2015). This was initially defined as 'the point where a rational, informed person has no preference between two (or more) available treatments' (Chard and Lilford 1998, p. 891; see Fried 1974; Lilford and Jackson 1995). The principle means that it is inappropriate to launch into a RCT of a new treatment solely on the basis that it would be interesting scientifically; some deliberation of the ethics of the treatment is needed. Moreover, it is inappropriate on the basis of weighing up the benefits and risks of the new treatment alone. Some comparison of the risks and benefits in relation to the other available treatments on offer, especially existing practice, is required.

This raises a question as to who the appropriate 'person' is to make this judgement – the clinician, researcher or patient – and whether this is to be viewed as an individual or collective point of view, e.g., by the doctor alone, or across current practice. A more nuanced formulation emerged in Freedman's conceptualisation of *clinical* equipoise, defined as when 'there is genuine uncertainty within the expert medical community – not necessarily on the part of the individual investigator – about the preferred treatment' (Freedman 1987, p. 141). Thus an individual's doubts in the face of current good practice or research evidence are not enough to warrant a randomised controlled trial, but researchers have to consider the views of the professional community collectively. This means that it is unethical to try out a RCT in the face of widespread evidentially-informed acceptance of one treatment and rejection of alternatives, and researchers cannot be overly dogmatic in their espousal of new treatments. The principle tends towards caution when deciding what research should be conducted.

Nevertheless, although this principle is of considerable importance, it is debated (London 2009; Gelfand 2013), particularly because it conflates the different ethical approaches of research and practice, between the physician and the researcher (Miller and Brody 2003; Veatch 2007; Miller and Joffe 2011). This tension is found at critical moments in medical research, as practitioners are under a duty to cure or heal, acting in the patients' best interests, whereas researchers may take a more distanced position, in establishing the effectiveness of different techniques or pharmaceuticals. There is a mismatch between the care of an individual patient and wider long-term gains for the population as a whole. For example, given the severity of the recent Ebola outbreak in West Africa it was considered by some (e.g., Adebamowo et al. 2014) to be unethical to establish a control group when testing new drugs, as all patients should have received any untested new treatments. Even though there was still genuine uncertainty about the new treatment, it was considered unethical to withhold it from anyone. Further, the degree of uncertainty may be disputed given the existing evidence, because it could be considered malpractice to carry out the new treatment if there is not genuine uncertainty, and what constitutes the boundary between certainty and uncertainty within medical knowledge becomes crucial, which in turn depends on the rigour of existing research: one researcher might think that the current research is inadequate or flawed and therefore consider a new treatment to be worthy of testing, whereas another might consider current research to be rigorous and dependable, and therefore the testing of a new treatment is inappropriate (e.g., Mirzadeh et al. 2014; Mirzadeh and Ponce 2015; Montgomery 2015).

Applying equipoise to education: the expert community and interim data

The principle of equipoise is not unknown in educational research, as noted above. Gorard (2013) discusses the principle, particularly arguing for the advantages of a 'waiting list design' (p. 134), in which a treatment is deferred for the initial control group, so that they can initially be compared to the intervention groups, but then get the benefit of its potential effects. Fives et al. (2015) also describe its benefits, suggesting that:

> a reasonable distinction can be made between what is taken as best practice in education on the one hand and on the other hand the social scientist's honest null hypothesis when considering whether an innovative pro- gramme will prove to be more effective than an alternative (p. 60).

In their research, the expert *education* community considered that a particular reading intervention was effective but the expert *research* community considered that there was no valid evidence to support this claim. In medical research, some would argue that the opinion of the *research* community should prevail, as equipoise is an illusion – the 'difference' position (e.g., Miller and Brody 2003). Fives et al. would disagree, considering that through negotiation the research design should be modified to ensure that participants were not deprived of the opportunity to benefit from the treatment. Their solution involves the different communities involved coming together to discuss and resolve their different ethical priorities.

This however might be a demanding task, as this situation can be considered an ethical quandary rather than simply a dilemma. Ethical dilemmas typically occur when the ethical criteria, such as the norms or rules involved, are clear but contradictory, for instance between lying to protect someone and telling the truth. Quandaries however can be said to occur when there are different sets of norms or rules at stake, so it is not clear what the criteria are that should apply, and some colleagues and I have been researching the nature of quandaries in practiced-based research (Fancourt et al. 2016). A dilemma is akin to a sports team having to make decisions how to play the game together, whereas a quandary is as if there is disagreement within the team as to what game they are playing. Teachers may well have a different view to the researchers or government agencies of the ethical issues involved, how they are constructed and how they might be resolved. Indeed, there is some recent research that considers how individuals, especially teachers, need to work across professional boundaries in 'value-laden practices' (Edwards 2010, p. 99; see also Edwards 2016) with university researchers (Fancourt et al. 2015), especially on collaborative research (Locke et al. 2013).

There was, however, a further complexity with such an approach in the CtG project, as, first, the schools were increasingly involved in aspects of the research and encouraged to conduct their own research, acting both as researchers and as practitioners, and second, they were also deemed to be the givers of consent on behalf of the pupils. They therefore would have had to reconcile three potentially different roles: researchers, practitioners and consent givers. As researchers, there might be good reasons for conducting a trial of a particular intervention, and as practitioners, there might be a general professional belief in the efficacy of the intervention, but as consent givers, the particular intervention might not suit an individual pupil for personal reasons, such as major anxieties caused by any process of testing. Within a school it might be that different staff took on these different positions, but this would of itself need a leadership decision about who should decide on these different priorities and how any conflict would be resolved. The quandary would thereby become either internalised within an individual or within the organisation, but then the micro-politics of school hierarchies could affect the decision-making process.

Despite its importance, the notion of equipoise has received little sustained attention in professional discussions of ethics in educational research. Neither BERA's (2011) ethical guidelines nor the American Educational Research Association's (2011) code of ethics use the term. BERA mentions some ethical issues raised by RCTs, touching on the question of beneficence:

Researchers must take steps to minimize the effects of designs that advantage or are perceived to advantage one group of participants over others e.g. in an experimental or quasi-experimental study in which the treatment is viewed as a desirable intervention and which by definition is not available to the control or comparison group respectively.

(BERA 2011, p. 7)

This partially addresses the problem, for instance by providing the 'treatment' to the control group after the research is completed, akin to Gorard's waiting list design, but arguably does not go far enough in that simply *minimising* the effects is insufficient. The risks should not exist at all, rather than merely being reduced. For example, in a comparison of literacy strategies, once a group of pupils has been taught using one approach which is shown to be ineffective, it would be difficult and arguably more detrimental to start again with another approach. Equipoise demands consideration of whether a treatment should run at all, rather than how best to alleviate any subsequent negative effects after the research has finished. This lack of attention in BERA's guidance may also account for its absence in many current guides to the design of RCTs in education. For instance, the Educational Endowment Foundation (2015), which seeks to promote greater use of and reliance on RCTs in education, sets out various ethical principles but makes no mention of equipoise, although this could be a valuable deliberative tool for potential researchers to balance the potential competing principles.

The second stage is that of the use of interim data. An implicit equipoise question arose: was there still 'genuine uncertainty' about a particular strategy if the interim data showed that it was currently ineffective? Hypothetically, if the analysis had shown that one of the interventions was having significantly negative effects on pupils' learning, the researchers could have cancelled that intervention, as discussed above. In medical research, 'knowledge of short-term outcomes may directly and legitimately affect the decision to continue or abandon a . . . trial' (Allardyce et al. 2012, p. 126). This might include a statistically insignificant number of patient deaths, if this is seen as too high (see Pocock 1992), though current practice is often for the researchers to tend to keep interim data confidential from the clinicians involved (Allardyce et al. 2012). The question of defining genuine uncertainty can therefore be seen as both an ethical and an epistemological one, which affects the procedures for statistical analysis, for instance, setting appropriate p-values for the interim data, or in terms of reliance on other forms of evidence and research (Lie and Miller 2011; see Sammons 1989).

Within the CtG project, the researchers' process of ethical deliberation would have benefited from applying this principle. This is not to suggest that the research was therefore unethical, but that the principle would have allowed for the differences between the question of beneficence/non-malfeasance and that of certainty/uncertainty to be made more explicit, and thus aid the decision-making process. It is hard to say if the interventions that were finally chosen would have been rejected, or that different decisions on the basis of the interim data would have been made, but the problem was that at these stages, the researchers did not explicitly identify any rules or guidelines for deliberating these issues.

In future school-based RCTs, the problem of the handing of interim data would potentially be played out through the triple roles identified above. Thus, it raises further questions for schools as researchers, as expert practitioners and potentially as givers of consent. It is not hard to imagine that interim research data on the proven efficacy of an intervention might lead to demands for its expansion as school practice, and to the abandonment of a control group, or vice versa if the intervention was shown to be harmful or less successful than the control treatment. In this situation, equipoise might provide a suitable start for the deliberations.

Conclusion

In conclusion, the initial impulse for the research, to raise the attainment of a type of pupil who has often been let down by the process of schooling, should be re-acknowledged. RCTs have a vital role – alongside other methodologies – to play in contributing to our understanding of how we might address these issues, including but not limited to de-bunking popular, expensive but un-evidenced strategies. This chapter has sought to reflect creatively on the ethical deliberations within one uniquely large research project by identifying the various ethical issues it raised, and how some of them might have been addressed more effectively. These issues themselves are not unique, potentially applying to other RCTs, and thus offer the opportunity for other researchers to respond imaginatively to the ethical complexities involved.

In particular, equipoise is reasserted as an important principle for thinking through the dilemmas, defined as genuine uncertainty within the expert community about a particular strategy. However, the debates within medical research and the differences between education and medicine caution against blindly applying it; it needs to be nuanced considerably in determining the nature and limits of genuine uncertainty, appropriate consent and the constituency of an appropriate expert community in education. These are questions to be developed and refined in relation to particular research. This principle is also important because it appears twice in the research process, first at the design stage and then once there are any interim data. This means that it is not an issue that can be simply addressed in the initial stages, but is one which researchers need to be ready to address throughout a project. In particular, its relationship with consent would benefit from more elaboration, especially in relation to who makes these judgements.

Finally, the ethical issues raised by the development of school-led RCTs also need further consideration, as the different roles of teacher and researcher, and potentially consent-giver, also need to be addressed. If teachers are to be mobilised to tackle educational inequality by conducting RCTs, then the principle of equipoise provides the start of a deliberative discussion about these issues, but cannot be applied uncritically in seeking to make judgements about the tangle of rights, responsibilities, benefits and uncertainties.

References

Adebamowo C., O. Bah-Sow, F. Binka, R. Bruzzone, A. Caplan, J. Delfraissy, D. Heymann, P. Horby, P. Kaleebu, J.-J.Muyembe Tamfum, P. Olliaro, P. Piot, A. Tejan-Cole, O. Tomori, A. Toure, E. Torreele, and J. Whitehead. 2014. "Randomised controlled trials for Ebola: practical and ethical issues". *Lancet*, 384: 1423–1424.

Allardyce, R., P. Bagshaw, C. Frampton, F. Frizelle, P. Hewett, P. McMurrick, N. Rieger, J. Smith, M. Solomon, and A. Stevenson. 2012. "Ethical issues with the disclosure of surgical trial short-term data". *ANZ Journal of Surgery*, 81(3): 125–131.

American Educational Research Association. 2011. *Code of Ethics*. Downloaded from: http://www.aera.net/Portals/38/docs/About_AERA/CodeOfEthics(1).pdf

Bentham, J. 1996. *An Introduction to the Principles of Morals and Legislation*. Oxford: Oxford University Press.

Brindley, S. and A. Bowker. (2013) "Ethics and school based practitioner research". *Educational Action Research*, 21(13): 289–306.

British Educational Research Association (BERA). 2011. *Ethical Guidelines for Educational Research*. London: BERA. https://www.bera.ac.uk/wp-content/uploads/2014/02/BERA-Ethical-Guidelines-2011.pdf?noredirect=1

Burgess, R. (ed.) 1989. *The Ethics of Educational Research*. London: Falmer.

Chalmers, D. 2011. "Viewpoint: Are the research ethics committees working in the best interests of participants in an increasingly globalised research environment?" *Journal of Internal Medicine*, 269(4): 392–395.

Chard, J. and R. Lilford. 1998. "The use of equipoise in clinical trials". *Social Science & Medicine*, 47(7): 891–898.

Churches, R. 2016a. *Closing the Gap: Test and Learn. Executive Summary*. Nottingham: National College for Teaching and Leadership.

Churches R. 2016b. *Closing the Gap: Test and Learn. Research Report*. Nottingham: National College for Teaching and Leadership.

Churches, R. and T. McAleavy. 2015. *Evidence That Counts – What Happens When Teachers Apply Scientific Methods to Their Practice*. Reading: CfBT.

Connolly, P., A Biggart, S. Miller, L. O'Hare & A. Thurston. 2017. *Using Randomised Controlled Trials in Education*. Los Angeles: Sage.

Educational Endowment Foundation. 2015. *EEF Ethics Policy*. https://education endowmentfoundation.org.uk/public/files/Evaluation/Setting_up_an_Evaluation/EEF_Ethics_Policy_2015.pdf

Edwards, A. 2010. *Being an Expert Professional Practitioner: The Relational Turn in Expertise*. Dortrecht: Springer.

Edwards, A. (ed.) 2017. *Working Relationally In and Across Practices: A Cultural-Historical Approach to Collaboration*. Cambridge: Cambridge University Press.

Fancourt, N., A. Edwards, and I. Menter. 2015. "Reimagining a school–university partnership: the development of the Oxford Education Deanery Narrative". *Education Inquiry*, 6(3). Online Journal: http://dx.doi.org/10.3402/edui.v6.27724

Fancourt, N., L. Foreman-Peck, and A. Oancea. 2016. "Ethical quandaries in practice-based research". Available from: https://www.researchgate.net/project/Ethical-quandaries-inpractice-based-research [Accessed 6 January 2017]

Fives, A., D. Russell, J. Canavan, R. Lyons, P. Eaton, C. Devaney, N. Kearns, and A. O'Brien. 2015. "The ethics of randomized controlled trials in social settings: can social trials be scientifically promising and must there be equipoise?" *International Journal of Research & Method in Education*, 38(1): 56–71.

Frankfort-Nachmias, C. and Nachmias, D. 1992. *Research Methods in the Social Sciences*. London: Edward Arnold.

Freedman, B. 1987. "Equipoise and the ethics of clinical research". *The New England Journal of Medicine*, 317(3): 141–145.

Fried, C. 1974. *Medical Experimentation: Personal Integrity and Social Policy*. Amsterdam, The Netherlands: North Holland Press.

Gelfand, S. 2013. "Clinical equipoise: actual or hypothetical disagreement?" *The Journal of Medicine and Philosophy*, 38(6): 590–604.

Goldacre, B. 2013. *Building Evidence into Education*. London: Department for Education.

Gorard, S. 2013. *Research Design: Creating Robust Approaches for the Social Sciences*. London: Sage.

Haggerty, K. 2004. "Ethics creep: governing social science research in the name of ethics". *Qualitative Sociology*, 27(4): 391–414.

Hammersley, M. 2008. "Paradigm war revived? On the diagnosis of resistance to randomized controlled trials and systematic review in education". *International Journal of Research & Method in Education*, 31(1): 3–10.

Hammersley, M. 2010. "Creeping ethical regulation and the strangling of research". *Sociological Research Online*, 15(4): 16.

Haynes, L., O. Service, B. Goldacre, and D. Torgerson. 2012. *Test, Learn, Adapt: Developing Public Policy with Randomised Controlled Trials*. London: Cabinet Office.

Homan, R. 2002. "The principle of assumed consent: the ethics of gatekeeping". In M. McNamee and D. Bridges (eds.) *The Ethics of Educational Research*, pp. 23–40. Oxford: Blackwell.

Israel, M. and I. Hay. 2006. *Research Ethics for Social Scientists: Between Ethical Conduct and Regulatory Compliance*. London: Sage.

James, M. 2013. "New (or not new) directions in evidence-based practice in education". London: BERA. Downloaded from: https://www.bera.ac.uk/promoting-educational-research/issues/dfe-review-of-evidence-in-education

Kaplan, I., S. Miles, and A. Howes 2011. "Images and the ethics of inclusion and exclusion: learning through participatory photography in education". *Journal of Research in Special Educational Needs*, 11(3): 195–202.

Lie, R. and F. Miller. 2011. "What counts as reliable evidence for public health policy: the case of circumcision for preventing HIV infection". *BMC Medical Research Methodology*, 11: 34.

Lilford, R. and J. Jackson. 1995 "Equipoise and randomisation". *Journal of the Royal Society of Medicine*, 88: 552–559.

Locke T., N. Alcorn, and J. O'Neill 2013. "Ethical issues in collaborative action research". *Educational Action Research*, 21(1): 107–123.

London, A. 2009. "Clinical equipoise: foundational requirement or fundamental error?" In B. Steinbock (ed.) *The Oxford Handbook of Bioethics*. http://www.oxfordhand books.com/view/10.1093/oxfordhb/9780199562411.001.0001/oxfordhb-9780 199562411-e-025

McNamee, M. and D. Bridges (eds.) 2002. *The Ethics of Educational Research*. Oxford: Blackwell.

Midgley, W., P. Danaher, and M. Baguley (eds.) 2013. *The Role of Participants in Education Research: Ethics, Epistemologies, and Methods*. Abingdon: Routledge.

Miller, F. G. and H. Brody. 2003. "A critique of clinical equipoise: therapeutic misconception in the ethics of clinical trials". *The Hastings Center Report*, 33(3): 19–28.

Miller, F. and S. Joffe. 2011. "Equipoise and the dilemma of randomized clinical trials". *New England Journal of Medicine*, 364(5): 476–480.

Mirzadeh, Z. and F. Ponce. 2015. "DBS with versus without MER: clinical equipoise or malpractice?" *Movement Disorders*, 30(3): 439–441.

Mirzadeh, Z., K. Chapple, M. Lambert, R. Dhall, and F. Ponce. 2014. "Validation of CT-MRI fusion for intraoperative assessment of stereotactic accuracy in DBS surgery". *Movement Disorders*, 29(14): 1788–1795.

Mockler, N. 2014. "When 'research ethics' becomes 'everyday ethics': the intersection of inquiry and practice in practitioner research". *Educational Action Research*, 22(2): 146–158.

Montgomery, E. 2015. "Validation of CT-MRI fusion for intraoperative assessment of stereotactic accuracy in DBS surgery". *Movement Disorders*, 30(3): 439.

Morrison, K. 2001. "Randomised controlled trials for evidence-based education: some problems in judging 'What Works'". *Evaluation and Research in Education*, 15(2): 69–83.

National College for Teaching and Leadership. 2016a. *Closing the Gap: Test and Learn. Technical Annex A: Statistical Analysis*. Nottingham: National College for Teaching and Leadership.

National College for Teaching and Leadership. 2016b. *Closing the Gap: Test and Learn. Technical Annex B: Provider Perspectives*. Nottingham: National College for Teaching and Leadership.

National College for Teaching and Leadership. 2016c. *Closing the Gap: Test and Learn. Teacher Led Randomised Controlled Trials – Digital Applications*. Nottingham: National College for Teaching and Leadership.

National College for Teaching and Leadership. 2016d. *Closing the Gap: Test and Learn. Teacher Led Randomised Controlled Trials – Feedback Case Studies*. Nottingham: National College for Teaching and Leadership.

National College for Teaching and Leadership. 2016e. *Closing the Gap: Test and Learn. Teacher Led Randomised Controlled Trials – Literacy Case Studies*. Nottingham: National College for Teaching and Leadership.

National College for Teaching and Leadership. 2016f. *Closing the Gap: Test and Learn. Teacher Led Randomised Controlled Trials – Numeracy Case Studies*. Nottingham: National College for Teaching and Leadership.

National College for Teaching and Leadership. 2016g. *Closing the Gap: Test and Learn. Teacher Led Randomised Controlled Trials – Organisation Case Studies*. Nottingham: National College for Teaching and Leadership.

National College for Teaching and Leadership. 2016h. *Closing the Gap: Test and Learn. Teacher Led Randomised Controlled Trials – Resilience Case Studies*. Nottingham: National College for Teaching and Leadership.

Parsons, S., C. Abbott, L. McKnight, and C. Davies 2015. "High risk yet invisible: conflicting narratives on social research involving children and young people, and the role of research ethics committees". *British Educational Research Journal*, 41(4): 709–729.

Pocock, S. 1992. "When to stop a clinical trial". *BMJ: British Medical Journal*, 305(6847): 235–240.

Robinson-Pant, A. and N. Singal 2013. "Researching ethically across cultures: issues of knowledge, power and voice". *Compare: A Journal of Comparative and International Education*, 43(4): 417–421.

Sammons, P. 1989. "Ethical issues and statistical work". In R. Burgess (ed.) *The Ethics of Educational Research*, pp. 31–59. London: Falmer.

Shamim F. and R. Qureshi. 2013. "Informed consent in educational research in the South: tensions and accommodations". *Compare: A Journal of Comparative and International Education*, 43(4): 464–482.

Shaw, T., D. Cross, L. Thomas, and S. Zubrick. 2015. "Bias in student survey findings from active parental consent procedures". *British Educational Research Journal*, 41(2): 1469–3518. http://dx.doi.org/10.1002/berj.3137

Taber, K. 2013. "The right medicine for educational research?" *Royal Society of Chemistry*. Downloaded from: http://www.rsc.org/Education/EiC/issues/2013 May/goldacre-education-research-report.asp

UK Government. 1996. *Education Act*. London: HMSO.

Veatch, R. 2007. "The irrelevance of equipoise". *Journal of Medical Philosophy*, 32(2): 167–183.

Walford, G. 2005. "Research ethics guidelines and anonymity." *International Journal of Research and Method in Education*, 28(1): 83–93.

Zeni, J. 2001. *Ethical Issues in Practitioner Research*. New York: Teachers College Press.

Part 3

New approaches to school-based educational research

Chapter 9

Teacher-researchers' expanding perceptions of research in a school–university collaborative research project

Els Laroes, Larike H. Bronkhorst, Sanne F. Akkerman and Theo Wubbels

Introduction

Around the world teachers are increasingly encouraged to engage in research in their schools, often in collaboration with university researchers, and the project Closing the Gap exemplifies this in the English context. An emphasis on evidence-based teaching, as is clear in the Closing the Gap project, can be seen in other countries, for example in the Dutch government initiated programme 'Onderwijsbewijs' (Education Proof). This programme funded 37 studies, most of which were randomized controlled trials in which schools and universities worked together to evaluate educational interventions. As for CtG, an important aim was not only to gather evidence on what works but also to introduce and encourage schools to participate in rigorous research. Other examples are a grant scheme of the Netherlands Organisation for Scientific Research for teachers who want to complete a PhD and the 'Academic schools' that are quite similar to the English Teaching Schools in wanting to give schools and teachers an active role in research, development and innovation, among others, through involvement in initial teacher education.

The study presented in this chapter involved ten teacher-researchers who participated in a collaborative research project lasting for three years between four secondary schools and an educational department of a university in the Netherlands. The project was based on a project-plan, which was required for funding, and written by university researchers and principals of the participating schools. The teacher-researchers across four schools conducted research in their respective schools on the same theme, i.e., development of the quality of teacher feedback, in collaboration with university researchers. As this theme and the research design were established in the project-plan, the teacher-researchers were faced with a predetermined theme, *'teacher feedback to students that works'*, and research design, as in the CtG project, an intervention study using a randomized experimental pre-test/post-test design with experimental and control groups. In this collaboration the evaluation aimed at teaching rather than measuring student learning, as was done in the CtG project. The ambition of the collaborative research stated in the project plan was to *'improve the actual teaching practice* (i.e., contribute to school development) *as well as to gain more in-depth scientific insights*' (i.e., contribute to scientific knowledge development) into '*the effects of different teacher professional development interventions on the quality of feedback given by teachers* (i.e., contribute to teacher professional development) *in the different schools*'.

Teachers who do research in their own practice are referred to as teacher-researchers (Cochran-Smith & Lytle, 1999; Leeman & Wardekker, 2014). Research by teachers in schools is often conducted in long-term collaborative projects with university researchers. Such projects usually not only have a research aim but also intend to develop teacher-researchers' research knowledge and skills and by doing so expect teacher-researchers to use research and research results in their teaching practice as they come to appreciate research more (Cochran-Smith & Lytle, 1999).

Scholars have investigated various aspects of what has been described as 'teacher research', focusing on the impact of conducting research on teachers (Cochran-Smith, Barnatt, Friedman & Pine, 2009), on changes in beliefs and classroom practices (Zeichner, 2003), on teacher-researchers' motivation for engaging in research (Worall, 2004) and/or on different views of university researchers on goals of research by teachers (Cochran-Smith & Lytle, 1999).

An important aspect of research by teachers yet to be uncovered, is how teacher-researchers actually perceive research and how their research perceptions develop over time when conducting research in collaborative projects. This is relevant as, first, the collaborative projects in which research by teachers is often conducted are expected to achieve sustained effects in terms of teacher-researchers developing an academic attitude, for which perceptions of research are central (Akkerman & Bruining, 2016). Second, perceptions may influence research practice. For example, Brew (2001) argues that every research practice rests on the underlying ideas researchers have about what research is and what researchers are doing when they carry it out. These underlying ideas have been shown to differ among academics (Åkerlind, 2008; Brew, 2001) and are influenced by active engagement in research, according to Healey, Jordan, Pell and Short's (2010) study of university students. Studying the development of research perceptions over time may allow us to evaluate the expectation that by conducting research themselves teachers come to perceive research differently. Third, perceptions of research affect collaboration. Brew (2001) found that researchers with markedly different perceptions were unable to communicate effectively. In line with Brew's finding, literature on research by teachers in collaborative partnerships suggests that teacher-researchers and university researchers can only collaborate effectively if they understand how each partner perceives educational research (Ebbutt, Worrall & Robson, 2000).

If teacher-researchers' perceptions of research guide their research practice as academics' perceptions of research have been shown to do, it is relevant and timely to explore how teacher-researchers' perceptions of research develop over time when conducting research in collaboration with university researchers.

Theoretical framework

Perceptions of research

We see perceptions of research as the way research is understood, regarded or interpreted. In the literature, various perceptions of research can be discerned as different positions on a continuum ranging from *informal exploration*, 'getting to the bottom of something' (Bruggink & Harinck, 2012), to *more formal inquiry*, 'solving or improving a problem in the professional practice' (Cochran-Smith et al., 2009), to *rigorous research*, 'developing a generally applicable theory', 'theorising' or 'creating new knowledge' (Åkerlind, 2008).

Perception of research has itself been an object of investigation. A review on academics' perceptions of research indicated that these perceptions can be described in terms of views on the research process, questions, intentions and outcomes (Åkerlind, 2008). Åkerlind (2008) identified differences in academics' perceptions of research for each of these aspects. For example, the research process was perceived as a technical, rigorous and scholarly process investigating a research question, identifying and solving a problem, a creative process discovering something new and addressing community issues. Similarly, perceptions of research outcomes ranged from outcomes as academic publications, concrete products and personal understandings to outcomes as benefits to the community. Brew (2001) also focused on academics' research perceptions, which she described in terms of a structural dimension concerned with what research is. In addition, she distinguished a referential dimension concerned with the meaning given to what is perceived. Brew found a variation in the desired achievement of research and describes a varying focus on research as making it possible to solve practical problems, exchange products, discover underlying meaning and potentially lead to theoretical transformations. Bruce, Pham and Stoodley (2004) described academics' perceptions of research by focusing on views of what constitutes the significance and value of research. These views are described in terms of what research must be or achieve in order to be valuable. They found that academics experience the significance and value of research in different ways, which can be described in terms of an expanding impact of research, from impact on the individual researcher, to the research team, the research community and the world.

The three studies described above all investigated what academics' research perceptions are at a certain moment in time. Even though engagement in research is assumed to influence research perceptions, we have not found studies that investigated the development of (academics') research perceptions over time.

Research by teachers

Research by teachers is increasingly seen as important internationally and also in the Netherlands. Based on earlier experiences with research by teachers in

English-speaking countries (e.g., Cochran-Smith & Lytle, 1999), Dutch schools and universities have initiated collaborative research projects in which teacher-researchers study their own practice.

Many researchers have pointed out that there is no consensus on the definition of 'teacher research' (Borko, Liston & Whitcomb, 2007; Cochran-Smith, 2002; Cochran-Smith & Lytle, 1999; Zeichner, 2003). In a review on the nature and value of research by teachers, Zwart, Smit and Admiraal (2015) show that teacher research is characterized differently in different studies. For example, Zwart et al. found that several scholars see critical inquisitiveness combined with a positive research attitude as central to teacher research. Others claim that teacher research entails the collaborative design of curriculum materials or consider teacher research merely a critical reflection tool that leads to innovation. Also, teacher research is seen in contrast with other types of educational research, for example, teacher research aims at examining educational practice instead of showing effects of interventions and improving practice rather than developing a generally applicable theory. Zwart et al. distinguish the four most common types of teacher research: action research, lesson-study, self-study and design-based study. Their review shows that although the nature and type of research is different, teacher research is mostly small-scale qualitative research into the school practice with limited generalizability of the findings. Likewise, in a review on teacher research, Zeichner (2003) reports that teachers use a variety of methods of doing research, including some not typically found within academic research communities such as action research, self-study or open-ended approaches.

Several aspects of research by teachers have been investigated, providing insight into, for example, the impact of doing research on teachers (Cochran-Smith et al., 2009) and into teacher-researchers' motivation for engaging in research (Worall, 2004). Little is known, however, about teacher-researchers' perceptions of research and how these perceptions develop. Moreover, by conducting research themselves, teacher-researchers are expected to develop a different perception of research, potentially resulting in a more positive attitude towards research, improvement of their research knowledge and skills and usage of research and research results in their educational practice (Coburn & Stein, 2010; Cochran-Smith & Lytle, 1999). Some scholars claim that research by teachers will lead to bridging the proverbial 'gap' between educational research and practice (Broekkamp & van Hout-Wolters, 2007; Levin, 2004).

In this study, we aim to describe teacher-researchers' perceptions of research and gain insight into how these perceptions develop during their engagement in research in a three-year collaborative research project in a school-university partnership. We describe teacher-researchers' perceptions of research in terms of their views on (1) what research is, i.e., descriptions of what *'research is'* and prescriptions of what research should be, i.e., what *'research ought to be'* and (2) what research can achieve or afford, i.e., descriptions of *'research makes it possible to'*, *'with research you can'* and prescriptions of what research should achieve/afford, i.e., *'research ought to make it possible to'*. The central research question is: how do teacher-researchers' perceptions of research develop during a three-year collaborative research project with university researchers? We expect that, by engaging in research, teacher-researchers' perceptions of research will change because of the increased familiarity with and knowledge about research through conducting research. This may result in a more positive perception of research, which is relevant as many studies have shown that teachers' appreciation of research is not favourable (Ebbutt et al., 2000; Gore & Gitlin, 2004; Shkedi, 1998). Knowing what teacher-researchers' perceptions of research are, and how these perceptions develop, can provide academics and teachers with tools to bridge the gap between research and practice.

Method

Context and participants

In each of the four schools involved, two or three teachers voluntarily took the role of teacher-researcher, which was conducted alongside their teaching. Within their school, these teacher-researchers formed a research group with a university researcher. The two university researchers involved were engaged as supervisors and each worked with teacher-researchers in two schools. The teacher-researchers designed, implemented and evaluated a professional development programme (henceforth 'intervention') aimed at improving teacher feedback in their school. They fine-tuned the design of the intervention and the research into its local effects and conducted this research in collaboration with a university researcher over a period of three years. The teacher-researchers in this project had a background of a master's degree in the subject they teach (rather than in educational studies), which might mean their view of research is influenced by the research norm in their subject areas. Consequently, their experience with research in social and behavioural sciences, i.e., the type of educational research in this project, was often limited. Table 9.1 shows an overview of the participating teacher-researchers per school, their background and participation in the project and the university researcher with whom they collaborated.

Interviews

Three group interviews with the ten teacher-researchers participating in the project were conducted over time for each of the four schools: at the start, in the middle and at the completion of the project. We conducted group interviews as the interaction in group interviews can stimulate elaboration and expression (Frey & Fontana, 1991).

The interviews were semi-structured. The first interview was conducted by the second author. To explore teacher-researchers' perspective on research, the

Table 9.1 Background of the participants and participation across the schools

School	TR	Gender	School subject	Previous research experience in social and behavioural sciences	Participation in project/ interviews	University researcher
A	TR1	Female	Dutch	-	Start to finish, all interviews	1
	TR2	Male	History	-	Start to finish, all interviews	
B	TR3	Female	Dutch	Course in learning to conduct research in school one year previous to project	Start to finish, all interviews	1
	TR4	Male	History	Course in learning to conduct research in school one year previous to project	Start to finish, absent at interview	1
C	TR5	Female	PE	Three years as teacher-researcher previous to project	Start to finish, all interviews	2
	TR6	Female	Social studies	Master's in sociology and previous year student teacher in project	Start to finish, all interviews	
	TR7*	Male	Math	Three years as teacher-researcher previous to project	Start to halfway, interviews 1 & 2	
	TR8	Female	Arts	-	Joined project at start of 3rd year, interview 3	
D	TR9	Male	Biology	-	Start to finish, all interviews	2
	TR10*	Female	Social studies	Master's in public administration and organizational sciences	Start to halfway, interviews 1 & 2	

* TR7 and TR10 left for reasons unrelated to the project.

interview included questions about how teacher-researchers designed their research and why they had chosen that way of working, about their concerns and challenges regarding research and about anticipated research findings. The second interview was conducted for each school and by the collaborating university researcher focusing on evaluating the research conducted in the previous year and looking forward to the teacher-researchers' research plans for the coming year. Although this interview was also semi-structured in that the interview scheme provided a number of topics, it was more open because of its evaluative and future-oriented nature. The third interview was again conducted by the second author and aimed at teacher-researchers' experiences in conducting research and the developments in their research throughout the project. In the interviews we questioned the teacher-researchers about what they were doing regarding research and why they chose to do so. Examples of follow-up questions are; 'I see, why do you do that, is that your research or what?' (interview 1). 'How do you see the research, what were your ambitions and are you satisfied?' (interview 2). 'Interesting. Are there any other things about research you found exciting to learn?' (interview 3). Such probing aimed to elicit answers that revealed the teacher-researchers' actions or theory-in-use, rather than their espoused theory (Argyris and Schön, 1974). As a result, the teacher-researchers described their actions, which may be governed by their theory-in-use, instead of describing their research perceptions by using words to convey what they would like others to think. We thus aimed to elicit answers revealing more implicit and perhaps less conscious views on research, which enabled us to deduce the teacher-researchers' research perceptions from the data.

The interviews were conducted at the respective schools and lasted about an hour and a half. They were audiotaped and transcribed verbatim.

Analysis

First, transcripts of the interviews were segmented, excluding statements that were not relevant to our research question. These were mostly statements about the content of the intervention on feedback, the actual schooling of colleagues during the intervention, the collaboration with the university and the super-vision of student teachers. Second, each interview, i.e., moment in time, was summarized in a matrix (Miles & Huberman, 1994). To account for possible differences between teacher-researchers within the schools (e.g., as a result of previous research experience) we analysed (the development of) teacher-researchers' perceptions on an individual level. These matrices contained a summary per interview of the teacher-researcher's views on (1a) what the teacher-researcher perceived research to be, i.e., 'research is', (1b) what the teacher-researcher thought research should be, i.e., 'research ought to be', (2a) what the teacher-researcher thought research can achieve or afford, i.e., 'research makes it possible to', 'with research you can' and (2b) what the teacher-researcher thought research should achieve/afford, i.e., 'research ought to achieve/afford'. Table 9.2 shows our description of the two aspects of the research perception and examples from the data.

Third, for each moment in time we identified teacher-researchers' *shared* perceptions of research, viz. shared by at least half of the teacher-researchers and contested by none. Shared perceptions of research were first summarized for each moment in time. Last, we compared the three shared matrices for each moment in time. This chronological analysis of the teacher-researchers' research perceptions resulted in an overview of the development of the teacher-researchers' shared perceptions of research over time (see Table 9.3). We illustrated the results with quotes, which we translated from Dutch into English.

Table 9.2 Description for the aspects of the research perception

Aspect[a]	Description	Examples from the data[b]
Research is	Research is defined by TR or described in terms of how TR sees research, what they think *research is.*	For our research we collect a lot of data, and every time we think of something new, we go back to the data and check this new insight. (TR5, interview 1)
Research ought to be	Research is described in terms of normative or ideal-typical value judgements. This can also be a prescription of what TR thinks *research should be.*	The research instruments should also be valid and reliable. (TR2, interview 1)
Research can achieve/afford	Research is described in terms of TRs' views on what they think *research can achieve or afford.*	Well with research you can show it, you know. Research findings prove that this works, so research shows that this is a good theme to focus on. (TR 9, interview 1)
Research should achieve/afford	Research is described in terms of normative or ideal-typical value judgements of what research should achieve. This can also be a prescription of what TR thinks *research should achieve/afford.*	Research always ought to start from a problem or a question. (TR1, interview 1)

a The aspects can be also be described in negative terms, such as contrasts or reversals.
b Utterances referring to research were signalled by: 1) phrases literally containing the word 'research', e.g., researcher, research plan, research question; and 2) words concerning research, e.g., analysis, data, qualitative, statistics, theory, university, validity.

The first author performed the analyses. To ascertain quality in all of the steps described, the first author provided a detailed description of the data and the analytic steps in the process of analysis (e.g., Poortman & Schildkamp, 2012). The steps and procedures were discussed with the second author, who reviewed all steps, decisions and interpretations.

Results

Table 9.3 provides an overview of the development of the teacher-researchers' shared perceptions of research over time. Below, we also describe instances wherein teacher-researchers' perceptions differ. For each aspect of the research, perception descriptions are followed by prescriptions of what research is and can achieve.

Development of perceptions of what research is and ought to be

All teacher-researchers perceived research as an iterative process that involves several research steps at all three moments in time. According to the teacher-researchers, these research steps consist of asking research questions, developing 'measurement' instruments for data collection (TRs 1, 2, 3, 4, 9, 10, T_1), analysing data to answer the research question and presenting the findings in a research report. All teacher-researchers said these research steps were 'theoretically grounded' (TRs 3, 4, 5, 6, 7, T_2) and described in the theoretical framework of the research plan before conducting the research. From the first to the second interview the perceptions of what research is expanded as the teacher-researchers added several aspects to the research process, for example, 'formulating a hypothesis' (TRs 1, 2, 3, 4, 5, 6, 7, T_2) and the research question 'which keeps changing' (TRs 1, 2, 3, 4, T_2), that they did not articulate at the start of the project. Expansions also concerned more elaborate descriptions of research instruments for data gathering and analysis mentioned by all teacher-researchers, for example, as described by TR3:

> We discussed how to analyse the questionnaires, you know: shall we group and code the concepts, or shall we score them individually. Well just some ideas that can guide the process of analysis. (TR3, T_2)

At the end of the project, their descriptions of the research process and steps were less detailed again.

We found development over time in how teacher-researchers perceived the research design. At the start of the project, all teacher-researchers perceived research as being an experimental design involving measurements and statistics. Four teacher-researchers characterized data collection as a means to measure differences over time, i.e., pre-/post-intervention (TRs 1, 2, 9, 10). Three

Table 9.3 Development of teacher-researchers' shared perceptions of research over time (T1, T2, T3)

Additions to previous research perceptions are in italics.

Aspects	Over time		
	Start of project T1	Middle of project T2	End of project T3
Research is	Research is an iterative process that involves research steps: asking research questions, collecting and analysing data to answer research questions and reporting on the findings. Research includes characteristics: theoretical grounding, methodical and systematic methods.	T1+ *Research is an iterative process wherein: research question keeps changing, hypothesis is formulated, research report is written including methods section, conclusions & future research. More elaborate descriptions of research instruments & analyses.*	T1
	Research is quantitative, longitudinal and large-scale: research is an experimental design involving pre-/post-tests and comparisons between experimental and control groups to show differences over time.	T1	*Research can be quantitative, longitudinal and large-scale: an experimental design involving pre-/post-tests and comparisons between experimental and control groups to show differences over time.*
			Research can also be qualitative, small-scale and short term to describe development over time.
Research ought to be	Research ought to be relevant to school practice: – investigate existing problems/ questions in school – provide clear results applicable in school practice	T1	T1+ *present relevant and usable results to participants*

	Research ought to meet basic scientific criteria:	Research ought to meet basic scientific criteria: T1+	Research ought to meet basic scientific criteria: T1&T2+
	– be reliable and transparent, i.e., justify research steps, use valid and reliable instruments – provide clear results that show pre-/post-intervention differences	– describe method and underpin findings – acknowledge references	– be systematic and methodical – provide trustworthy results – relate findings to theories
Research can achieve/ afford	Research makes it possible to generate findings that: – show change in relevant teacher behaviour – illustrate the effectiveness of interventions – prove what works – show how participants evaluate the intervention	Research makes it possible to generate findings that: T1+ *Research can also provide results that describe:* – development of relevant teacher behaviour – knowledge development of participants	Research makes it possible to generate findings that: T1&2+ *Qualitative research makes it possible to generate findings that:* – describe knowledge development of participants – describe development of relevant teacher behaviour – underpin school policy – contribute to teacher professional development and school development
Research should achieve/ afford	Research should provide results that: – show pre-/post-intervention differences – show causal relations		*With qualitative research you cannot provide evidence of effectiveness*

teacher-researchers (TRs 1, 2, 3) mentioned that research entails measuring differences between experimental and control groups. One of these three teacher-researchers, however, made an explicit provision with respect to the reliability of such experimental designs regarding measuring differences on the level of students and stated that research could also be qualitative in nature because that is more reliable within the school context:

> I think perhaps that it is even more interesting to look at the intervention qualitatively, I also think that is more reliable, you know you just take a teacher, or a couple of teachers, and you just follow them as in what were they like before the training and what did the training look like. (TR3, T_1)

Halfway through the project, most teacher-researchers' view of research being an experimental design involving measurements and statistics had not changed. Three teacher-researchers from one school, however, considered 'taking on a qualitative approach' in which they would no longer use the questionnaire they designed as an 'instrument for measuring effectiveness' of the intervention but as 'input for our goals' (TR 5, 6, 7, T_2). This can be seen as an indication that in their view research can also have a qualitative design. At the end of the project, we found that all teacher-researchers' views of what research is had expanded by additional views of what research could also be. All teacher-researchers described that, compared to the longitudinal and large-scale research in the project, research in schools can also be short-term and small-scale.

Throughout the project, all teacher-researchers perceived that research should be relevant to the school practice and should meet basic scientific criteria. According to them, the required relevance for the schools can be realized in various ways. First, throughout the project, all teacher-researchers indicated that research should investigate 'questions' (TR 9, 10, T_1), 'research questions' (TRs 3, 4, T_2) or 'problems' (TRs 1, 2, T_3) in the schools. Second, research results should be applicable in the school practice, which in the opinion of TR1 is not the case as research results 'hardly ever reach the school', and if they do, nobody knows 'how to apply them' (TR1, T_1).

Last, three teacher-researchers from one school argued that research should provide 'clear results', even though only positive results are seen as valuable to the schools. These teacher-researchers are aware that they 'obviously' want positive results in terms of improved teacher behaviour:

> TR5: As a researcher that's perhaps not so interesting as long as you have a nice or clear result . . . Obviously, I want that those teachers, that it's added value, that you improve the quality of education within the school.

> TR6: Do you mean that, suppose we find like, this type of session doesn't work at all, and we've learned how to change it, then you really have a result as well? Is that what you mean?

TR7: As researcher you certainly have a result.

TR6: As researcher you definitely have an outcome.

TR5: Yes.

TR6: Even if it's a very negative one.

TR5: Yes.

TR7: But then we're very dissatisfied. [T_1]

At the end of the project, the relevance of research to the school practice remained an important norm for all teacher-researchers, which they sometimes described by contrasting research in a generic sense to their own research. According to them, their own research should 'really fit' with the school practice, whereas research often does not (TRs 1, 2, T_3). Also, their research should present relevant and usable results to participants, but those results do not have to be 'academic' (TR6, T_3).

All teacher-researchers perceived that research should meet basic scientific criteria, but the way they described these criteria developed over time. At the start of the project, all teacher-researchers mentioned criteria research should meet in general terms, such as 'be reliable'. Halfway through the project, the teacher-researchers detailed what research should be, e.g., 'describe methods section and underpin findings' (TRs 1, 2), 'acknowledge references' (TRs 9, 10). At the end of the project we found that teacher-researchers still described what they perceived research should be in a detailed way, such as 'be systematic and methodical' (TRs 5, 6, 8), 'relate findings to theories' (TRs 1, 2, 3, 4), 'provide trustworthy results' (TR 5, 6, 8, 9).

Looking at the development of their perceptions of what research is, the teacher-researchers perceived research as an iterative process involving research steps, which they described more extensively halfway through the project. All teacher-researchers started the project perceiving research design as quantitative, longitudinal and large-scale and at the end their perception expanded to research also being qualitative, short-term and small-scale. Similarly, their perception of what research should be developed in terms of an increasing degree of detail in which they described the basic criteria research should meet, while relevance for the school practice was a stable factor in the teacher-researchers' perception of what research should be.

Development of perceptions of what one can and should achieve by research

At all three moments in time, all teacher-researchers perceived that research could show change in relevant teacher behaviour, as the following quotes illustrate:

With our research we check if teachers have developed in terms of feedback behaviour. (TR 7, T_1)

I think you can research what changes in the teachers' feedback behaviour. (TR 3, T_2)

Our research showed there was little development in terms of teacher feedback regarding self-regulation. (TR 8, T_3).

Regarding the provision of results showing effectiveness, however, teacher-researchers' perception of what research can achieve changed over time. At the start of the project, all teacher-researchers stated that research makes it possible to generate findings that illustrate the effectiveness of interventions and described that research can provide 'evidence' that 'proves what works' (TRs 1, 2, 9, 10, T_1) and can 'show' and 'measure effects' (TRs 1, 2, 3, 4, 9, T_1) in relevant teacher behaviour as a result of the interventions. As TR9 put it:

We set up an intervention because we want to improve them [teachers], and obviously we want to measure that with a pre-test and a post-test at the end, you know to measure the effects of the intervention. [TR9, T_1]

Five teacher-researchers suggested that research can also provide insight into how participants perceive and evaluate the intervention and show 'what kind of intervention works well according to the participants' (TRs 5, 6, 7, 9, 10). Although they would like to show differences in relevant teacher behaviour as a result of the interventions, three of these teacher-researchers from one school (TRs 5, 6, 7) question whether this is possible. TRs 5, 6, 7 described this as:

TR7: Teachers who improve their teaching, change their behaviour. That only makes sense if students perceive it too. And the question is, whether you can measure that. Which doesn't mean that it didn't actually happen . . . It could be that the research shows that the teachers didn't score differently on the instruments. But that obviously doesn't mean that nothing changed.

Interviewer: Yes, and what do you expect?

TR5: I think that the pre-test and post-test will show a difference in terms of cognition. But I just don't know, I hope that perhaps it is visible on the videos [of teacher behaviour], but yes it's difficult to prove something like that . . .

TR6: That's really what we have been trying to do last year, to develop a measuring instrument that can actually show these kind of things. But I think we didn't find anything conclusive and I don't know if such an instrument exists, either, I mean the perfect measuring instrument with which you can show every improvement. [T_1]

Halfway through the project, the same three teacher-researchers expressed the view that research can also achieve different results, e.g., 'appreciation' and 'knowledge development' of participants in the intervention. (TRs 5, 6, 7, T_2). TRs 3, 4 from school B showed a similar development regarding their perception of the kind of results that research can achieve. At the start of the project, TR3 stated that research could 'show results of the intervention' by 'measuring' development of teacher behaviour. Halfway through the project TR4 spoke about 'visualizing' development of teacher behaviour, while at the end of the project TR3 specified that with qualitative research you can 'describe' the development of teacher behaviour. At the end of the project most teacher-researchers specified that qualitative research could also provide valuable results that can underpin school policy (TRs 1, 2, 3, 4) and contribute to teacher professional development and to school development (TRs 3, 4, 5, 6, 8). This is how TR8 described their development:

> We moved to more qualitative research (TR6: That you just look at individual participants. TR5: Yes) And we started looking more, not only at the participant appreciation, but also at possible results, irrespective of how much you can or can't prove. I think that's very valuable. (TR8, T_3)

Only one teacher-researcher saw results achieved by qualitative research differently. Although TR9 stated that qualitative designs can also provide results, he perceived that such a design couldn't provide the 'quantifiable results' he desired:

> The reason why we repeated the questionnaire, well I just couldn't resist the temptation to see whether after three years we could measure an effect, which again wasn't the case . . . So we focused on teachers that were open to learning, because I think that then you would be able to measure and show something about the effect. I still think it's very important that research measures effects. (TR9, T_3)

TR9 persisted in his view that research should provide measurable results that show the effectiveness of the intervention, which relates to his perception of what research should achieve.

The earlier described relevance of research and its results to the school practice remained stable over time, but we found that the teacher-researchers perceived the type of results research should achieve differently over time. At the start of the project, most teacher-researchers indicated that research ought to show pre-/post-intervention differences (TRs 5, 6, 7, 9, 10). Halfway through the project, two teacher-researchers from one school specified that research should 'prove' the effectiveness of the intervention (TRs 9, 10), while the other teacher-researchers perceived that research could also provide 'valuable' results, such as 'development of teacher behaviour' (TRs 1, 2, 3, 4) and 'knowledge development of teachers' (TR 5, 6, 7), without showing causal relations. Gradually, towards the end of the project, all teacher-researchers (except TR9) no longer described the type of results research should achieve, but they described the type of results different research designs could achieve, as we illustrated above.

Summarizing the development of the teacher-researchers' perception of what research can achieve or afford, all teacher-researchers started the project perceiving that research could show the effectiveness of interventions. Over time, they perceived that with the type of research they used, you could generate different types of results, such as knowledge development of participants, but you couldn't prove such causal relations. The teacher-researchers' perception of the type of results research should achieve also developed over time. At the start of the project the teacher-researchers suggested that research *should* provide evidence of effectiveness, while gradually their perception of research results expanded as the teacher-researchers later suggested that research *could* achieve different types of results, which can be relevant to the school practice as well.

Discussion

Our research question was: how do teacher-researchers' perceptions of research develop during a three-year collaborative research project with university researchers? At all three moments in time teacher-researchers perceived research as a cyclical process involving several research steps, by which one can show results that should be relevant to the school practice, which according to the teacher-researchers means investigating problems in the schools and achieving results that are applicable in school practice. Also, teacher-researchers perceived that research should meet basic scientific criteria, such as being reliable, valid, systematic and methodical. These results resemble the views expressed by the trial coordinators in schools and reported in Chapter 7 of this volume.

The teacher-researchers' perceptions of research correspond with how educational research is defined in the literature (Creswell, 2008). Similar to Creswell's (2008) definition of educational research, the teacher-researchers perceived research as a process of steps used to collect and analyse data to answer a research question. Teacher-researchers' detailed descriptions of research contrast with earlier findings of Vrijnsen-de Corte, Den Brok, Kamp and Bergen (2013), who found that teacher-researchers in Dutch professional development schools hardly referred to what research and the research process should look like and spoke of research in very general terms. The teacher-researchers in this project were explicit and specific about what research ought to be and gave detailed descriptions of research activities. This may be due to the teacher-researchers in this project being actively involved in conducting research themselves, supported by university researchers, for three years. Also, our interview questions were directed at teacher-researchers' actions, instead of asking for perceptions directly, which also may have evoked more detailed responses.

Teacher-researchers' research perceptions in our project developed over time in three respects. First, the perception of what research is was described in terms of increasing methodological detail and with detail regarding which basic scientific criteria should be met (particularly visible at T_2). The teacher-researchers' research-expanding perceptions seemed to be connected to (previous) experience with conducting research in social and behavioural sciences. For example, one teacher-researcher already perceived that research can also be qualitative at T_1, which could be due to her previous research experience. The increased details in their perceptions suggest an increased familiarity with and knowledge about research through conducting research.

Second, while at the start of the project teacher-researchers perceived that research is quantitative and experimental, at the end of the project they perceived that research can also be qualitative and more action-oriented. This development concurred with their expanded perception of the type of results research can achieve, as the teacher-researchers perceived that, in addition to achieving results regarding effectiveness, one can achieve different types of results with qualitative research (particularly visible at T_3). The teacher-researchers' expanded perceptions of research could be explained in terms of growing insight into the different values of various research designs, reflecting Cochran-Smith's (2002) claim that different perceptions of research often concern discussions about the value of different types of research designs. At the end of the project, the teacher-researchers perceived that with qualitative research you could generate certain results, but not all the kinds of results they initially aspired to. This result reflects awareness of the complexity of the educational practice and the type of research that is possible in the school context described in the literature (Biesta, 2007; Leeman & Wardekker, 2014).

Third, while at the start of the project teacher-researchers suggested that research results *should* provide evidence of effectiveness, gradually their perception of research results expanded as the teacher-researchers described that research *could* achieve different types of results, which can be relevant to the school practice as well (particularly visible at T_3). Teacher-researchers' initial perception of research could be explained by the project-plan, wherein the research design was predetermined. However, given that the predetermined theme of the intervention, feedback, was fiercely discussed by the teacher-researchers, we assume that the lack of discussion on the research design may indicate that the teacher-researchers' initial research perception was similar to the one described in the project-plan. It should be noted that, because of the project-plan, the teacher-researchers started doing a different type of research (experimental) compared to what is described in the literature as typical research conducted by teachers (Zwart et al., 2015).

Our teachers developed their understanding of what research is and can imply, which was one of the aims of the CtG project and was also a result reported in the first study in of this volume by teachers who were part of the early adopters programme. It is interesting that some of the teachers on the CtG project (Chapter 7 in this volume) moved from perceiving research in more qualitative action research terms towards: firstly, a group that saw qualitative and quantitative research as valuable and complementary to each other and secondly, those, particularly in the early adopter scheme, who saw RCTs as now the most valuable form of research. In the research presented in this chapter, teachers tended to move in the opposite direction from seeing research mainly as quantitative, and finding out what works, to valuing the insights qualitative research can provide. This difference may have been caused by a different starting position of the participating teachers. The CtG teachers seemed to have more experience with teacher research than the teachers in our study who on top of that initially were prompted in the research plan to think about participating in randomized controlled trial studies.

Implications for educational practice

We found that teacher-researchers initially perceived research as large-scale quantitative experimental research. Our findings suggest that such a perception of research may actually be counterproductive to reducing the distance teachers experience between research and practice. In accordance with our expectations, teacher-researchers' engagement in research led to a richer and more positive perception of research. In light of these findings, engaging teachers in research could be a stepping stone to bridge the gap between research and practice. The results furthermore might help educational researchers who collaborate with teacher researchers better understand their school counterparts and thus strengthen the collaboration effectiveness.

References

Åkerlind, G. S. (2008). An academic perspective on research and being a researcher: an integration of the literature. *Studies in Higher Education, 33*(1), 17–31.

Akkerman, S., & Bruining, T. (2016). Multi-level boundary crossing in a professional development school partnership. *Journal of the Learning Sciences, 25*(2), 240–284.

Argyris, M., & Schön, D. (1974) *Theory in Practice: Increasing Professional Effectiveness.* San Francisco: Jossey-Bass.

Biesta, G. (2007). Why 'what works' won't work: Evidence-based practice and the democratic deficit in educational research. *Educational Theory, 57*(1), 1–22.

Borko, H., Liston, D., & Whitcomb, J. A. (2007). Genres of empirical research in teacher education. *Journal of Teacher Education, 58*(1), 3–12.

Brew, A. (2001). Conceptions of research: a phenomenographic study. *Studies in Higher Education, 26*(3), 271–285.

Broekkamp, H., & van Hout-Wolters, B. (2007). The gap between educational research and practice: a literature review, symposium, and questionnaire. *Educational Research and Evaluation, 13*(3), 203–220.

Bruce, C., Pham, B., & Stoodley, I. (2004). Constituting the significance and value of research: views from information technology academics and industry professionals. *Studies in Higher Education, 29*(2): 219–38.

Bruggink, M., & Harinck, F. (2012). De onderzoekende houding van leraren: wat wordt daaronder verstaan. *Tijdschrift Voor Lerarenopleiders,* 47–48.

Coburn, C. E., & Stein, M. K. (Eds.). (2010). *Research and Practice in Education. Building Alliances, Bridging the Divide.* Plymouth: Rowman & Littlefield Publishers.

Cochran-Smith, M. (2002). What a difference a definition makes; highly qualified teachers, scientific research, and teacher education. *Journal of Teacher Education, 53*(3), 187–190.

Cochran-Smith, M., & Lytle, S. L. (1999). The teacher research movement: a decade later. *Educational Researcher, 28*(7), 15–25.

Cochran-Smith, M., Barnatt, J., Friedman, A., & Pine, G. (2009). Inquiry on inquiry: practitioner research and student learning. *Action in Teacher Education, 31*(2), 17–32.

Creswell, J. W. (2008). *Educational Research: Planning, Conducting, and Evaluating Quantitative and Qualitative Research.* Upper Saddle River, NJ: Pearson Education, Inc.

Ebbutt, D., Worrall, N., & Robson, R. (2000). Educational research partnership: differences and tensions at the interface between the professional cultures of practitioners in schools and researchers in higher education. *Teacher Development, 4*(3), 319–338.

Frey, J. H., & Fontana, A. (1991). The group interview in social research. *Social Science Journal, 28*(2), 175–187.

Gore, J. M., & Gitlin, A. D. (2004). Visioning the academic–teacher divide: power and knowledge in the educational community. *Teachers and Teaching, 10*(1), 35–58.

Healey, M., Jordan, F., Pell, B., & Short, C. (2010). The research–teaching nexus: a case study of students' awareness, experiences and perceptions of research. *Innovations in Education and Teaching International, 47*(2), 235–246.

Leeman, Y., & Wardekker, W. (2014). Teacher research and the aims of education. *Teachers and Teaching, 20*(1), 45–58.

Levin, B. (2004). Making research matter more. *Education Policy Analysis Archives, 12*(56). Available online: http://epaa.asu.edu/epaa/v12n56/ [Accessed on: 10th October 2015].

Miles, M. B., & Huberman, A. M. (1994). Matrix displays: some rules of thumb. *Qualitative Data Analysis: An Expanded Sourcebook.* Thousand Oaks, CA: Sage (pp. 239–244).

Poortman, C., & Schildkamp, K. (2012). Alternative quality standards in qualitative research? *Quality & Quantity, 46*(6), 1727–1751.

Shkedi, A. (1998). Teachers' attitudes towards research: A challenge for qualitative researchers. *International Journal of Qualitative Studies in Education, 11*(4), 559–577.

Vrijnsen-de Corte, M., Den Brok, P., Kamp, M., & Bergen, T. (2013). Teacher research in Dutch professional development schools: perceptions of the actual and preferred situations in terms of the context, process and outcomes of research. *European Journal of Teacher Education, 36*(1), 3–23.

Worrall, N. (2004). Trying to build a research culture in a school: trying to find the right questions to ask. *Teacher Development, 8*(2–3), 137–148.

Zeichner, K. M. (2003). Teacher research as professional development P-12 educators in the USA. *Educational Action Research, 11*, 301–326.

Zwart, R. C., Smit, B., & Admiraal, W. F. (2015). A closer look at teacher research: a review study into the nature and value of research conducted by teachers. *Pedagogische Studiën, 92*(2), 131–149.

Chapter 10

The future promise of RCTs in education

Some reflections on the Closing the Gap project

Paul Connolly

Introduction

In reading the preceding chapters it is encouraging to note that the debates surrounding the use of randomised controlled trials (RCTs) in education are beginning to move on. As noted by Menter and Thompson (Chapter 3), it is regrettable that one of our main methodology textbooks in education within the UK is still encouraging our next generation of educational researchers to believe that RCTs are 'fundamentally flawed' and that they 'belong to a discredited view of science as positivism' (Cohen et al., 2011: pp. 314, 318). However, the debates covered in this volume reflect a much more constructive and nuanced engagement with the issues and challenges faced by the use of RCTs in education. Moreover, using the Closing the Gap: Test and Learn project (CtG) as a case study has allowed for a meaningful exploration of the potential and limitations of RCTs as they have been employed in practice.

CtG has been a significant project in the context of the UK but it is not unique. CtG is not one trial but comprises seven core parallel trials. There is now a significant tradition of successfully completing trials of this size, and larger, in the UK that have involved various forms of collaboration with schools. Indeed, when these current CtG trials were underway (mid-2015), our own research found that there had already been 746 RCTs published internationally since 1980, with a quarter of these (26%) involving over 1,000 participants (Connolly, 2015). Within this, we found 83 unique RCTs in the UK and Ireland that had been successfully completed and published. However, it is precisely because CtG is not unique in this regard that it makes it much more valuable as a practical case study for exploring the use of RCTs in practice in education.

The purpose of this chapter is to draw out and reflect upon some of the key issues arising from the preceding chapters, using CtG as a vehicle to highlight several more general points regarding the role of RCTs in educational research. In doing this it is important to declare from the outset that I am not an impartial commentator on this debate. Rather, as Director of the Centre for Evidence and Social Innovation (CESI) at Queen's University Belfast and founding Director of the new National Campbell Centre for the UK and

Ireland, I am a strong advocate for the use of RCTs in education. Indeed, CESI has either completed and/or is currently in the process of running over 50 RCTs in the fields of education and social care. However, my advocacy of the greater use of trials is not uncritical, and we have learnt much over the last decade regarding the issues and challenges facing the use of RCTs in practice. It is this experience, elaborated more fully elsewhere (Connolly et al., 2017), that I will seek to draw upon in the discussion that follows.

The role of RCTs in educational research

The rather trenchant nature of debates that have taken place over the last decade surrounding the use of RCTs in education, as illustrated by Cohen et al. (2011), are more a reflection of broader political rather than methodological concerns. Politically, it is the case that RCTs have tended to assume a privileged position in various policy circles over the last decade or so, especially in the US (Lather, 2010). The prevalent discourse of RCTs as representing the 'gold standard' of educational research has been particularly damaging and has raised quite legitimate concerns regarding the potential marginalisation of other forms of research, as highlighted by Menter and Thompson (Chapter 3). In this regard, Higgins (Chapter 5) is quite right to stress that the RCT is just one of many tools available to educational researchers, designed to do a very specific job. As he also makes clear, the RCT is an absolutely necessary but not sufficient research design for drawing conclusions about the effectiveness of education practice.

The basic logic of the RCT is compelling and illustrates why they are necessary when attempting to understand the effectiveness of educational interventions. Ultimately, if we are interested in determining whether an intervention has had a tangible impact on improving the learning of students, we need some measure of where they started (the baseline or pre-test) and then where they have progressed to (the post-test). It is only by tracking the actual change in educational outcomes of the students (whether in terms of their knowledge, understanding and/or skills) that we will have any objective measure of whether the intervention has led to change amongst the participating students and the magnitude of that change. However, educational outcomes amongst students are likely to change over a period of time and for a wide variety of reasons. If we just tracked changes in a cohort of students participating in an educational intervention, then we would have no basis for determining how much of that change has been due to the effects of the intervention and how much may have been due to the plethora of other intervening factors that will have impacted upon them but have nothing to do with the intervention. It is for this reason that we need a control group of similar students who we can also track over the same period of time. Having a control group allows us to determine whether the changes experienced by the students participating in the intervention are above and beyond those that we would have expected to have happened in any case (as represented by the control group).

Of course, the validity of this comparison of students in the 'intervention group' with those in the 'control group' rests on the assumption that we are comparing like with like. More specifically, the basic premise of the RCT is that we can be as sure as possible that the only systematic difference between the two groups of students is that one has received the educational intervention whilst the other has not. It is because of this premise that we can then conclude with some confidence that any differences in the changes experienced by both groups must be due to the effects of the intervention as all other potential factors will be broadly balanced across the two groups. This is why the random allocation of students to intervention and control groups (whether individually or as whole classes or schools or other type of grouping) is so critical to an RCT as the process of random allocation, assuming the sample size is large enough, will tend to ensure that all other potentially mediating factors are balanced across the two groups and that they are thus well matched. It is for this reason that random allocation is thus not just regarded as an 'optional extra' but is fundamental to the design of an RCT. As soon as this element of the design is compromised then there is a strong likelihood that biases are introduced to the trial. It is also for this reason that we tend to be obsessive about the process of randomisation and with reporting it clearly, in detail and entirely transparently.

However, whilst the logic of the RCT design allows us to draw robust conclusions regarding whether a particular educational intervention has had an effect, on its own it can tell us very little about *why* that effect has occurred (or has not occurred as the case may be). Such questions regarding why an intervention has had an impact or not are equally important in the study of the effectiveness of educational practice. However, they require very different methods that shift the focus towards: the perspectives and experiences of participants; the complex sets of social processes associated with the intervention; and the contexts within which they occur. In this sense, if RCTs are the 'gold standard' for determining whether an intervention has had an effect, then qualitative methods – and particularly in-depth ethnographic case studies – are the 'gold standard' for helping us understand causal mechanisms and processes and thus for understanding why. In making this point, it is worth noting that Higgins' argument about RCTs being a necessary but not sufficient method for drawing conclusions about effective educational practice is equally applicable to these other methods. Thus, for example, it is not difficult to find evaluative studies in education that have sought to understand the effectiveness of a programme using solely qualitative methods. The fundamental problem here is that in the absence of evidence from an RCT or equivalent design, we have no way of knowing whether the intervention has actually been effective in the first place. Whilst our qualitative research may have produced very plausible and compelling theories for making sense of the impact of the educational intervention, these may be completely misguided in explaining outcomes that do not actually exist (Bonnell et al., 2012).

The rhetoric and reality of RCTs

Beyond the issue of what role RCTs perform within the wider context of educational research, there is the more fundamental question regarding whether it is actually possible to undertake RCTs in education and, if so, how far they can be meaningfully led by or involve the active participation of teachers. As several chapters in this present volume have documented, the present case study of CtG clearly demonstrates that not only are RCTs quite possible in the field of education but there was little resistance found towards them and, on the contrary, there appears to be a 'considerable appetite' amongst schools (Chapter 6, p. 120). This certainly resonates strongly with our own experience at the Centre for Evidence and Social Innovation at Queen's University Belfast where we have run a large number of trials in schools over the last decade. Whilst some work is required in talking through the basic logic underpinning RCTs, once this is done we have also found very little resistance on the part of teachers and schools. Indeed, our experience is that the emphasis on effectiveness and outcomes tends to align closely with the everyday concerns of teachers. Teachers thus tend to be continuously reflecting upon their particular pedagogical approaches and seeking out new and potentially more effective methods. They also tend to be natural experimenters and engaged in an ongoing process of comparing the results obtained from adopting one method with those attained previously with another. Perhaps most significantly, we have come across very few teachers who have been afraid of asking the question 'what works?' or who have been concerned with research efforts to determine the effectiveness of particular approaches.

None of this is to suggest that teachers or schools are unaware of the complexities associated with such issues. When a teacher asks the question 'what works?' they will be clearly aware that any answer cannot simply be applied to each and every student in their class but is about the effectiveness of specific approaches *on average*. They will also tend to be very clear that the effectiveness of educational programmes and interventions is likely to vary across contexts and from one group of students to the next. This is why they will often be concerned with asking and seeking to answer the more specific question of: 'what is most likely to work best for my particular class or year group?' All these points apply, equally, to the many parents and students we have engaged with over the last decade. Very few people we have worked with have failed to appreciate the complex and context-specific nature of how students learn and develop. However, they also recognise that there is a need to start somewhere and that, however partial and fallible the evidence might be, it is helpful to learn from what appears to have been effective (or not) elsewhere. These concerns regarding the notion of 'what works', and the inability to take a grounded and pragmatic approach to the evidence claims generated through trials, does therefore appear to be a peculiarly academic one.

Beyond this, the experience of CtG also clearly suggests that the role of teachers and schools within RCTs need not necessarily be relegated to objects of research but that they can be active participants and co-producers of such research. This was particularly the case for the subgroup of schools involved in designing and conducting mini RCTs. As outlined in several of the previous chapters, with the support of small grants from NCTL, these 'Early Adopters' planned and successfully completed 50 mini trials. As would be expected, such efforts on the part of the schools required capacity building and support but clearly demonstrated the potential of teachers to play a strong and collaborative role in the use of RCTs in education. Moreover, and as Menter and Thompson note in referring to this subgroup of schools, those 'with the most advanced understanding of experimental methods also developed the most sophisticated contextual qualitative methods for a closer understanding of the reasons for positive or negative effect sizes' (Chapter 3, p. 70).

However, and in contrast to the relative success of these mini RCTs, Menter and Thompson have raised some concerns regarding the limited room for flexibility or creativity regarding the larger trials run through the CtG programme. The key point here is that there is no reason why teachers and schools (and parents and students) cannot play a full role as active participants and co-producers of RCTs, even large trials. Having said this, there is a need to understand the nature of trials and thus where in the research process such contributions can be made. In this sense, and based upon our own experience within the Centre for Evidence and Social Innovation, it is quite possible to work collaboratively with teachers and schools, and with parents, students and local communities, to jointly identify priorities and the focus of an educational intervention and to develop and pilot that intervention. We have also shown how it is possible to work together to jointly identify the outcomes to be measured and the specific design to be employed for the RCT. Moreover, we regularly work collaboratively with key stakeholders to make sense of and interpret the findings that arise from our trials and to agree the best mechanisms for reporting these.

Thus, flexibility and innovation can be built into the entire process of a trial – from initial conception and design through to its execution and then reporting – and it is also equally possible for teachers and schools to be centrally involved as co-leaders of this. However, the one element of a trial where it is necessary to maintain a standard approach is in the actual delivery of the intervention concerned. In this regard, whilst there is complete flexibility in relation to what intervention is developed, once it has been agreed it does need to be delivered as originally intended. To understand the reason for this we need to return to the basic logic of a trial as described earlier. If we were to find a difference between outcomes amongst students in the intervention group compared to the control group at post-test, then we can only attribute this difference to the effects of the intervention if we are clear about what that intervention has been. This, in turn, requires us to identify what the key elements of the intervention should be and then to ensure that these are adhered to for the duration of the programme. Only when this has been done can we be confident in generating claims regarding the effects of a particular educational approach. Moreover, the whole point of RCTs is to identify which interventions tend to be more effective for which groups of students and in which contexts so that those that have been found to be effective can be replicated by others. This is simply not possible if there is complete flexibility and where teachers for a given intervention can adapt it as they wish. In such circumstances, whilst an intervention may have been found to be effective overall, there will be no way of knowing which practices, amongst the wide variety that emerged from the teachers adapting the intervention in differing ways, were those that were critical in achieving the effects.

This, then, is why there tends to be an emphasis within RCTs on specifying exactly what the nature of the intervention is that is to be evaluated, often through setting out its core elements in a programme or manual, and then in measuring how well the intervention was actually delivered against these original intentions. There are, however, three caveats to this focus on what has tended to be termed 'programme fidelity'. The first is that where interim findings suggest that an intervention may be actually causing harm then there is an ethical imperative to stop the intervention at that point; a practice that resonates with some of the issues raised by Fancourt (Chapter 8). The second point is that this focus on specifying the nature of the intervention does not, in itself, require that the intervention is strictly prescribed. It is quite possible, and valid, to develop an intervention that is only based on a broad set of principles or values to be adhered to or a few key parameters within which teachers or schools must work. So long as these are then followed, an RCT design will still be capable of determining whether the application of such principles or values is sufficient to have an effect. The third and final point to note is that there is an important role to be played by RCTs in formative evaluation. Higgins sets this out clearly, in Chapter 5, in relation to the different emphases of pilot, efficacy and effectiveness trials. In this sense, considerable room for flexibility and innovation remains if RCTs are seen as just specific stages of a longer-term process of developing and refining educational interventions. Whilst there is a need to adhere to the core elements of an intervention at the point that it is being delivered and its effectiveness evaluated, once the findings are known there is every opportunity to adapt and refine the intervention subsequently.

The design and administration of RCTs

One of the key lessons we have learnt through our work in undertaking RCTs through the Centre for Evidence and Social Innovation over the last decade has been the importance of starting small and building up from pilot studies and efficacy trials towards eventual larger-scale RCTs. Some of the early trials we were commissioned to run were funded by The Atlantic Philanthropies through its Disadvantaged Children and Youth Programme on the island of

Ireland. The emphasis of this programme was on encouraging a shift towards early intervention and prevention by funding a relatively large number of NGOs and community-based organisations to develop and deliver evidence-based interventions. One of the requirements of the funding was that the interventions needed to be evaluated through the use of an RCT so that, over time, the Disadvantaged Children and Youth Programme would contribute to the development of a robust evidence base to inform future efforts and investments.

Further details of the Programme and evaluations of its impact over the last decade are available on The Atlantic Philanthropies' website (http://www. atlanticphilanthropies.org/themes/children-youth). There is little doubt that the Programme, overall, has achieved significant impact and has led to the prioritisation of early intervention and prevention and also a focus on outcomes-based accountability by the respective governments in Northern Ireland and the Republic of Ireland. However, there were also some clear lessons to be learnt that arose particularly from the early stages of the Programme where there was a focus on developing new interventions against tight timeframes and then moving directly to relatively large-scale RCTs to evaluate their effectiveness. This, in turn, led to concerns regarding such issues as: the premature evaluation of interventions before they had been sufficiently developed; the selection of inappropriate outcomes and measures for RCTs that did not adequately reflect the actual aims of the intervention(s) concerned; and difficulties experienced at times in managing large-scale trials and ensuring ongoing engagement of schools and their commitment to either delivering the programmes as intended and/or their willingness to continue to participate in the trials to the end.

Through the experience we have gained over the last decade, we have learnt the importance of beginning small, of taking our time in working with teachers and schools and other educational providers to better understand the nature of the problems and issues that we wish to focus on and in identifying and developing interventions that are most appropriate to address these. We have also learnt how important it is to develop interventions that are evidence-based and theoretically-informed and how useful logic models are in helping to develop a shared understanding not only of the nature of the issues at hand but also of the theory of change that will underpin the intervention seeking to address these. Perhaps most importantly, and as indicated above, we have learnt the importance of starting with small pilots and efficacy trials to test 'proof of concept' before beginning to scale up to larger trials, not least of all because there is a world of difference between delivering an intervention in a tightly-controlled and well-supported handful of schools and attempting to roll the intervention out across a whole region or nationally.

My reading of the previous chapters suggests that some of these same issues are also evident in the development and delivery of the CtG programme. For example, there appears to have been relatively little time provided for the development and piloting of the seven core interventions before subjecting them to large-scale RCTs. There are also concerns raised regarding the appropriateness of the two core outcome measures applied uniformly to all the interventions and an acknowledgement by Churches et al. (Chapter 2) that some of these interventions were never intended to achieve change in relation to these two particular outcomes. There is also a lack of clarity regarding the randomisation processes adopted for the main trials. Moreover, and again an issue that is fairly typical of large-scale trials that are not tightly controlled, attrition appears to have been relatively high, ranging from 22 to 48 per cent of pupils across the trials.

Overall, and considering the above points, it is not surprising to find that six of the seven large-scale trials found no effects. Given the space restrictions of the present volume, it is clearly not possible for the chapter authors in this present volume to report the full findings of the various trials here. However, the main report of the CtG programme available online does not provide much additional information (Churches, 2016). In this regard, there are clear and extensive guidelines that exist – through the internationally-developed and agreed CONSORT Statements – for how to properly report trials (see: http://www.consort-statement.org). In light of the earlier discussion regarding the basic logic of trials, it should come as no surprise to note that such guidelines require accurate, comprehensive and transparent reporting of all key aspects of a trial to allow for a full assessment of the reliability and validity of the findings reported from an RCT. Such guidelines include the need to report: the exact processes used for randomisation; the precise levels of attrition and where they occurred in the process; data on the characteristics of the intervention and control groups at pre-test to allow assessment of their comparability; the statistical methods used for the main analysis and any additional analyses planned; full details on the outcomes used that should all be pre-specified; and specific information on each of the interventions and how they were actually delivered with sufficient details to allow replication. In relation to CtG, whilst the main report includes some of these details, key information is currently missing. It is noted however that, at the time of writing, the main report had only recently been published and it is therefore hoped that there are plans to report the findings of each of the trials more fully in due course.

Conclusions

It is clear from the chapters in this book that CtG has been an important programme nationally. It has provided further evidence that RCTs are not only entirely possible in education but that there is little resistance to them and, on the contrary, there is a significant appetite amongst teachers and schools to participate in them. The evidence from CtG, especially from the impressive number of mini trials conducted, is that schools can also play an active role in co-designing and undertaking pilot trials themselves. However, and as also noted, there are also lessons to be learnt regarding the particular approach adopted to the design and delivery of the CtG programme, especially in relation to the tight time pressures involved and the decision to move directly to relatively large-scale trials for interventions that, for the most part, had not previously been subject to trials. This latter point is important in that whilst six of the seven core interventions were well established in terms of their delivery in schools, they had not benefited from the process of pilot testing or efficacy trials. This is a significant limitation as many of the problems and issues faced by the current CtG trials (e.g., ill-defined outcomes; high levels of attrition; inconsistencies in the randomisation processes; and problems associated with fidelity of delivery) could have been identified and addressed early and, most importantly, before the considerable investment and expense incurred through large-scale trials. In this regard, and just as we have learnt through our own engagement in RCTs over the last decade, starting small and working carefully through the stages of pilot tests and efficacy trials before subjecting interventions to larger-scale effectiveness trials not only helps mitigate many of these problems but also creates a more appropriate context for the development of meaningful collaborative partnerships between researchers, schools, parents and students where RCTs can be genuinely co-produced.

This latter point is critical and reflects the way in which RCTs are increasingly becoming high stakes tests of interventions. In this regard, positive findings from an RCT can be extremely beneficial in providing robust evidence to secure further funding and support for a specific intervention. However, and conversely, there is a growing trend for particular interventions to be evaluated by one RCT and then for their future to rest upon a positive result from that trial. In cases where the findings from the RCT are inconclusive and/or provide no evidence of effectiveness, there is the risk that further funding and support for that intervention will simply be withdrawn. This makes it all the more imperative that we avoid the pressure to move too quickly and prematurely to large-scale RCTs. However, it also emphasises the need to contextualise the findings of individual trials within the wider evidence-base provided by other trials of that intervention or similar interventions.

With the increasing number of RCTs being completed in education, this is where systematic reviews and meta-analysis can play an increasingly important role. Even where we are dealing with a clearly-defined intervention that has been subject to several RCTs, meta-analyses still tend to reveal considerable variations in the size of the effects found from one trial to the next. Such variations partly reflect differences in the interventions themselves as well as variations in the differing contexts within which the intervention has been delivered and also the differing characteristics of the students it has been delivered to. However, they also partly reflect simple randomness between samples. There will be cases, therefore, where an intervention is likely to be effective but where, simply because of the random way in which a particular sample has been chosen for an RCT, the findings of that trial are inconclusive or even negative. At the very least, this is where it is important not to dismiss a specific intervention based on the findings of just one trial but to contextualise the trial findings through a broader meta-analysis that can pool the data from several trials of the same (or similar) interventions. However, the promise of systematic reviews and meta-analyses is much more than this. With the ever-increasing number of RCTs now being published, there are more opportunities to pool data from several trials of similar interventions to begin to analyse the variations that exist. This, in turn, will provide greater opportunities to begin to assess in which contexts particular interventions tend to be more effective and also for what subgroups. Moreover, we will increasingly be able to note the key elements of each intervention and use meta-analyses to assess what particular elements, and combinations of elements, of interventions are most significant in achieving positive outcomes and, again, in what contexts and for whom?

References

Bonnell C., Fletcher, A., Morton, M., Lorenc, T. and Moore, L. (2012) 'Realist randomised controlled trials: a new approach to evaluating complex public health interventions', *Social Science & Medicine*, 75 (12): 2299–2306.

Churches, R. (2016) *Closing the Gap: Test and Learn, Research Report Winter 2016*. London: National College for Teaching and Leadership. Available online: https://www.gov.uk/government/uploads/system/uploads/attachment_data/file/495580/closing_the_gap_test_and_learn_full_report.pdf

Cohen, L., Manion, L. and Morrison, K. (2011) *Research Methods in Education*, 7th Edition. London: Routledge.

Connolly, P. (2015) 'The trials of evidence-based practice in education', Keynote address, British Educational Research Association Annual Conference, 15–17 September, Queen's University Belfast. Available online: https://www.youtube.com/watch?v=svuMXlAsaCE

Connolly, P., Biggart, A., Miller, S., O'Hare, L. and Thurston, T. (2017) *Using Randomised Controlled Trials in Education*. BERA/Sage Research Methods in Education Series. London: Sage.

Lather, P. (2010) *Engaging Science Policy: From the Side of the Messy*. New York: Peter Lang.

Chapter 11

What's not to like about RCTs in education?

Trevor Gale

Introduction

It is a sad truth that I am a sympathiser of Pavlov's dogs (1927). Whenever I hear mention of phrases such as 'evidence-based' policy and practice, 'what works' and RCTs (Randomised Control Trials) in education, my instant response is to dig up those foundational tenets of methodology: ontology and epistemology. This chapter, then, is a kind of archaeological dig, an excavation of the preceding chapters and of the research community's understandings of what we know about research and the ways in which we know it. It is an attempt at reflection and, I hope, provocation. It is a personal narrative and, I hope, with experiences and understandings that resonate with the research dispositions of others. So let me begin.

My first real struggle with questions of ontology and epistemology in research was as a postgraduate student in a methodology class, reading the likes of Karl Popper and Thomas Kuhn and being reintroduced to 'the nature of reality . . . different kind[s] of knowledge . . . [and] different set[s] of standards for evaluating knowledge claims' (Schwandt 1989: 379). It was there that I first encountered Habermas, the Frankfurt School and critical social science, being taken in by its political commitments and dialectic method.[1] It was there too that I first came across turtles as the basis for an alternative worldview, at the start of one of my compulsory readings, which has stayed with me ever since:

> There is a story about an Englishman who was told by his Indian friend that the world rested on a platform which rested on the back of an elephant which in turn rested on the back of a turtle. The Englishman asked his

---

1 As Leo Bartlett, my lecturer, said to me at the time, 'the person you are is the researcher you are'. Leo later appointed me to my first academic post and I have since learned that 'the person you are is the academic you are'. There is a reality worth acknowledging here: although we are similar, more so to some than to others, we are not all the same and what a jolly good thing that is.

friend, "And what does the turtle rest on?" "Another turtle," came the reply. "And that turtle?" asked the Englishman. "Ah, Sahib," said the friend, "after that it is turtles all the way down."

(Schwandt 1989: 379)

I admit to thinking at the time, what a strange thing to include in an article on research methodology. It didn't help that Schwandt didn't return to explain what he meant by his oblique reference to the Hindu mythological/cosmological concept of infinite regression, other than by way of introduction to 'getting to the bottom' of different approaches to research. To me it seemed devoid of scientific rigour, even of common sense, and not the sort of thing that education research was meant to be about. It also felt condescending – despite the claim to friendship – representing the colonised other as infantile. But what struck me most was what I perceived as the juxtaposition of narrative and research. In my mind narrative was reserved for fiction, humour and the everyday. Research was supposed to be far more serious, more precise, more analytical in explaining the world, particularly in relation to things like what and how to teach and how to know the extent to which these make any difference.

I later came to understand narrative as a distinct way of knowing and of representing knowledge. As a teacher educator I saw its value in helping my predominantly white middle-class young female students move beyond deficit accounts of disadvantaged young people and their communities. Narrative was the vehicle I used in *Rough Justice* (Gale 2005) written with this audience in mind: to confess and share my own middle-class ignorance and insensitivities, hoping that this would encourage my readers to do similarly, to explore how the 'helping' professions and their social institutions position people living in poverty and to create a space for young people living on the streets to speak for themselves about how they understood their lives and their decisions. My ambition was for these personal stories to enable my audience to grasp the reality of the lived experiences of differently positioned others – which, in their inexperience and affluence, they had a habit of misrecognising and/or denigrating – revealing their lives in a way that quantitative social science seemed unable to do. My hope was that my students would identify with the narrative's personal qualities. In my reckoning, narrative afforded them access to a certain reality, an ontology, which a traditional scientific method did not, could not. It allowed them to know things previously excluded from their frames of reference.

My ears were pricked again by narrative when widening participation policies were reintroduced into Australian higher education in 2008.[2] In the new policy regime universities were required to ensure that, by 2020, 20 per cent of their student population would be from a low socioeconomic background. Narrative

---

2 For a history of widening participation policies in Australian higher education, see Gale and Tranter (2011).

became a useful vehicle to research and capture the lived experiences of young people from particular social groups who were marginalised and excluded from higher education. Interestingly, many vice-chancellors then felt compelled to share their own personal stories of socioeconomic disadvantage and hardship as a way of demonstrating their empathy with these accounts and to parade their own social justice credentials. Their shift in narrative from elitism to meritocracy is akin to the respective critiques provided by Piketty (2014) and Dorling (2010) (see Gale et al. 2017); the narratives of vice-chancellors are now more merito-cratic with often quite explicit messages of 'if I can do it [access university] so can you', 'we want the brightest and best, wherever they can be found' and so on, without any apparent regard for knowledge as a form of cultural capital (Bourdieu 1986) – the inheritance of the dominant – or for different, changed and changing circumstances.

Narrative is not the preserve of the marginalised. It is also the stuff of education politics and policy making[3] but it tends to be on the periphery in the realm of knowledge and knowledge production (Connell 2007). It is often associated with indigenous peoples in the global south (Kunnie & Goduka 2006) and, like my initial reading of turtles as an explanation for everything, is regarded as somewhat simplistic as a research methodology. And yet there are some quite sophisticated accounts of doing indigenous research (e.g., Martin & Mirraboopa 2003) with quite clear and robust ontological and epistemological positions. For example, most Indigenous Australian researchers subscribe to a relational ontology, not unlike Actor Network Theory (ANT), in which the nature of reality is named as 'Country . . . the waters, the earth, the air we breathe, the flora, the fauna; it is everything connected to and in our environment' (Blair 2015: 194). The way to know this reality is through 'stories of relatedness' (Martin 2008: 84).

I have taken a leaf out of Schwandt's 'book' in introducing this chapter in a collection about Randomised Control Trials (RCTs) in education by beginning with narrative, that is, starting from a position that is about as far removed from RCTs as one might imagine – as far as turtles are from models of inquiry – and yet the issues for narrative research and RCTs are not antithetical, as I hope will become apparent. As introductions go, it is also rather long although my intention is also for it to provide some disjuncture from other chapters, a kind of pedagogy of discomfort (Boler & Zembylas 2003; Zembylas 2008). So[4] I have deliberately written in the first person and deliberately tried

---

3 For example, see Gale and Cross (2007) on 'the politics of (re)learning how and what to teach in Australia'.

4 In other circumstances I would have used 'thus' instead of 'so' but I want to draw attention to how easily we move from one thing to another and, through the judicious use of language, disguise the move as logical, even scientific, in order to hide any tenuous aspects of our conclusions. I confess to doing this myself but I have used 'we' here to signal that I am not alone! The significance of moving 'from one to another' will become more apparent further on.

to engage research personalities – by which I mean that research is a subjective exercise on the part of researchers and needs to be recognised and named as such[5] – because it seems to me that RCTs seek to maintain an objectivity, a claim to a non-political or non-ideological stance, which is beyond their grasp and this needs to be drawn out into the open.

The chapter is arranged in three parts: the privileging of the physical world as the dominant reality; the privileging of causal relations in epistemic claims; and the privileging and ethics of RCTs as the gold standard for educational research. I use these themes to review the Closing the Gap (CtG) project as reported in this collection. A lot more could be said about this research and its record discussed in the preceding chapters, but I am conscious of the space available to me and also that others have a similar brief and hopefully they will do justice to the parts that I cannot address or do not address very well. All of this is against the backdrop of how researchers in the CtG project approach the question of what can be done to improve the academic achievement of students in schools, particularly p those who face educational disadvantages and do not perform very well on standardised tests, and particularly whether a specific 'intervention' can affect a positive change. In the background too is the proposition that research in schools is part of the answer, including the possibility of teachers as researchers and of building capacity within schools to produce 'the evidence'. As part of this, I am particularly taken by Steve Higgins' (Chapter 5, this volume) claim that 'causal warrant' methodologies, like RCTs, are 'necessary but not sufficient in educational research', because I think this speaks directly to issues of ontology and epistemology, which I hope to address.

My virus has a mind of its own – on the ontological question of necessity

As a first move in that direction, then, it is important to understand that RCTs do not regard the physical and the social as different worlds. From a RCT perspective, they are one and the same reality.[6] More accurately, the social world is assumed to have no distinguishing features that would warrant demarcating it from the physical or the 'natural' world (Taylor 1985).[7] In this sense, the

---

5   See Bourdieu and Wacquant (1992) on reflexive objectivity.
6   It is as if the interpretive, cultural, linguistic and postmodern turns, the legitimation crisis and the crisis of representation have passed RCTs by (St. Pierre 2006: 243).
7   There is also a small 'p' political or pragmatic element to subsuming the social within the physical. Dewey (1899) took this route – albeit his strategy was more epistemological than ontological – in the creation of Laboratory Schools as a way of gaining legitimacy for educational research in academic contexts (specifically in the University of Chicago), marshalling the methods and approaches of the physical sciences and applying them within educational psychology. That legacy continued with the establishment of national associations of education researchers so that educational research was defined largely as psychological research; educational research by association (Lingard & Gale 2010).

natural world is more than just the physical things of nature. There is a claimed common sense – a naturalness – about its reality that is hegemonic (Gramsci 1971).[8] This is different from the ontology of 'Country'[9] and even Actor Network Theory (ANT), which stress a relatedness between animate and inanimate objects; indeed they question whether objects can be inanimate, since they are dripping with meaning.

Instead RCTs are informed by an ontology that universalises the reality of the physical across the social world. This is not a claim that is made explicit but it is so nonetheless because RCTs are deemed by their users to be equally applicable in physical and social worlds by the simple fact of their use in both. And it is not the case that RCTs are agnostic with respect to ontological propositions, thereby rendering their use valid in both social and physical realms.[10] Instead, they are derived from and favour a particular view of reality – which is 'out there' to be discovered (by particular methods of discovery) – of what things are and how they are related (e.g., Hammersley 2013). Like all methods of research, RCTs are imbued with beliefs about the nature of the research 'problem', how it can be researched, what will count as data and so on. They are methods for producing knowledge based on what is deemed to count as knowledge. They are designed to produce certain knowledge outcomes (e.g., related to 'interventions'), albeit there can be some variation in these outcomes.

It is important to understand, then, that RCTs and related 'evidenced-based' approaches to research have been conceived within the field of medical science (e.g., Pirrie 2001). They were designed to research things like viruses (e.g., influenza, Ebola, etc.), randomly assigning a 'treatment' or an 'intervention' to a sample or experimental group and having a control group that does not receive the intervention. The effectiveness of the intervention is inferred by comparing the two groups to determine the 'counterfactual' condition.[11] It is not just the virus that is at stake here. It is the interaction of the virus with the body's physiology and the treatment. Also, being a randomised intervention, there is a claim that the results have more general applicability and a high degree of validity (Ainsworth et al. 2015). This works for things like viruses because they do not have a mind of their own but are of the same 'mind' (e.g., see Taylor 2002). They tend not to select people to infect based on some social marker that distinguishes some people from others. Any turtle will do.[12] But

---

8   See also Taylor on how the pervasiveness of this ontology is bound up with human agency (1985), modern individual identity (1989) and the collective social imaginary (2004).

9   Or a 'country-view' a la 'worldview'.

10 Have you noticed how my register has slipped back towards a more scientific mode? Are you being more fully persuaded?

11 See Slavin (2002) for a fuller definition of RCTs.

12 The fact that some research reported in this volume employed a modified form of randomisation (e.g., Chapter 2) could be seen as evidence that researchers themselves do not believe that any turtle will do, and thus RCTs are ontologically inadequate when employed in the field of education.

while viruses have no regard for social distinctions (cf. Bourdieu 1984), people have a mind of their own (see Taylor 2002 on predictability, changing self-understandings, etc.), which means they can and do act in ways that are unexpected, although not always![13] A key ontological debate in sociology has hinged on this very interplay between structure and agency and how these seemingly conflicting social realities can be reconciled (e.g., see Giddens (1984) on 'structuration'; Bourdieu (1990) on 'the habitus').

The language of the research reported in this collection, then, is ontologically telling. Students, teachers, schools were 'exposed to interventions . . . [they] receive treatment' (Chapter 2) with just a little bit of 'pollution' and 'contamination' of control groups by experimental groups (Chapter 3) – spillage. This medical discourse and approach is adopted unproblematically it would seem, given the express desire for 'learning lessons from medicine and health care . . . [and for interventions that are] modelled on medicine and the health sciences' (Chapter 6, p. 114). The rationale for rolling out RCTs in schools would appear to be for Teaching Schools 'to parallel the role of Teaching Hospitals' (Chapter 6, p. 114). Presumably, then, students' learning difficulties are akin to viruses (and other forms of disease and illness). Indeed, the model of inquiry is premised on students having a problem or 'symptoms' that require treatment, facilitated by assessments that demonstrate students' absence or diminished forms of cultural capital.[14] These students are pathologised first by naming their problem (often expressed in terms that match the solutions at hand)[15] and then by being treated with an intervention by some external agency or person (i.e., the types of interventions in the CtG project). All being well, they should recover.[16] Any change – it is after all an experiment – is deemed to be the effect of the intervention because that is the only thing seen to be different from the control group; the logic of which represents a leap of faith of elephant proportions. Thus, students are regarded as not having a mind of their own. When they are exposed to the same circumstances they are presumed to respond in the same ways.

That is the RCT reality. No account is taken in the research design of other influences on student learning (Berliner 2014) beyond discounting these through the use of control groups. No account is taken of the circumstances of those doing the intervening: teachers 'exposed to loads of different CPD,

---

13 There is a classic exchange in the film *The Life of Brian* when Brian admonishes the crowd for its crowd mentality in mindlessly following him: 'You've got to think for yourselves. You're all individuals. You're all different', he proclaims from on high, to which a sole unidentifiable voice in the crowd replies, 'I'm not'.

14 This is one reason why you rarely see interventions in elite schools; another concerns the politics of doing so, although they are related.

15 Policy makers are also adept at naming problems that match the solutions at hand. See Gale (1994) on 'story telling and policy making'.

16 Or not, as Chapter 2 notes, 'the majority of the interventions [in the CtG project] showed no effect greater than existing good practice'.

loads of different agenda, loads of different information coming at them' (Chapter 2). Except when RCT advocates realise that people are different from each other and so they engage in fancy statistical footwork to 'reduce between-participant variation' (Chapter 2). And except when teachers who engage in RCTs realise that context makes a difference to how interventions work (or do not work) and so they make decisions about ' "what works" in their own contexts' (Chapter 1) and then 'adapted interventions to suit' (Chapter 2). In fact, more often than not 'the importance of context is often ignored and can lead to the simplistic adoption of a "what works" approach to policy making' (Chapter 3). But even when acknowledged, there is a danger for context to be regarded as just another variable to factor in, to control for, understood as a difference in circumstances rather than as a social and cultural space in which ways of being, doing and understanding vary. In an RCT worldview, context is not the equivalent of what Bourdieu would call 'field' (social sites of positions and stance, of manoeuvre and struggle). Rather, context matters to the extent that: If you take the student out of one set of circumstances and put him/her in another set of circumstances, s/he will flourish. A few days in the sun will do you good.

But 'being a student is quite different from that of being a patient – being a student is not an illness, just as teaching is not a cure' (Biesta 2007: 8). In order to adequately research teaching and learning, we need research methodologies that first recognise:

> how humans understand themselves and their world is an essential or primary property of their existence, not one that can be bracketed out in the quest to explain them. Secondly, because humans' self-interpretations influence their actions and behaviour, any account that excludes this variable cannot be adequate.
>
> (Abbey 2000: 154; sec. Taylor 1985)

And if RCTs in education are not ontologically adequate, then they are probably not necessary.

Just a little bit pregnant – on the epistemological question of sufficiency

Because RCTs see no difference between physical and social worlds or regard the social world as operating in the same way as the physical world, they tend to search for the same kinds of knowledge they imagine to exist in the physical world. In fact, with ontological matters held constant, research is reduced to matters of epistemology. I am being a bit sloppy here in personifying RCTs as if they can be attributed with human characteristics, which they cannot. Of course I mean those who employ RCTs, which have been designed with this purpose in mind. But my sloppiness is illustrative of the ways in which RCTs also operate, in reverse, to strip personal characteristics from research subjects (Taylor 1985) – they are not to be known for their differences beyond their membership of one of two groups, and perhaps a little bit about their contexts (i.e., circumstances, often socioeconomic). As I mention above, RCTs provide a method for producing knowledge based on a particular view of what counts as knowledge. Specifically, their experimentation is designed to produce knowledge about cause and effect relations, nothing personal. That is, 'if we know this, then we know that', 'if we introduce this intervention, it will change things in a particular way'. There is an assumed unambiguous and linear relationship between the first and the second, from the first to the second. Pavlov's (1927) theories of stimulus and response provide a good example.[17] Another example: in education and governments around the world, there is now an imagined and clear line of sight from what teachers do and what students learn, which means we can hold teachers accountable for the poor academic achievement of students and, in turn, hold teacher educators to account for the poor teaching of teachers (Gale & Parker 2017). It is a 'representational epistemology' (Biesta 2010), presenting the world as a series of cause–effect relations that mirror reality.

There is a very appealing aspect to having such knowledge: the ability to predict what will happen on the basis of what we know now and/or what we have seen happen before. The trouble is, the evidence indicates that the randomised control trial in education 'falls short of its own claims to be controlled, exact and unambiguous' (Thomas 2004; Parlett & Hamilton 1987), so that it 'does not enable the establishment of causal connections' (Thomas 2004; Goldstein 2002). This is similar to what CtG researchers also found. Even though there was a desire to implement 'evidence-informed practice using designs with strong causal inference' and a 'trials methodology' focus on 'stronger causal evidence' (Chapter 4), 'the majority of the interventions showed no effect greater than existing good practice' (Chapter 2). And yet several CtG project teachers saw benefit for some students in continuing with the interventions despite the official overall position that they did not have much effect (Chapter 1). They exercised their professional judgement!

Some blame teachers' 'personal theories' or bias – seen as the product of their inculcation into the teaching profession and an over-reliance on what has previously passed as educational research – for the poor showing of RCTs in the CtG project, because these teachers allowed their 'existing [preconceived] understandings of cause and effect in the classroom' to influence the research design (Chapter 5).[18] Of course, bias is not just the preserve of teachers. It is integral to what it means to be a researcher and thus to their methods, which

---

17 I want it noted that my sympathies are with Pavlov's dogs (see my opening sentence) not with the applicability of his theories in the field of education.
18 I will come to the exclusivity of this stance in the next section.

– to reiterate – are designed to generate specific kinds of knowledge; they are inherently and *deliberately* biased. They take a position on an issue: that it is worth researching, that something should be done (e.g., closing the gap). They are not and cannot be neutral and objective. How we confront the influence of researchers on research outcomes, then, turns on the different approaches and assumptions of the natural and social sciences. RCT researchers seek to deal with bias by removing the effect of the researcher 'through systematic data collection and analysis' and other (unspecified) control mechanisms (Chapter 5). But as social researchers we can build into our research a 'reflexive objectivity' (Bourdieu & Wacquant 1992) to enable us to name and better understand our involvement in privileging particular research aims and objectives and forms of evidence, interpretation and knowledge. As teacher educators, we can foreground reflexive objectivity with teachers too, to encourage the formation of *deliberative* not just 'deliberate' professionals (Gale & Molla 2017).

At their best, RCTs 'provide a *retrospective* assessment of whether the policy, intervention or approach was actually responsible for any changes in outcomes for learners' (Chapter 5, emphasis added). From this perspective, these assessments add to the evidence base, which is then used by RCT researchers to predict outcomes in the future. And yet there is no evidence that such prediction is valid. Just because it happened once does not mean it will happen again or in the same way, especially in the social world. As Biesta (drawing on Dewey's practical epistemology) observes, research 'can tell us what worked but cannot tell us what works . . . [in fact] we cannot and should not expect that situations will stay the same over time, and we should definitely not expect this in the social realm' (2007: 15–16). This is because social systems are recursive and non-deterministic, in contrast to the closed systems assumed in the natural sciences (Biesta 2010). Thus, 'prediction . . . cannot be a goal of social science as it is of natural science' (Taylor 1985: 48).

Even when there is evidence of change, without this predictability, without being able to establish a strong causal link to interventions, the warrant for RCTs in education has the appearance of being just a little bit pregnant.[19] In fact, you can be pregnant or not pregnant but never somewhere in between. Providing evidence *of* change but not evidence *for* change is a half-baked RCT outcome. And it makes claims like the following ring a little hollow:

> 'Scientific' knowledge about cause and effect in education are essential tools for the professional educator. Not to be open to the evidence from research with strong causal warrant is problematic as it implies professionals are limited to opinion and judgement, with only limited knowledge about

---

19 Lou Mannheim in the movie *Wall Street*: 'You can't be just a little bit pregnant when you are talking bankruptcy. You can't be just a little bit bankrupt. You are either bankrupt or not bankrupt'.

the effectiveness of what they do in relation to specific ends (e.g., reading or proficiency in mathematics).

(Higgins, Chapter 5)

Given such provocation, I have to ask what knowledge teachers in the CtG project were able to glean from their research, apart from the realisation that they were not able to 'scientifically' discern whether their interventions had any significant effect. That is, teachers can engage in RCTs with no discernible benefit, although to be fair, not being able to show an effect is still an outcome worth knowing – as several chapter authors acknowledge. But the lack of a determinable effect of an intervention does not bode well for governments aiming to amass evidence for 'what works' and on which to base policy and practice. And I would also point out that in the absence of RCTs, teachers' knowledge and judgements are not necessarily limited to opinion. Professional learning opportunities aside (see Doecke et al. 2008), there is a long history of teacher involvement in research (Chapter 7) and of other educational research that has had significant effects (e.g., see DETYA 2000, an Australian Government report bulging with evidence of the impact of educational research), although not all of it 'scientific' in the limited sense of that term used above. The choice for professional educators is not RCTs or nothing. In terms of not being 'sufficient' (Chapter 5), RCTs in education are certainly that.

Doing a Bradbury – on the ethical questions of distinction and exclusion

This then raises the issue of the distinction (the privileged status; cf. Bourdieu 1984) that RCTs have been afforded by governments as the new gold standard for educational research (Goldstein 2002; St. Pierre 2006; Holmes et al. 2006), to the point that in some quarters they have become synonymous with educational research itself; the consequence of a 'regime of truth' (Foucault 1980) that operates to ensure that one account of education research is positioned as the only account.[20] In this reckoning, if education does not engage with research with a strong causal warrant, all you have left is opinion. Then there is only one contestant left on the podium – gold it is! Australians would call this, 'doing a Bradbury'.[21]

This privileging of RCTs in education (and in other social fields) is a phenomenon particular to post-industrial nations, at a time of:

20 See my earlier footnote about the preeminence of psychology in establishing educational research as a legitimate academic endeavour.
21 At the 2002 winter Olympics, Steven Bradbury won gold for Australia in a short course speed ice skating event after being a distant last until the final corner, 10 metres from the finish line, when all six of his more fancied opponents ahead of him fell, allowing Bradbury to skate past and claim gold.

governments increasingly attempting to set research agendas and research priorities with implications for valorised methodologies and theories, either implicit or explicit within these political agendas. For example . . . the Bush government in the USA attempted to construct 'empirically randomised control trials' as the 'gold standard' for assessing educational research and for evaluating all research applications . . . The situation in the UK has been similar.

(Lingard & Gale 2010: 33)

The reasons for doing so are (1) ostensibly 'grounded in political and professional concerns about underachievement and educational equity' (Chapter 8); (2) for purposes of efficiency and effectiveness, so that 'time and money were not wasted on irrelevant or ineffective strategies' (Chapter 8); (3) both pursued in the belief that much education research is unscientific and based in values, opinion and 'bias' that have a disregard for evidence (Hammersley 2005; Ainsworth et al. 2015; Pring 2015). In fact, advocates of RCTs at government level have called for their use in educational research *precisely* because they are presumed to yield knowledge superior and more reliable than other methods (e.g., see Chapter 3; Goldacre 2013; Hammersley 2005). Hence, the UK Government's advocate for RCTs in education – Ben Goldacre, a medical doctor, broadcaster and academic – predicts:

a huge prize waiting to be claimed by teachers. By collecting better evidence of what works best, and establishing a culture where this evidence is used as a matter of routine, we can improve outcomes for children, and increase professional independence.

(Goldacre 2013: 7)

I have already noted that RCT claims to its elevated importance and usefulness in education are dubious, certainly as evidenced in the CtG project, but so are claimed increases to teacher independence. On this Higgins (Chapter 5) assures us that the:

involve[ment of] schools and teachers in selecting the focus for experimental inquiry and in managing and conducting the process of the trials themselves . . . is sufficient to counter Biesta's (2007) claim that 'scientific' approaches *necessarily* create a democratic deficit in educational research.

But this misses Biesta's (2007) point that the problem with RCTs in education is not so much with teacher participation in RCTs – both in determining their focus and in conducting the research – but with teachers' exclusion from theorising the nature of education, even before decisions are made about how knowledge about this reality can be generated.

The democratic deficit in RCTs, which Biesta identifies, is in relation to ontology not epistemology, more specifically in the privileging of epistemology over ontology. It is a fault of generalising the reality of the physical world over the social world noted above. It is: 'The great vice of the tradition [of scientific knowledge] . . . that it allows epistemology to command ontology' (Taylor 1990: 264); RCTs are used irrespective of the nature of the reality being researched, whereas 'questions of correct method are contingent upon the object under study; they cannot be determined in advance' (Abbey 2000: 189). As Biesta concludes:

> This is why the 'what works' agenda of evidence-based practice is at least insufficient and probably misplaced in the case of education, because judgment in education is not simply about what is possible (a factual judgment) but about what is educationally desirable (a value judgment).
>
> (Biesta 2007: 10)

Judgements of fact are matters for epistemology; judgements of value are matters for ontology.

The gold standard of RCTs in education is further tarnished when we consider the paradox of going to all this trouble to little effect or – if RCT treatments are believed to deliver improvements for students – of restricting access to treatments to some (the experimental group) while excluding others (the control group). How do these things get through ethics committees (see Chapter 8 in particular)? In fact, if such research was proposed in Australia and the students were Indigenous, it probably never would (see AIATSIS 2012 for the *Guidelines of Ethical Research in Australian Indigenous Studies*). Which brings me to the more substantive ethical issue of 'epistemological equity' (Dei 2010). The political advocacy of RCTs as the gold standard in educational research and the related posturing of RCT researchers to claim top position on the dais, are also about the rejection of other ways of knowing the social world. But their rejection is not just of other ways of knowing. By 'rejecting another epistemology . . . we are also rejecting the people who live that epistemology' (St. Pierre 2006: 257).

Conclusion

As a sociologist of education I imagine the social world in terms C. Wright Mills (1959) refers to as relations between 'private troubles' and 'public issues' – or perhaps I am a sociologist because I imagine the social world in these ways (see footnote 1). Other sociologists are inclined to name these relations as micro and macro, and even meso (i.e., just a little bit pregnant!). I am less inclined to use such nomenclature because it tends to emphasise structure over agency and also because it separates out from each other the social realities it attempts to name. For Mills, private troubles and public issues are different readings of the same social reality, they are embedded in each other. Thus, for me, important questions are why RCTs in education have become so prominent, to the extent that they have captured the research and policy imaginations of governments. How are the public issues and private troubles of student achievement related? Or how does the social reality speak of both?

I think the current economic crisis of post-industrial nations, in which industrial dominance has slipped from the grasp of 'western' nations and a global knowledge economy in which they might be preeminent, presents as a tantalising solution (Brown et al. 2011), the only solution. 'If we can no longer produce the goods, we need to live by our wits.' Smart schools, smart cities, smart states. Education has become a central mechanism for government to achieve its ends, not unlike the introduction of compulsory schooling at the start of the industrial revolution (Williams 1961).[22] Now progress towards this end is measured through PISA results and other standardised tests, which allow governments to compare and chart and scheme and worry and bring back traditional ways of doing education – like grammar schools and apprenticeship models for preparing teachers – which must have worked because 'we got to where we are doing it that way, didn't we?' Today's UK politicians fall into the same n=1 trap as Australian vice-chancellors (see above); that is, 'it worked for me, it will work for others'.

This account of public issues also provides an explanation for how it is that on one particular day there are far too many students from disadvantaged backgrounds who do not aspire to higher education, when the day before their aspirations were not even contemplated. In Australia, that was the day the government reintroduced widening participation policies to increase student enrolments – not in the face of pent-up demand, as in previous expansion periods, but because the supply of graduates was not sufficient to build a knowledge economy (Gale & Tranter 2011). On relations of private troubles and public issues:

> I could equally write about my own troubles on finishing school, of facing the prospect of missing out on accessing HE given my average academic results and all but non-existent financial resources. Yet these troubles were reframed by an incoming Whitlam Government's restructuring of 1970s Australian HE, including the creation of more university places thereby redefining minimum entry requirements – the removal of tuition fees and the introduction of a means-tested allowance. Had I graduated from school the year before, I would have been 'out in the cold'. Instead, HE access was transformed just at the moment I sought entry. As Mills explains,

22   The most recent agenda to expand higher education participation is like no previous expansion phase. The closest parallel is with the introduction of compulsory schooling (Gale 2015).

'the sociological imagination enables us to grasp history and biography and the relations between the two within society' (1959: 6).

(Gale 2015: 259)

In this context of precarious global ambitions, RCTs offer governments and schools the prospect of more precise instruments to engineer their populations into forms of human capital, which will enable them to claim a controlling stake in a knowledge economy and thus retain disproportionate positions of global power. Quite apart from the political and theoretical problems associated with a knowledge economy (Brown et al. 2011) and human capital (Feher 2009), RCTs can never deliver on this precision because they operate on a false premise: that the social world is the same as the physical world. But it isn't, and we must continue to point out the difference not just as a point of order, of ontology, but also as a matter of equity, of epistemology, for those who are the subject of others' interventions.

Acknowledgements

I am grateful to Stephen Parker for reading and commenting on earlier versions of this chapter, drawing my attention to other literatures and pushing my thinking on these important matters; to Julie Rowlands who said it was good and urged me to keep going; and to Ian Menter who invited my contribution and patiently waited for the outcome. Any errors of fact and fiction are mine.

References

Abbey, R. (2000). *Charles Taylor*. Teddington, UK: Acumen Publishing.
Ainsworth, H., Hewitt, C. E., Higgins, S., Wiggins, A., Torgerson, D. J., & Torgerson, C. J. (2015). Sources of bias in outcome assessment in randomised controlled trials: a case study. *Educational Research and Evaluation*, *21*(1), 3–14.
Australian Institute of Aboriginal and Torres Strait Islander Studies 2012 [AIATSIS] (2012). *Guidelines for Ethical Research in Australian Indigenous Studies*. Canberra: AIATSIS. Available at: http://aiatsis.gov.au/sites/default/files/docs/research-and-guides/ethics/gerais.pdf (Accessed on 12th March 2017).
Berliner, D. C. (2014). Exogenous variables and value-added assessments: a fatal flaw. *Teachers College Record*, *116*(1), 1–31.
Biesta, G. (2007). Why 'what works' won't work: evidence-based practice and the democratic deficit in educational research. *Educational Theory*, *57*(1), 1–22.
Biesta, G. J. J. (2010). Why 'what works' still won't work: from evidence-based education to value-based education. *Studies in Philosophy and Education*, *29*(5), 491–503.
Blair, N. (2015). Aboriginal education: More than adding different perspectives. In N. Weatherby-Fell (Ed.), *Learning to Teach in the Secondary School* (pp. 189–208). Port Melbourne, Victoria: Cambridge University Press.

Boler, M., & Zembylas, M. (2003). Discomforting truths: the emotional terrain of understanding difference. In P. P. Trifonas (Ed.), *Pedagogies of Difference: Rethinking Education for Social Change* (pp. 107–130). London: Routledge Falmer.

Bourdieu, P. (1984). *Distinction: A Social Critique of the Judgement of Taste* (R. Nice, Trans.). London: Routledge & Kegan Paul.

Bourdieu, P. (1986). The forms of capital. In J. G. Richardson (Ed.), *Handbook of Theory and Research for the Sociology of Education* (pp. 241–258). Westport, Connecticut: Greenwood Press.

Bourdieu, P. (1990). *The Logic of Practice* (R. Nice, Trans.). Cambridge: Polity Press.

Bourdieu, P., & Wacquant, L. J. D. (1992). *An Invitation to Reflexive Sociology.* Cambridge: Polity Press.

Brown, P., Lauder, H., & Ashton, D. (2011). *The Global Auction: The Broken Promises of Education, Jobs, and Incomes.* Oxford: Oxford University Press.

Connell, R. W. (2007). *Southern Theory: The Global Dynamics of Knowledge in Social Science.* Crows Nest, New South Wales: Allen & Unwin.

Dei, G. J. S. (2010). *Teaching Africa: Towards a Transgressive Pedagogy.* Dordrecht: Springer.

Department of Education, Training & Youth Affairs [DETYA] (2000). *The Impact of Educational Research.* Canberra: Commonwealth of Australia. Available online: http://www.voced.edu.au/content/ngv%3A33846. (Accessed on 13th March 2017).

Dewey, J. (1899). *School and society.* Chicago, IL: Chicago University Press.

Doecke, B., Parr, G., North, S., Gale, T., Long, M., Mitchell, J., Rennie, J., & Williams, J. (2008). *National Mapping of Teacher Professional Learning 2008 Report.* Canberra: Commonwealth Department of Education, Employment and Workplace Relations (DEEWR).

Dorling, D. (2010). *Injustice: Why Social Inequalities Persist.* Bristol: The Policy Press.

Feher, M. (2009). Self-appreciation; or, the aspirations of human capital. *Public Culture, 21*(1), 21–41.

Foucault, M. (1980). *Power/Knowledge: Selected Interviews and Other Writings, 1972–1977* (C. Gordon, L. Marshall, J. Mepham, & K. Soper, Trans. C. Gordon, Ed.). New York: Pantheon Books.

Gale, T. (1994). Story telling and policy making: the construction of university entrance problems in Australia. *Journal of Education Policy, 9*(3), 227–232.

Gale, T. (2005). *Rough Justice: Young People in the Shadows.* New York: Peter Lang Publishing.

Gale, T. (2015). Widening and expanding participation in Australian higher education: in the absence of sociological imagination. *The Australian Educational Researcher, 42*(2), 257–271.

Gale, T., & Cross, R. (2007). Nebulous gobbledegook: the politics of influence on how and what to teach in Australian schools. In A. Berry, A. Clemans, & A. Kostogriz (Eds.), *Dimensions of Professional Learning: Professionalism, Practice and Identity* (pp. 5–21). Rotterdam: Sense.

Gale, T., & Tranter, D. (2011). Social justice in Australian higher education policy: an historical and conceptual account of student participation. *Critical Studies in Education, 52*(1), 29–46.

Gale, T., & Molla, T. (2017). Deliberations on the deliberate professional: Thought-action provocations. In J. Lynch, J. Rowlands, T. Gale, & A. Skourdoumbis (Eds.),

Practice Theory: Diffractive Readings in Professional Practice and Education (pp. 247–262). Abingdon: Routledge.

Gale, T., & Parker, S. (2017, forthcoming). The prevailing logic of teacher education: privileging the practical in Australia, England and Scotland. In M. Peters, B. Cowie & I. Menter (Eds.), *A Companion to Research in Teacher Education*. Dordrecht: Springer.

Gale, T., Molla, T., & Parker, S. (2017). The illusion of meritocracy and the audacity of elitism: expanding the evaluative space in education. In S. Parker, K. Gulson, & T. Gale (Eds.), *Policy and Inequality in Education* (pp. 7–21). Singapore: Springer.

Giddens, A. (1984). *The Constitution of Society: Outline of the Theory of Structuration.* Cambridge: Polity Press.

Goldacre, B. (2013). *Building Evidence into Education.* Available online: http://media.education.gov.uk/assets/files/pdf/b/ben%20goldacre%20paper.pdf (Accessed on 7th March 2017).

Goldstein, H. (2002). *Designing Social Research for the 21st Century.* Inaugural professorial address, University of Bristol, 14 October.

Gramsci, A. (1971). *Selections from the Prison Notebooks* (Q. Hoare & G. N. Smith, Trans.). New York: International Publishers.

Hammersley, M. (2005). The myth of research-based practice: the critical case of educational inquiry. *International Journal of Social Research Methodology, 8*(4), 317–330.

Hammersley, M. (2013). *The Myth of Research-based Policy and Practice.* London: Sage.

Holmes, D., Murray, S. J., Perron, A., & Rail, G. (2006). Deconstructing the evidence-based discourse in health sciences: truth, power and fascism. *International Journal of Evidence-Based Healthcare, 4*(3), 180–186.

Kunnie, J., & Goduka, N. I. (Eds.). (2006). *Indigenous Peoples' Wisdom and Power: Affirming Our Knowledge Through Narratives.* Aldershot: Ashgate.

Lingard, B., & Gale, T. (2010). Defining educational research: a perspective of/on presidential addresses and the Australian Association for Research in Education. *Australian Educational Researcher, 37*(1), 21–49.

Martin, K. (2008). *Please Knock Before You Enter: Aboriginal Regulation of Outsiders and the Implications for Researchers.* Tenneriffe, Brisbane: Postpressed.

Martin, K., & Mirraboopa, B. (2003). Ways of knowing, being and doing: a theoretical framework and methods for indigenous and indigenist re-search. *Journal of Australian Studies, 27*(76), 203–214.

Parlett, M., & Hamilton, D. (1987). Evaluation as illumination: a new approach to the study of innovatory programmes. In R. Murphy & H. Torrance (Eds.), *Evaluating Education: Issues and Methods* (pp. 57–73). London: PCP.

Pavlov, I. P. (1927). *Conditioned Reflexes: An Investigation of the Physiological Activity of the Cerebral Cortex.* London: Oxford University Press.

Piketty, T. (2014). *Capital in the Twenty-First Century* (Trans. A. Goldhammer). Cambridge, MA: The Belknap Press of Harvard University Press.

Pirrie, A. (2001). Evidence-based practice in education: the best medicine? *British Journal of Educational Studies, 49*(2), 124–136.

Pring, R. (2015). *Philosophy of Education Research* (3rd ed.). London: Bloomsbury.

St. Pierre, E. A. (2006). Scientifically based research in education: epistemology and ethics. *Adult Education Quarterly, 56*(4), 239–266.

Schwandt, T. A. (1989). Solutions to the paradigm conflict: coping with uncertainty. *Journal of Contemporary Ethnography, 17*(4), 379–407.

Slavin, R. E. (2002). Evidence-based education policies: transforming educational practice and research. *Educational Researcher, 31*(7), 15–21.

Taylor, C. (1985). *Philosophy and the Human Sciences: Philosophical Papers 2.* Cambridge: Cambridge University Press.

Taylor, C. (1989). *Sources of the Self: The Making of Modern Identity.* Cambridge: Cambridge University Press.

Taylor, C. (1990). Rorty in the epistemological tradition. In A. Malachowski (Ed.), *Reading Rorty* (pp. 257–275). Oxford: Blackwell.

Taylor, C. (2002). Understanding the other: a Gadamerian view on conceptual schemes. In J. Malpas, U. Arnswald, & J. Kertscher (Eds.), *Gadamer's Century: Essays in Honor of Hans-Georg Gadamer* (pp. 279–297). Cambridge, MA: MIT Press.

Taylor, C. (2004). *Modern Social Imaginaries.* Durham, NC: Duke University Press.

Thomas, G. (2004). Introduction: evidence and practice. In G. Thomas & R. Pring (Eds.), *Evidence Based Practice in Education.* Maidenhead: Open University Press. (pp. 1–18).

Williams, R. (1961). *The Long Revolution.* London: Pelican.

Wright Mills, C. (1959). *The Sociological Imagination.* Oxford: Oxford University Press.

Zembylas, M. (2008). Engaging with issues of cultural diversity and discrimination through critical emotional reflexivity in online learning. *Adult Education Quarterly, 59*(1), 61–82.

Afterword

Ann Childs and Ian Menter

This book has provided a detailed account of the Closing the Gap: Test and Learn project from its policy origins to its implementation. It captures the diverse range of outcomes from the project, those intended from the RCT trials but also some outcomes that emerged and evolved over the course of the project. Further, the book explores debates about the use of RCTs in education, focussing on CtG as a case study, and engages with the wider issues about the burgeoning use of RCTs in educational research. Our concluding remarks attempt to draw out some key themes that run through the book's chapters to show how and the extent to which teachers were mobilised as researchers and how this analysis speaks to the future of research-informed practice in schools.

Three key themes seem to emerge consistently from Chapters 1–7 and these are: the emergence of teacher agency during the course of the project; the development of new forms of research collaboration within and between schools; and the development of teachers' knowledge of RCT methodology.

Firstly, evidence from the book shows that teachers were mobilised as researchers and showed considerable agency in taking on such roles. Although Chapter 1 initially raised some doubts about the space for teacher agency within the CtG project, agency certainly emerged through the development of the Early Adopters scheme, which supported trial coordinators and schools to appropriate the RCT methodology in order to run their own mini RCTs and set their own agendas for research within their schools and alliances. Indeed, as one member of the EDT team said:

> It has signalled what teachers are capable of and they can use a number of research methods and not just the ones they are more familiar with and have used in the past . . . I think it is where people have tried to do it themselves, on a small scale, *that we have seen the most learning* (our emphasis).
>
> (Chapter 1, p. 31)

Secondly, the flourishing of both teacher agency and enhanced research collaboration within and between schools is described in detail in Chapter 7.

Here some respondents talked about enhanced collaboration within their schools and alliances and the formation of new partnerships and collaborations with schools they had never worked with before. Furthermore, some respondents spoke about developing closer links with local HEIs and their Local Authority. Concomitant to this was the development of new research structures in schools such as the formation of development teams, new roles such as 'research leads' (p. 87) and 'specialist leaders of education in professional learning communities' (p. 153). Collaboration also flourished in the sharing of research across alliances through dissemination conferences and writing research reports. Indeed, the spirit of collaboration was fostered from day 1 in the project, as Chapter 4 demonstrates, from schools and teachers being involved collaboratively in the process of selecting the interventions through the implementation of the nationwide programme, and all of this relied on collaboration between Teaching Schools and other schools in the alliance. Thirdly, Chapters 1 and 6 show teachers becoming more knowledgeable about the use of RCTs in education whether they were involved in the main project or in the Early Adopter scheme. For some, RCTs were seen to be another tool they could use as they developed research-informed practice. However, others, particularly those in the Early Adopter scheme, became converts to using RCTs as their only method for research-informed practice. The significance of this developing knowledge, agency and collaboration was explored more thoroughly in relation to the three invited chapters in Part 3, but such was the confidence, collaborative spirit and knowledge built up in the system that it led to one respondent envisaging schools becoming specialists in areas of research much like specialist hospitals and, in doing so, becoming leaders in research, just as some have become leaders in teacher education within the context of the 'school-led system'.

As well as the three themes identified above, the three invited contributions in Part 3 also raise key issues and challenges for mobilising teachers as researchers and the use of RCTs in schools. Chapter 9 from Laroes et al. sheds interesting light on the changing perspectives of a group of teacher-researchers on what constitutes research. Chapter 9 claims that the teacher-researchers seem to move in an opposite direction from the teacher-researchers in CtG, that is from a very positivist perception of educational research, consistent with the RCT methodology adopted by their project, to a more nuanced appreciation of the contribution that qualitative evidence can provide in educational research. In CtG it is certainly the case that some of the teachers, particularly those involved in the Early Adopters scheme, became real advocates for the use of RCTs in their own schools. As one such teacher said:

the action researchers have become RCT[er]s, I think they have become more significant. (MM)

(Chapter 7, p. 147)

But there were also other voices too that saw RCTs, much as Higgins does in Chapter 5, as part of a toolbox and that 'RCTs will never replace the need for teachers to try things out and evaluate things for themselves' (p. 148). Furthermore, there were some, as said above, that went even further and were much less concerned with the actual results of the RCT trials if they had seen at first hand the benefits of the interventions with their pupils in their school. Therefore, we see rather more similarities than Laroes et al. suggest with some teacher-researchers in both groups still seeing RCTs as the only valid method but with some others also seeing the importance of qualitative research.

Many of the issues Connelly's chapter raises resonate with the themes emerging of teacher agency and the value of collaboration. However, Connelly also makes other methodological points about RCTs which resonate with points on the use of RCTs in education by Thompson and Menter (Chapter 3), Higgins (Chapter 5) and Fancourt (Chapter 8). Firstly, he echoes Higgins' points about the need for both RCTs and qualitative research to be part of a researcher's toolbox:

> Higgins (Chapter 5) is quite right to stress that the RCT is just one of many of the tools available to educational researchers designed to do a specific job.
>
> (Chapter 10, p. 198)

This is a point some of the teachers in the CtG project made too. Secondly, Connelly makes an important point about the importance of fidelity in the delivery of interventions in RCTs. He points out that teachers are natural experimenters which, in CtG, was demonstrated very clearly by teachers in the Early Adopter scheme. However, Connelly also raises some potential threats to fidelity arising from teacher agency in the implementation of the interventions in RCTs when teachers use their professional judgement to adapt interventions. In Chapter 2 and Chapter 3 there is evidence in CtG of teacher adaptation of the interventions for their context – an understandable response given that the teachers were experienced and expert professionals. Connelly's response is very clear on this issue:

> the one element of a trial where it is necessary to maintain a standard approach is in the actual delivery of the intervention concerned. In this regard, whilst there is complete flexibility in relation to what intervention is developed, once it has been agreed it does need to be delivered as originally intended . . . If we were to find a difference between outcomes amongst students in the intervention group compared to the control group at post-test, then we can only attribute this difference to the effects of the intervention if we are clear about what that intervention has been. This, in turn, requires us to identify what the key elements of the intervention

should be and then to ensure that these are adhered to for the duration of the programme.

(Chapter 10, p. 201)

However, Connelly does go on to say that 'it is quite possible, and valid, to develop an intervention that is only based on a broad set of principles or values to be adhered to or a few key parameters within which teachers or schools must work' (p. 202). Therefore, there seems to be more room for teacher agency in the design phase, but fundamentally Connelly is arguing that interventions do need to be delivered with fidelity and that the teacher agency alluded to in Chapters 1 and 2 was a potential threat to the outcomes of the RCTs.

A second key methodological issue Connelly highlights is the importance of the process of randomisation as essential in RCTs, and here he would have liked to have seen more transparency in the descriptions of how randomisation was achieved in CtG. However, interestingly, in order to overcome the challenges he identifies in running successful large-scale RCTs, Connelly proposes that the early stages should involve collaboration in developing smaller-scale RCTs before scaling these up. On collaboration he says:

> it is quite possible to work collaboratively with teachers and schools, and with parents, students and local communities, to jointly identify priorities and the focus of an educational intervention and to develop and pilot that intervention. We have also shown how it is possible to work together to jointly identify the outcomes to be measured and the specific design to be employed for the RCT. Moreover, we regularly work collaboratively with key stakeholders to make sense of and interpret the findings that arise from our trials and to agree the best mechanisms for reporting these.
>
> (p. 201)

Connelly's vision of collaboration here gives genuine space for teacher agency and for mobilising teachers as researchers to involve collaboration within and beyond the boundaries of their schools. On the reasons for starting small-scale, he says:

> In this regard, and just as we have learnt through our own engagement in RCTs over the last decade, starting small and working carefully through the stages of pilot tests and efficacy trials before subjecting interventions to larger-scale effectiveness trials not only helps mitigate many of these problems but also creates a more appropriate context for the development of meaningful collaborative partnerships between researchers, schools, parents and students where RCTs can be genuinely co-produced.
>
> (p. 205)

CtG started big, as acknowledged by Connelly and others in the book, because of its tight timescale, but it could be argued that the support and collaboration reported in the Early Adopter scheme did achieve the more small-scale collaborative approach that Connelly is advocating.

Thirdly, the issue of validity and transferability of the findings from RCTs emerges as a key issue in many of the chapters. Connelly identifies 'a growing trend for particular interventions to be evaluated by one RCT and then for their future to rest upon a positive result from that trial' (p. 205). He argues for those engaged in RCT design to resist the temptation to scale up before proper small-scale trialling has been completed. He also argues that in order to establish wider validity there is also 'the need to contextualise the findings of individual trials within the wider evidence-base provided by other trials of that intervention or similar interventions' or through the use of meta-analyses (p. 205). Higgins also deals with issues of validity, particularly external validity, which requires 'in my view, either extensive replication to understand the range of contexts where it (the intervention) can be successful or professional judgement and interpretation based on the limited inference from a single trial' (p. 98). Churches et al. (Chapter 2) also echo the need for replication in order to establish the efficacy of an intervention in a number of contexts with a wider range of pupils. Higgins' additional call for teachers to use professional judgement, when results from only one trial are available, was echoed to some extent in the CtG project in this teacher's words:

> And then we'll do a six-week trial of that, that's data driven, and then if it makes a difference in the six weeks then obviously it's working and we'll continue with it. If it doesn't make a difference in those six weeks then we know it isn't working in our context. And it's not that the research is incorrect, it just doesn't work in our context. (IF)
>
> (Chapter 6, pp. 151–152)

Here again the teacher seems to be bringing agency and professional judgement to bear on the results of their RCT. Professional judgement also surfaced in other ways in that some of the respondents went one step further in being prepared to ignore the RCT trial results if, in their professional judgement, the intervention worked with their pupils. Gale's chapter, coming as the final contribution to this book, offers an in-depth and significant challenge to the use of RCTs in educational research. Unlike other chapters that discuss the issues and challenges of running RCTs, Gale goes much further in questioning their very existence. His powerful critique is summed up as follows:

> RCTs can never deliver on this precision [what works] because they operate on a false premise: that the social world is the same as the physical world. But it isn't, and we must continue to point out the difference not

just as a point of order, of ontology, but also as a matter of epistemology, for those who are the subject of others' interventions.

(Chapter 11, p. 220)

Superficially, there seems to be some agreement and concern between Gale and Connelly about RCTs becoming the "gold standard" of educational research (Chapter 10, p. 198). Connelly's and Higgins' responses are to argue for both RCTs and other forms of research as valuable in their different and complementary ways:

In this regard, Higgins (Chapter 5) is quite right to stress that the RCT is just one of many tools available to educational researchers, designed to do a very specific job. As he also makes clear, the RCT is an absolutely necessary but not sufficient research design for drawing conclusions about the effectiveness of education practice.

(Chapter 10, p. 198)

Gale's argument takes a much more political stance and first examines why RCTs have become so prominent in government policy across the world:

the current economic crisis of post-industrial nations, in which industrial dominance has slipped from the grasp of 'western' nations and a global knowledge economy in which they might be preeminent, presents as a tantalising solution (Brown et al. 2011), the only solution.

(p. 219)

Gale goes on to argue that a return to:

traditional ways of doing education – like grammar schools and apprenticeship models for preparing teachers . . . must have worked because 'we got to where we are doing it that way, didn't we?' Today's UK politicians fall into the same n=1 trap as Australian vice-chancellors (see above); that is, 'it worked for me, it will work for others'.

(p. 219)

Therefore, in Gale's view the power of the role of RCTs and their perceived ability to demonstrate 'what works' explains why 'RCTs have been afforded by governments as the new gold standard for educational research (Goldstein 2002; St Pierre 2006; Holmes et al. 2006), to the point that in some quarters they have become synonymous with educational research itself' (p. 216). There is indeed evidence in that some of the schools in the Early Adopters scheme did see RCTs as the only game in town. Whereas the argument from Connelly and Higgins is based on the need for methodological pluralism, Gale's arguments see the universal advocacy and adoption of RCTs in educational

research as a power grab where RCTs have 'become synonymous with educational research itself; the consequence of a "regime of truth" (Foucault 1980)
that operates to ensure that one account of education research is positioned as
the only account' (p. 216). These are absolutely fundamental differences of view
between these authors.

Gale's second area of significant critique is that RCTs do not regard
the physical and social world as different worlds 'and favour a particular view
of reality – which is "out there" to be discovered (by particular methods of
discovery) of what things are and how they are related (e.g. Hammersley, 2013)'
(p. 211). Gale goes on to argue RCTs might be appropriate in the physical
world but in the social world 'people have a mind of their own (see Taylor
2002 on predictability, changing self-understandings, etc.), which means they
can and do act in ways that are unexpected, although not always!' (p. 212).
He sees RCTs as regarding students 'as not having a mind of their own' and
that 'when they are exposed to the same circumstances they are presumed to
respond in the same ways' (p. 212). Finally, Gale also fundamentally questions
whether it is possible to say that any change can be validly ascribed to
interventions because the intervention is 'the only thing seen to be different
from the control group'. He sees this as 'a leap of faith of elephant proportions'
and goes on to describe many contextual factors that he perceives undermine
the results from RCTs. These are serious charges and ones that are not either
easy or straightforward to answer. Connelly to a certain extent addresses Gale's
issue about RCTs being blind to the individuality of students:

> When a teacher asks the question 'what works?' they will be clearly aware
> that any answer cannot simply be applied to each and every student in
> their class but is about the effectiveness of specific approaches *on average*.
> They will also tend to be very clear that the effectiveness of educational
> programmes and interventions is likely to vary across contexts and from
> one group of students to the next. This is why they will often be concerned
> with asking and seeking to answer the more specific question of: 'what is
> most likely to work best for my particular class or year group?' Very few
> people we have worked with have failed to appreciate the complex and
> context-specific nature of how students learn and develop.
>
> (Chapter 10, p. 200)

There is evidence in the book that some of the teachers did take a more
nuanced and critical approach to RCTs. As said in Chapter 1, there is significant
evidence of teachers at the classroom level using their professional judgement
and agency to continue to use the intervention independent of any result
(positive or negative) from the RCT. However, there is also evidence that
suggests that this level of criticality did not pervade all levels in the school and
that senior managers were more likely to be influenced by the RCT results
for the reasons outlined in this chapter. Furthermore, if teachers are involved

in the collaborative way Connelly advocates above, or indeed go further to design and carry out RCTs themselves, then there is some opportunity for them to see, at first hand, the methodological and ethical challenges RCTs present. RCTs are now a part of the research landscape and it could be argued that teachers can only be critical and aware of their strengths and limitations if they are involved in their design and implementation. Evidence from both CtG and from Chapter 9 shows some teachers developing an awareness of the value of other forms of qualitative research to complement the findings from an RCT. If teachers do become involved in truly collaborative RCTs in the way that Connelly outlines, they may be able to engage more knowledgably in policy debates about the use of RCTs in educational research, drawing on their first-hand experiences. However, we acknowledge that this is a hope rather than the reality suggested in the chapters of this book.

In summary, the CtG project and the evidence within these chapters shows considerable mobilisation and agency for teachers as researchers in: understanding RCT methodology and, in some cases, designing their own mini RCTs; developing research collaborations including the emergence of new roles, structures and forms of dissemination within and beyond their schools and alliances. There is no doubt that for many the experience of being involved was valuable, but it is reasonable to ask whether the project provided value for money. This is a question which is impossible to answer here, but it seems RCTs are here to stay and Connelly's vision of small-scale local collaborative research, which also includes qualitative research, between teachers and other partners seems to be a stronger, more sustainable way forward. Involving teachers in the designing and implementation of RCTs at least provides the chance that they will be able, then, to engage with the ongoing debates about the use of RCTs in educational research rather than have them imposed from above.

In conclusion, it is our view that a great deal of professional learning took place through this very large-scale and imaginative attempt to involve hundreds of schools in a research-based initiative. That learning was achieved by hundreds (perhaps thousands) of teachers and hundreds of school leaders, by those of us in the teams that comprised the consortium that were involved in implementing the project and, we hope, by the politicians and policy makers who devised it originally. Finally, we also hope that this book can help to spread that learning to a wider, indeed international, group of professional educators and researchers.

Index

Note: 'N' after a page number indicates a note; 'f' indicates a figure; 't' indicates a table.